Hitler's Alpine Headquarters

Hitler's Alpine Headquarters

JAMES WILSON

Pen & Sword
MILITARY

First published in Great Britain in 2005
New updated edition published in 2013 by
PEN & SWORD MILITARY
an imprint of
Pen & Sword Books Limited
47 Church Street
Barnsley
South Yorkshire
S70 2AS

ISBN: 978 1 78303 004 0

A CIP catalogue record for this book
is available from the British Library

Typeset in Optima by Chic Graphics

Printed and bound in India by
Replika Press Pvt. Ltd.

Pen & Sword Books Ltd incorporates the Imprints of
Pen & Sword Archaeology, Atlas, Aviation, Battleground, Discovery,
Family History, History, Maritime, Military, Naval, Politics, Railways,
Select, Social History, Transport, True Crime, and Claymore Press,
Frontline Books, Leo Cooper, Praetorian Press, Remember When,
Seaforth Publishing and Wharncliffe.

For a complete list of Pen & Sword titles please contact:
PEN & SWORD BOOKS LIMITED
47 Church Street, Barnsley, South Yorkshire, S70 2AS, England
email: enquiries@pen-and-sword.co.uk
website: www.pen-and-sword.co.uk

Contents

Foreword

Since *Hitler's Alpine Retreat* was first published in 2005 I have enjoyed two seasons working as a tour guide in beautiful Berchtesgaden. Eagle's Nest Historical Tours, owned by David and Christine Harper, has an enviable worldwide reputation as specialist in presenting historically intensive tours on the history of the region during the Third Reich. This small, independent, personable company really sets the standard on what for many, is a particularly sensitive subject. While all tours are delivered in English, the clientele is truly international. All levels of interest are catered for; from the four-hour history intensive afternoon group tour, to the private eight-hour all day tour. I was delighted to spend two summers in Berchtesgaden, 2009 and 2010, when I worked with David and Christine.

These two periods, while extremely enjoyable, enabled me to expand my knowledge on the history of the area under the Nazis. Spending so much time in the area also allowed access to people and locations that would otherwise be impossible. The acquisition of additional photographic material, my experiences in Berchtesgaden, and the kind and encouraging comments expressed by readers of *Hitler's Alpine Retreat*; these are the factors that have compelled me to write *Hitler's Alpine Headquarters*.

Author's Comment

At the risk of leaving myself open to criticism, I should point out that from the outset it has been my intention not to express any political opinions in this work. Furthermore, I have deliberately attempted neither to promote nor denounce any individual or group; rather it has been my intention to present the facts and to allow the reader to draw their own conclusions.

This intention might best be explained by way of the following scenario. Imagine yourself a member of the working class living in 1920s Germany. While the defeat of 1918 still haunts the nation, the resulting shattered economy, uncontrolled rampant inflation and widespread unemployment are even harder to bear. The end of 1923 sees the beginning of sustained economic growth. This growth continues until halted by the catastrophic effects of the World Depression in 1930. Germany, perhaps more than any other country, is hardest hit.

Let us move forward, it is 1933 and the Nazis are in power, now try to imagine how you might react to a relentless, and as yet, never previously encountered sophisticated propaganda campaign. While there is no escaping the powerful symbolism of the new regime, there are frequent broadcasts applauding the achievements of the new political and social order. Where the government of the Weimar Republic failed; the Nazi Party's 'Four Year Plan', introduced in 1933 to tackle unemployment and economic problems is now bearing fruit and changing people's lives.

It is now 1935 and the restrictions of the Versailles Treaty are being openly flouted, not least by the re-emergence of the military, and all it seems without any foreign reaction. Finally, there is a definite feeling of renewed national pride as the new government declares itself responsible for all the improvements in everyday life, with promises of better to come. Exciting times by any stretch of the imagination, don't you think! With that in mind, notwithstanding the terrible hidden agenda as yet to unfold, can we be sure, given the same set of circumstances that we would have reacted any differently. Who are we to judge?

For the majority of people living in Germany in the early 1930s it has been said that there were only two choices; Communism, or National Socialism. In the end National Socialism would dominate. A commonly held view of National Socialism at the time was that it was; 'Something good with some bad side effects, or something bad with some good side effects'.

Finally, and in order to better understand the captions that accompany the following images, it should be explained that all text appearing in '**bold type**', whether this appears as just part of the caption, or indeed the entire caption, is a translation of the original German text taken from that particular postcard. The reader should also understand that each caption has been composed to compliment and enhance the image to which it relates; this is a deliberate effort on my part in an attempt to replicate how these images would have been presented to the German public and the rest of the world at the time of their original release.

Introduction

The Alpine cottage that would eventually be known as Haus Wachenfeld was first occupied in 1861 by Michael and Elisabeth Renoth. The property changed hands twice between 1891 and 1922. On 8 March 1922 the house was bought by Frau Margarete Winter-Wachenfeld, a merchant's widow from Buxtehude near Hamburg. Frau Winter's maiden name had been Wachenfeld; thus the property was named Haus Wachenfeld. Constructed in traditional Alpine style, this humble cottage would later achieve notoriety as the country home of none other, than Adolf Hitler. However, in order to fully appreciate the importance of Haus Wachenfeld (later known as the Berghof) and the role this beautiful mountainous region would play in the life of Adolf Hitler, we must go back to that point in time when Hitler first came to the area. Hitler visited Berchtesgaden and the Obersalzberg for the first time in April 1923. He came to see his old friend and mentor Dietrich Eckart. Eckart, as editor of *Auf gut Deutsch!* (In Good German!), an anti-Semitic periodical, was wanted for questioning regarding the anti-Semitic nature of his writing. Eckart had selected the Obersalzberg as a hiding-place in his efforts to avoid arrest. At that time Eckart was using the alias Dr Hoffmann, in an attempt to keep his whereabouts secret from the authorities. Hitler, for his part, and in an effort not to lead the police to Eckart, came to the area using the name Herr Wolf.

At the end of his visit, Hitler was, in his own words, 'completely captivated' by the region. Back in Munich and later that year, Hitler and the other Nazi leaders found themselves charged with high treason as a result of their unsuccessful attempt to seize power, (known as the Munich Beer-Hall *'Putsch'* (Revolt)) on 9 November 1923. The authorities, having successfully suppressed the 'revolt' arrested Hitler two days later on 11 November. Hitler was discovered at the family home of his friend, Ernst 'Putzi' Hanfstaengl at Uffing near the Staffelsee, some seventy kilometres (forty-five miles) south-east of the Bavarian capital where he was found recovering from injuries sustained during

the uprising. The would-be Führer (Leader) was held in Landsberg Prison until trials began the following year.

Adolf Hitler was charged with high treason. Should he be found guilty the maximum penalty for high treason at that time was the death penalty, failing that, life imprisonment. Amid much public interest trials began in Munich on 26 February 1924. Of the accused, Adolf Hitler would emerge the dominant figure. Franz Gürtner, Bavarian Minister of Justice personally saw to it that the judiciary was lenient during the Hitler trails. Gürtner, a member of the *Deutschnationalepartei* (German Nationalist Party) was a supporter of right-wing extremist politics. It was thanks to Gürtner's influence and protection and the fact that all five judges had been selected for their sympathetic leanings towards the Nazi cause, that Hitler was permitted to speak in his own defence, interrupt proceedings at will, and to cross-examine witnesses at length. While going against all normal legal procedure, this highly irregular activity was nonetheless permitted by the presiding judge, Georg Neithardt. Hitler seized upon the interest of both the national and international press covering the event. His lengthy statements were printed verbatim in daily newspapers, not only in Germany, but around the world.

1. Panorama of the Obersalzberg before the destruction.
This fabulous image shows the entire Nazi complex located on the Obersalzberg at the height of its development and following the completion of all building works. As the caption states, this is how the region appeared prior to the air-raid on the morning of 25 April 1945 which resulted in the destruction of many of the buildings seen here.

The identification of the buildings relates to the numbers as they appear on the original image; 1. Post Office in the prohibited area. 2. Nursery. 3. Chauffeur's living quarters. 4. Large garage. 5. Gatehouse to prohibited area. 6. Barracks/Economics building. 7. Barracks/Drill hall of bodyguard. 8. Parade ground/Underground shooting range. 9. Barracks/Living quarters. 10. Hotel Platterhof. 11. Hotel Platterhof staff living quarters. 12. Obersalzberg administration. 13. Model house for architectural planning. 14. Kindergarten. 15. Berghof. 16. Reich's security service and Gestapo.

Grasping his opportunity, Hitler displayed ability, inspirational oratory, and unrivalled political awareness as he proclaimed the Party's ideas through his numerous 'speeches' throughout the trials. Furthermore, he highlighted the many 'injustices to', and 'sufferings of' the German people as a direct result of the unfair Versailles Treaty. He railed against the Weimar Republic and the 'November Criminals'; those who had overseen Germany's surrender in 1918. A mastery of inspired, hard-hitting oratory would see Adolf Hitler emerge from the trials, part victim, part hero, but more importantly, a true patriot. Hitler had turned the tables on his political opponents and pricked the public consciousness. The trials of those involved in the Beer-Hall 'Putsch' ended on 1 April 1924. Adolf Hitler for his part had turned defeat into victory by appearing on the front page of every newspaper in Germany, and beyond. A court appearance had actually worked in Hitler's favour. He had used it like a spot-lit platform to deliver the Party's ideology to the masses; moreover, the proceedings had presented Hitler as a gifted politician, one worthy of attention.

While he openly admitted attempting to overthrow the national government, Hitler went further; he accepted full responsibility for the attempted *Putsch*. His claim; that his was not an act of treason, but indeed that of a patriot, did not fall on deaf ears. Hitler, or the Führer (Leader) as he was now hailed, for his part in the *Putsch* received a five year prison sentence, that being the minimum penalty if convicted on a charge of high treason. However, once again, due to lenient authorities and the intervention of 'friends in high places' the conditions he faced while in Landsberg Prison were far from unpleasant. Hitler was treated as something of a celebrity; to the extent that he was permitted to entertain friends in his private room or to wander around the prison grounds with his fellow inmates. Thus, with most of his time unoccupied, Hitler engaged himself in dictating the bulk of the first part of his book *Mein Kampf* (My Struggle) to his friend

2. Panorama of the Obersalzberg after the destruction.
In comparing this image with the previous postcard appearing on pages 8 and 9, we can see the devastation inflicted upon the region in 1945 is almost limitless.

and fellow prisoner, Rudolf Hess. As he reflected upon the trials, Hitler later concluded that political success might be achieved without violent confrontation. Thereafter, he decided, the Nazis would pursue political power by legal means. Having served only a small part of his five year sentence, Adolf Hitler was released from Landsberg Prison on 20 December 1924. Hitler's early release had been secured by his protector, Franz Gürtner, Bavarian Minister of Justice. Gürtner later persuaded the Bavarian government to lift the ban on the NSDAP and to allow Hitler to resume public speaking.

Following his release Hitler returned to Berchtesgaden, spending time there with friends and benefactors. Hitler's time was now occupied addressing small groups (although at that time he was banned from such activity under the terms of his prison release) and dictating the second part of *Mein Kampf*. Already spending a considerable amount of his time on the Obersalzberg, Adolf Hitler, having agreed a figure with the owner, began renting Haus Wachenfeld on 15 October 1928. The house, typically Bavarian in style, offered fabulous views towards the Untersberg across the valley and beyond into neighbouring Austria, the birthplace of the new tenant. The Obersalzberg is located a short distance above the town of Berchtesgaden. It is an area of outstanding natural beauty; here, Hitler could relax, collect his thoughts and develop strategy for the continuing political struggle. Later, during the war, in reference to these early years spent on the Obersalzberg Hitler remarked; 'those were the best days of my life', praise indeed for someone whose domestic life prior to settling in the area had been more than a little turbulent. The following years saw the Nazis develop and introduce unprecedented, propaganda-fuelled political campaigning methods. Steadily increased use of the cleverest, and for its time incredibly subtle propaganda, would result in the Nazi Party making inroads into mainstream politics. This, backed-up where necessary with the muscle-power of the SA, saw off challenges from the Party's greatest rivals, the Communists.

Hitler wasted little time; in late 1928 during the first period of the rental agreement, he approached Frau Margarete Winter-Wachenfeld to enquire if she might consider selling the property. With the sale of Haus Wachenfeld agreed, legal proceedings on the

purchase began on 17 September 1932. Hitler would describe this region as his *Wahlheimat,* 'the homeland of his choice'. Adolf Hitler was appointed German Chancellor on 30 January 1933. The legalities in connection with the purchase of Haus Wachenfeld were completed on 26 June 1933. Hitler, since being appointed Chancellor, had become a very wealthy man. He received enormous sums in royalties from the sales of *Mein Kampf.* Moreover, the book was now compulsory reading under new legislation. As time passed, and as head of state, Hitler later received royalty payments due to the fact that his head appeared on postage stamps. Using personal funds from the sales of *Mein Kampf,* Adolf Hitler bought Haus Wachenfeld for the sum of 40,000 Gold Marks. This single, yet seemingly unremarkable act would ultimately lead to great changes in the area. The foundations of the later-to-be-constructed Berghof (mountain farm) and the already existing idea of the Hitler cult would come together on the Obersalzberg.

Haus Wachenfeld now underwent several stages of renovation and reconstruction, most of which were planned and paid for by Hitler himself. The Nazi Party then moved to persuade the Bavarian authorities to donate pieces of land in the immediate area towards the development of the newly planned complex. This, together with the compulsory purchase of farmland adjoining that of the Führer's property would eventually form an enclosed area of some ten square kilometres at its conclusion. Initially, and on Hitler's instructions, these purchases were carried out correctly and generously. However, as time passed and with the involvement of Martin Bormann, reluctant landowners faced a stark choice; accept payment, failing that, forced eviction or imprisonment. Bormann employed the very unpopular Gotthard Färber as enforcer during this period of acquisition of land on the Obersalzberg. By 1937 Bormann had succeeded in buying out or evicting all the residents. The entire Obersalzberg now underwent dramatic change; the once peaceful farming area became a large, well ordered and well guarded estate. Of this area, Hitler owned only Haus Wachenfeld and the grounds in which it stood.

Throughout the early years and during the many periods he spent on the Obersalzberg, Hitler enjoyed an almost carefree lifestyle. Here, in peace and comfort, he could escape the daily grind of political administration and public duties, which, for the most part, he disliked. The Führer delighted in long walks in the region. In these surroundings, Adolf Hitler projected an image of someone who loved nature and the great outdoors, a man of the people who enjoyed a simple and informal lifestyle. When in the company of ladies he was always extremely polite, the perfect host who amused everyone with his sharp sense of humour. Between 1923 and 1936, Hitler spent periods of anything between two and six months every year at his beloved mountain retreat.

The Obersalzberg quickly became a place of pilgrimage; literally thousands of people arrived on an almost daily basis. These adoring multitudes from every corner of the Reich wanted to see the place where their Führer lived, and perhaps, as was sometimes the case, be greeted by Hitler personally close to Haus Wachenfeld. After 1934 the masses were no longer permitted unrestricted access to the Obersalzberg, although the number of visitors to Berchtesgaden itself continued unabated. Subsequently the entire mountain became a more heavily restricted, high security area. After 1936 only those possessing special permits had access to the Obersalzberg, with no less than three checkpoints having to be passed. Leaving Berchtesgaden, the visitor was required to produce the necessary pass to gain entry to the outer security zone at the SS guardhouse located by the Schießstättsbrücke. Halfway up the mountain road one encountered a second checkpoint permitting access to the middle security zone. The last checkpoint, within sight of the Berghof, controlled access to the central, most secure zone. As time passed, other members of the Nazi hierarchy, including Martin Bormann and Hermann Göring, set about acquiring their own properties on the Obersalzberg close to the Führer. In 1938 Hitler would invite Albert Speer to come and live on the mountain.

Adolf Hitler's appointment as Chancellor on 30 January 1933 would see Haus Wachenfeld, the Obersalzberg, and the town of Berchtesgaden instantly elevated to become areas of high status in the Nazi realm. The Obersalzberg would quickly evolve to become Hitler's second seat of government; when not in Berlin it was on the Obersalzberg that the Führer made his decisions. It is therefore hardly surprising that major development followed. From 1936, and under Martin Bormann's supervision, many grand projects were undertaken, including an improved road leading from the town of Berchtesgaden up to the estate. Additionally, many new buildings were constructed on the mountain to enhance the lifestyles of those who spent time in and around the Berghof, providing food, recreation and security, (including a large SS barracks). Hitler's much loved Haus Wachenfeld also underwent major redevelopment during the period 1935-36. The new Berghof that was painstakingly constructed around Haus Wachenfeld was indeed something worthy of the Führer, large and tastefully furnished, yet not ostentatious. It was here that Adolf Hitler entertained 'invited guests', these included; royalty, foreign heads of state, and diplomatic envoys. On the other hand, if 'summoned', rather than 'invited' to the Berghof, an individual might be forgiven if harbouring any doubts as to the level of hospitality they could expect upon arrival.

This period of massive construction on the Obersalzberg produced; the large SS complex, kindergarten, chauffeurs' quarters, garages, economics building, the new Hotel Platterhof, administration buildings and much more. At the same time in the vicinity of Berchtesgaden itself more buildings were already appearing, these included; a Reich Chancellery, a youth hostel, an enormous army barracks, and a new railway station. A small airport constructed at Ainring near Freilassing in 1933, served many who travelled to see the Führer on the Obersalzberg; upon arrival at the airport visitors were then chauffeur driven the remaining relatively short distance, about thirty-five kilometres (twenty-two miles) to Hitler's country residence.

Throughout the war years Adolf Hitler made repeated visits to his mountain retreat, enjoying the peace and relaxation he had always found there. Not until 1943 when the possibility of Allied air-raids in the area became a real danger was the decision taken to build a system of underground bunkers on the Obersalzberg. These vast excavations through solid rock, although never quite completed, were a remarkable undertaking. The bunkers themselves provided comfortable living quarters and ample store-rooms. They were supplied with water, electric power, communications, heating and ventilation systems, everything necessary to withstand a prolonged attack. An extensive network of tunnels, all with emergency exit points and fortified entrances connected these bunkers, while externally anti-aircraft positions were improved and numbers increased. Additionally, smoke-generating equipment had been installed to 'cloak' the valley in the event of an air-raid; hiding all probable targets beneath a dense man-made fog.

On the morning of Wednesday, 25 April 1945, with most of the Nazi leadership in Berlin; some 359 Allied aircraft dropped approximately 1,232 tons of bombs on the

Obersalzberg, causing extensive damage to the vast majority of buildings situated there. Just five days later, on 30 April, the Führer committed suicide in his Berlin bunker. Within a week of Hitler's demise the war in Europe ended on 6 May 1945. After the Second World War some of the less severely damaged buildings on the Obersalzberg were repaired and taken over by the US military. In 1952 the bomb damaged remains of the Berghof were blown up. The Bavarian State only regained control of the mountain area following the departure of the Americans in 1995.

Today, a new Documentation Centre stands near the former site of the now disappeared Hotel Platterhof; this provides an audio-visual history of the area during the Third Reich. Visitors to the centre also have an opportunity to enter part of the aforementioned tunnel/bunker system. Another section of this system can be entered through the delightful Hotel zum Türken, a traditional, family-owned hotel established in the early 1900s. Due to its proximity to Hitler's Berghof, this property was confiscated by the Nazis in late 1933 and used to accommodate the *Reichsicherheitsdienst* (RSD; Reich Security Service) who were responsible for Hitler's personal security. Not until 1949, and under unique circumstances, were the original owners permitted to reclaim the property, following repairs and refurbishment the hotel re-opened for business in late 1950.

When one considers that the Third Reich lasted little more than twelve years, and that for the latter half of that period the regime was engaged in world conflict; the amount of construction carried out on the Obersalzberg and surrounding area alone between 1936 and 1945 almost defies belief. The execution of these grandiose building programmes in themselves, clearly indicates the importance of the region to the Nazis, yet more so their Führer, Adolf Hitler, as his home, his spiritual retreat, and his southern headquarters. Despite the enormity of the projects undertaken in the area during the Third Reich, and the equally devastating efforts of the Allies to destroy those projects, the Obersalzberg and Berchtesgaden retain their almost magical charm; both remain as popular and beautiful today as they ever were.

James Wilson
January 2013

Propaganda Postcards

The use of postcards for patriotic and propaganda reasons, in so far as Germany is concerned, dates from the early 1900s. The introduction of faster photographic techniques and production methods at that time permitted the distribution of postcards on a scale as never before. During the First World War, many firms (including the famous W. Sanke of Berlin) produced large numbers of posed studio images in postcard form depicting many of Germany's better known, high ranking military figures.

The arrival of the latest technological advances in military hardware, such as aircraft, U-boats and airships into that conflict, contributed to the production of numerous postcards publicizing the new generation of young military hero. These were the men gaining fame and honour at what was then the 'cutting edge' of modern warfare. The availability of these postcards throughout Germany created an interest in collecting the sharp photographic images resulting from the latest processes.

Later, in 1933 when the Nazis came to power, the value of using postcards for propaganda purposes was fully realized and consequently used to maximum advantage and effect. The Propaganda Ministry of Dr Joseph Goebbels was highly efficient; it had been determined that the postcard image could be personal, even intimate and strong in human interest. Here was a medium that could influence and inspire. With this in mind, the gargantuan machine that was the Propaganda Ministry went into overdrive, producing images of popular figures both political and military.

3. The Führer in front of his country house on the Obersalzberg.
Adolf Hitler, idolized Chancellor of Germany accompanied by his aides creates something approaching hysteria as he walks along the road near his beloved Haus Wachenfeld. Large crowds such as this were a common sight on the Obersalzberg in the early days; young and old with arms outstretched they salute their Führer in an almost uncontrolled burst of enthusiasm.

4. Munich – The House of German Art. Franz Triebsch - Portrait of the Führer.
This study of the Führer completed in 1941 depicts Hitler as the determined
and charismatic military leader. The original painting was exhibited in the
House of German Art in Munich; here it is yet another example of Hoffmann's
work in producing postcards from original works of art.

There followed a fantastic number of postcards showing the then rapidly expanding
armed forces on manoeuvres with the latest equipment. So great was the interest that many
military units were assigned their own photographer. These men were obliged to submit their
work to the Propaganda Ministry where all images were selected and approved prior to
production and release. If not selected for use as a postcard image the work of the unit

photographer often found its way onto the pages of one or more of the many popular military magazines or newspapers of the day. Publications such as; *Der Adler* (the air force magazine), *Die Kriegsmarine* (the naval magazine), *Die Wehrmacht* (combined armed forces magazine), *Das Schwarze Korps* (the SS magazine) or *Signal* (the largest selling wartime picture magazine in Europe, also under the control of Dr Goebbels) featured much of the work of these men.

Military, patriotic and politically motivated postcards were widely available throughout the Third Reich with outlets on virtually every street corner. The Nazi Party had a ready source of revenue through this medium, in addition to the almost unimaginable propaganda value it provided. Many such postcards were distributed in other countries through the various German embassies before the Second World War, thus many examples turn up bearing foreign stamps and postmarks.

On the political side it has to be said production was almost limitless, particularly where Hitler himself was concerned. Of all political and military figures of the twentieth century, Adolf Hitler probably remains the single, most photographed and filmed personality of all. Many such images (some the work of Hoffmann, Hitler's personal photographer) then reproduced in postcard form depict Hitler in incalculable situations and locations, for example speaking at rallies, meeting the people, with other heads of state, in his Berlin Reich Chancellery, or relaxing at the Berghof. The variety is staggering. As with the majority of German postcards of the period these are high quality photographic prints and not, as one might imagine, machine printed examples, (these do exist, but on a lesser scale).

The idea that Germany's infrastructure had been completely destroyed in 1945 through Allied 'saturation bombing' is open to challenge, in so much that all the materials and equipment necessary for the production of postcards were still in place, right up until the last days of the war. Unit photographers were still in a position to acquire film, to have that film processed, to obtain photographic paper for printing and return the work to Berlin for approval.

In retrospect, this, combined with the fact that the government departments responsible for the design and production of new postage stamps were still operating, now seems inconceivable. This indicates that quantities of paper were available, electric power was in place and printing machinery functional. The idea that such things had been maintained at a time when priorities surely lay elsewhere, shows just how detached these bureaucrats were from the reality around them. That said, it also reveals how much emphasis had been placed on the postcard image, the believed effect it had in inspiring ordinary people and subsequently its contribution to maintaining a nation's morale.

The Nazis utilized this medium with great dexterity to promote strength, a political idea and a way of life, using intensive and invasive propaganda techniques that were very much ahead of their time. Many of their methods of political campaigning and use of the media for electioneering purposes have been adopted by numerous post war politicians around the world. No other nation had come to recognize the potential or appeal of the postcard image for purely propaganda purposes during that period.

Nevertheless, it must be said that other countries did produce patriotic postcards. However they had little impact and were never produced on such a scale as in Hitler's Germany. We must conclude therefore, on the evidence of the remaining postcards from the Nazi period, that the quantity and variety of these images together with the demand for them, even by today's standards, was almost inexhaustible.

Section One

Humble Beginnings

P ostcards numbers 5 to 10 deal with the early life of Adolf Hitler, his family, where he was born and how these things were later used to deliver the idea of Hitler, the man of humble origin who knew hardship and pain, but who, having ultimately triumphed, remained a man of the people.

Klara Hitler

Klara Hitler, undoubtedly the most important female figure in the life of Adolf Hitler. He was her favourite, and she, the mother he adored. This postcard shows the distinct physical resemblance between mother and son; Hitler certainly inherited his mother's piercing gaze. Klara Pölzl was born in Spital, about seventeen kilometres (eleven miles) south of Gmünd, on 20 August 1860. The families of both Hitler's parents had their origins in the Waldviertal region of Lower Austria; this rural wooded landscape inhabited mainly by peasant farmers at that time is located approximately 140 kilometres (88 miles) north-west of Vienna. The Führer's mother has been described as quiet, polite and hard working; when aged twenty she entered domestic service in Vienna.

5. Mother of the Führer.

On 7 January 1885 Klara Pölzl married Alois Hitler (1837-1903), her second cousin. This was not an uncommon practice in the area at that time; however, an episcopal dispensation had to be obtained before the marriage could take place. Alois Hitler was a difficult man, and the marriage was not a particularly happy one, but Klara did all she could to make a home for herself and her husband who worked as a customs officer along the Austrian-German border. They had six children together, four of whom died in childhood; Gustav 1885-87; Ida 1886-88; Otto, born and died Autumn 1887; Adolf 1889-1945; Edmund 1894-1900; and Paula 1896-1960. Adolf was his mother's favourite. While the boy feared his father, who often put young Adolf in his place via word or belt, or both; Klara was gentle, possessive, protective and indulgent. Such extremes could hardly fail to have an impact on Adolf Hitler during his formative years.

Alois Hitler retired from the customs service in 1895. However forty years' regimented lifestyle had left its mark and he found it difficult to settle. Leaving Passau, the border town where Alois had held his last post, the family lived briefly in Hafeld-am-Traun, then Lambach, before moving to Leonding, a village outside Linz. Hitler's father, having suffered respiratory problems for some time, died as the result of a lung haemorrhage on 3 January 1903. The following year Hitler's mother moved the family to Urfahr, a suburb of Linz. Klara, herself not a particularly strong or healthy person went on to develop breast cancer. Hitler, then in Vienna, on learning that his mother was terminally ill immediately returned home to be by her side. Klara spent the last weeks of her life being lovingly nursed by her devoted son; she died on 21 December 1907.

Hitler was absolutely devastated by the death of his mother; the bonds between them had always been very strong. Klara Hitler was laid to rest beside her husband in the small graveyard at Leonding. Hitler would spend the next five years wandering aimlessly around Vienna; until rescued from depression and obscurity by the outbreak of the First World War. Following his appointment as Chancellor in 1933, further visits of the Führer to the graves of his parents in the quiet graveyard near Linz were subject to the usual accompanying publicity; portraying the dutiful son paying his respects. Hitler's only surviving sibling, Paula, made her home in Berchtesgaden after the Second World War where she lived quietly until her death on 1 June 1960. Paula Hitler is buried in Berchtesgaden's Bergfriedhof cemetery, where her final resting place remains carefully tended.

Alois Hitler

Alois Hitler, the father of the future German Chancellor was born in the village of Strones in Lower Austria on 7 June 1837; the result of a liaison between one Johann Georg Heidler, a miller, and Maria Anna Schicklgruber, a peasant girl. The names 'Heidler' and 'Hitler' (a later form of spelling the family name) actually sound very similar when spoken, this may account for early spelling variations and inaccuracies. The couple married five years later in May 1842 at Döllersheim, but it was not until 1876, when he was almost forty years old, that the birth of Alois Schicklgruber would be legitimized; henceforth Alois would use the family name Hitler.

Having served an apprenticeship as a cobbler, Alois, then eighteen, left the area and joined the Imperial Customs Service near Salzburg; thereafter he spent most of his working life serving as a customs officer in and around the area of Braunau am Inn, in Lower Austria. By 1875 Alois Schicklgruber had risen to the rank of Inspector of Customs, a supervisory position bringing responsibilities and, elevating the former peasant's son into the lower middle class. The Führer's father, while carrying out his

6. Father of the Führer.

duties both honestly and efficiently was popular with colleagues and superiors alike. It must be said that, given his background, Alois had actually done extremely well for himself in a world then dominated by a strict social class system.

Alois Hitler would marry three times during his lifetime; in 1864 he married Anna Glasl-Hörer, the daughter of a fellow customs official. Anna was fourteen years older than Alois and the relationship was not a particularly happy one ending in legal separation in 1880. Following a long illness Anna died in 1883. A month later, Alois married again. Franziska Matzelsberger, a hotel cook, had already borne him a child, Alois Jr, outside wedlock in 1882, then Angela in 1883, three months after they were married. Sadly, within a year Franziska had succumbed to tuberculosis.

On 7 January 1885 and, as previously discussed, having acquired the necessary episcopal dispensation required for a marriage between second cousins, Alois married for the third and last time. Klara Pölzl and Alois Hitler were married in the Pommer Inn in Braunau am Inn; the very building where Klara would give birth to her third child Adolf, on 20 April 1889. Alois retired from the customs service in 1895 to receive a pension on which the family could live fairly comfortably. Unable to settle, and finding

7. The room of Adolf Hitler's birth in Braunau am Inn (Upper Austria).

It was in this room that Klara Hitler gave birth to her son Adolf, on 20 April 1889.

While obviously celebrated by his immediate family, the event of Hitler's birth was otherwise without significance. It is therefore reasonable to assume that this photograph, if contemporary, would have been taken for other reasons, or at a later date; consequently we cannot be certain that the room appears exactly as it would have done in April 1889.

8. Braunau am Inn, Salzburger Vorstadt.

Braunau am Inn, a small Austrian town close to the German border. The house on the right, Gasthof Josef Pommer, 15 Salzburger Vorstadt, is where Adolf Hitler was born at 6.30 on the evening of 20 April 1889. Apart from the introduction of modern traffic etc., the scene remains virtually unchanged.

9. Braunau am Inn, Adolf Hitler's birthplace.
As Hitler achieved political success it was inevitable that the place where he was born would also acquire status. Here we see the building adorned with flags and Party symbols. To the left of the doorway stands an SS man, on the right a member of the SA.

retirement difficult, Alois and family moved several times. In 1899 Alois Hitler finally settled in a comfortable house with a garden in the village of Leonding just outside Linz.

The father of the future German Chancellor was an obstinate and unsympathetic man and his relationship with young Adolf was not a happy one; the latter often bearing the brunt of his father's displeasure by way of almost daily beatings. While perhaps sounding brutal, this was common practice at the time; the belief, 'spare the rod and spoil the child' was an idea adhered to by many. The fact that Alois Hitler had found the transition from a regimented working lifestyle to a civilian lifestyle particularly difficult would undoubtedly have added to an already strained relationship between the former customs official and his rebellious son; that, together with his occasional bouts of heavy drinking would have led to even greater domestic disharmony. When young Adolf declared that he wished to pursue the life of an artist, his father, who was planning a life for his son as a civil servant, reacted in the usual way.

Klara Hitler, who had always cared for the two children from her husband's previous marriage, Alois Jr and Angela as if they were her own, having already lost four children; Gustav 1885-87; Ida 1886-88; Otto 1887-87; and Edmund 1894-1900, before Adolf was born, may have overcompensated by lavishing too much attention on the young Adolf. On 3 January 1903 while taking his usual morning walk, Alois Hitler, on entering his local tavern Gasthaus Stiefler, complained of feeling unwell. He sat down and died almost immediately of a pleural haemorrhage. Alois Hitler was buried in the quiet churchyard within sight of the family home two days later. Adolf Hitler, then almost fourteen, reportedly broke down and wept bitterly on seeing his father's body; the unrelenting struggle between domineering father and rebellious son was finally at an end.

10. The Führer's parents' house in Leonding.
This postcard shows the house purchased by Hitler's father in late 1898, some three years after his retirement from the customs service. Alois Hitler paid 7,700 Kronen for the property situated at 16 Michaelsbergstrasse in Leonding. The village of Leonding is five kilometres (three miles) southeast of Linz. The Hitler home was situated opposite St Michael's Church and cemetery. The Führer's parents are buried in St Michael's cemetery. Following the unexpected death of her husband on 3 January 1903, Klara Hitler and her children continued to live in the house until 1904. Leaving Leonding in 1904 the family to Urfhar, a suburb of Linz; Adolf Hitler always considered Linz his hometown.

Following a timely visit to Leonding and his parents' graveside on 12 March 1938, and, with the annexation of Austria imminent, the Führer proclaimed the establishment of the Greater German Reich from the balcony of the Rathaus in Linz later that same day. While there is nothing on the reverse of this image to help date it, the presence of the Nazi flag on the side of the building would indicate that this postcard was produced when Hitler had achieved some notoriety.

Elternhaus des Führers in Leonding

Creating the Führer

Postcards numbers 11 to 15 reveal something of the transformation of Adolf Hitler from a rather awkward individual, obviously not at ease in front of the camera, to that point where his persona almost leaps from the image grasping the viewer's attention. Hitler had worked hard on these problems, these imperfections in the image he wished and needed to project together with his personal photographer, Heinrich Hoffmann. The results, over a relatively short period of time were staggering. Postcards such as these played no small part in creating the belief that in Hitler the German people had found a strong leader, one who would improve their lives in so many ways. These simple postcards projecting Hitler as the consummate political leader gave little indication of the effort involved in their creation, or their true intention. A form of propaganda used so skilfully by the Nazis that its impact was neither apparent, nor accurately assessed during the period of the Third Reich; only when the regime had passed away would its influence be fully understood.

The Führer's unsurpassed popularity reached its zenith during the 1930s. Hitler's appeal transcended traditional class divisions still very much in existence at that time to attract support from a complete cross-section of society; workers, intellectuals and the upper classes, even to members of the German royal family offered their allegiance.

Crown Prince Wilhelm openly supported Hitler during the 1932 presidential elections and Prince Auguste Wilhelm, another of the Kaiser's sons, joined the Nazi Party in 1930, later serving as a *Gruppenführer* (Lieutenant-General) in the SS. Having witnessed Communism's rough attempts to establish itself in Germany, many of the nobility became alarmed at the prospect of such ideology winning popular approval. These genuine fears influenced the decision of many of the aristocracy, amongst them Prince Philipp von Hessen, nephew to the Kaiser and great-grandson of Queen Victoria, to support Hitler.

On one hand, world economic depression and crippling reparations resulting from a particularly harsh Versailles Treaty coupled with inept German government; on the other, Hitler's personal magnetism, charisma and a gift of brilliant oratory combined with an ability to exploit and make political profit from the least opportunity. These explosive ingredients, together with a mastery of previously unseen and innovative electioneering tactics would see Adolf Hitler appointed German Chancellor on 30 January 1933.

11. Reich Chancellor Adolf Hitler. While lacking the impact of later examples, this rather gloomy study of Hitler was probably photographed soon after his having been appointed Reich Chancellor.

It is well known that Edward, Prince of Wales, later King Edward VIII harboured Nazi sympathies. Edward abdicated (in part forced upon him, in part self-inflicted) on 11 December 1936, in favour of the woman he loved, Mrs Wallis Simpson. On 22 October 1937, both visited Hitler at the Berghof then as Duke and Duchess of Windsor. At the same time, powerful elements certainly still existed in England who would have preferred to see Edward on the throne rather than his brother George, who was generally perceived as lacking in both character and personality when compared with Edward. The suggestion has been put forward that had England been defeated during the Second World War, Edward would almost certainly have regained his throne and remained a close friend of Nazi Germany.

12. Reich Chancellor Adolf Hitler.
This obviously posed studio photograph portrays Hitler as rather rigid, and looking somewhat uncomfortable. Nonetheless, a stern gaze deliberately directed away from the camera and the wearing of full uniform helps to achieve a calculated semblance of authority. The Führer is observed holding his ever-present dog-whip; something Hitler carried constantly as a means of personal protection in the early days.

13. Uncaptioned.
An altogether much more self-assured and confident look. This Hoffmann study of the Führer reveals something of Hitler's intense mesmerizing gaze, a characteristic remarked upon by many who met him.

14. Reich Chancellor Adolf Hitler.
A most compelling image projecting the man of destiny. Hitler's expression and bold posture challenges the camera to capture the moment.

15. Uncaptioned.
Hitler reads the *Völkischer Beobachter* (Nationalist Observer); this was the official Nazi Party newspaper that had been acquired in 1920. The headline reads; '*Large Remembrance Meeting in Lipper Land Today*'. The Lipper Land is a region in Nordrhein-Westfalen.

Munich:
City of Struggle & Triumph

Postcards numbers 16 to 34 relate to those places having the greatest significance in Adolf Hitler's early political life. With the exception of Landsberg Prison, all were located in the Bavarian capital, Munich. From the Sternecker Bräustübl, where Hitler first encountered the *Deutscher Arbeiterpartei* (DAP; German Workers' Party) in September 1919, to the impressive buildings around the Königsplatz, the centre of Nazi power in Munich when victory had been achieved. By July 1921, less than two years later, Hitler had won the internal battle for control of the party, by then renamed the *Nationalsocialistische Deutscher Arbeiterpartei* (NSDAP; National Socialist German Workers' Party) and emerged its undisputed leader. *München – Hauptstadt der Bewegung* (Munich – Capital of the Movement) was how the Nazis described Munich. This popular slogan appeared as a caption on numerous postcards, then later as part of the postmark on anything posted in the city during the Third Reich.

16. Aerial view of Munich.

This superb aerial photograph shows the historic centre of the city of Munich. The twin-towers of the Frauenkirche (Church of Our Lady) dominate the image. The tall spire to the right of the Frauenkirche houses the famous Carillon; part of the new Rathaus located on the Marienplatz, built in 1909. The spire to the right of the Rathaus is that of St Peter's Church (built in the 12th century) Munich's oldest parish church. Munich suffered heavy bombing during the Second World War; with over forty-five percent of its buildings destroyed. However, all buildings of historical importance have been painstakingly rebuilt. To the left of the twin-towers of the Frauenkirche, the building with the colonnaded façade is the National Theatre. The Feldherrnhalle is situated close to the National Theatre.

17. Anton Drexler.

Anton Drexler (1884-1942) one of the leading founders of the *Deutscher Arbeiterpartei* (DAP; German Workers' Party). Drexler was born in Munich on 13 June 1884. A locksmith and toolmaker by trade, Drexler did not serve during the First World War; following medical examination he was deemed unfit. Drexler, together with journalist Karl Harrer, engineer and economic theoretician Gottfried Feder, and journalist/writer Dietrich Eckart founded the *Deutscher Arbeiterpartei*, a remnant of the earlier and once quite powerful Pan-German Fatherland Party following the armistice in 1919. Hitler, on attending a meeting of the fledgling *Deutscher Arbeiterpartei,* was impressed more by Drexler's ideas than his oratory. Adolf Hitler became member No. 55 of the DAP on 19 September 1919.

While Hitler identified and fully agreed with the party's ideology, he saw their agenda as lacking the necessary impetus and energy to carry it forward. The DAP asserted the idea of a Jewish-capitalist-Masonic conspiracy; something with which Hitler was in total agreement. It has been said that these first encounters with the DAP provided the spark that ignited Hitler's feelings of anti-Semitism.

Hitler's drive and excellent oratory soon led to his appointment as chairman of the German Workers' Party. In April 1920, and at Hitler's suggestion, the German Workers' Party became the *Nationalsocialistische Deutscher Arbeiterpartei* (NSDAP; National Socialist German Workers' Party). By July 1921 Adolf Hitler was the undisputed leader of the NSDAP with Drexler promoted honorary chairman; a purely symbolic position of no real importance. Drexler left the party in 1923 at a time when the NSDAP was proscribed; he took no part in the Beer-Hall *Putsch.* Following Hitler's release from Landsberg Prison and the subsequent reorganization of the party in 1924/25, Drexler played no part in it; in fact he opposed Hitler. A form of reconciliation did come about in 1930. Anton Drexler rejoined the Nazi Party in 1933 following Hitler's appointment as Chancellor. At the time of his death on 24 February 1942, Anton Drexler was, for the most part, a forgotten man.

18. Foundation corner of the NSDAP in the Sternecker Braüstübl Munich.

The notice on the table reads; 'At this table the Reich Chancellor Adolf Hitler founded the NSDAP.' The Sternecker Braüstübl located in Sterneckerstrasse im Tal, near the Isartor (Isar Gate, 14th century) was indeed the birthplace of the National Socialist German Workers' Party; it was here that Adolf Hitler's political life began on 12 September 1919. This postcard shows that part of the building where the Party held its first meetings. Here the area has been set aside as a shrine to the founder, Adolf Hitler, and other leading Nazis.

19. Adolf Hitler's cell in the prison fortress Landsberg am Lech.

Located on the first floor, room number seven is where Hitler served a small part of the five year sentence he received for his role in the *Putsch* (revolt). Hitler's period of incarceration in Landsberg Prison began on 11 November 1923 following his arrest, and ended on 20 December 1924. Franz Gürtner, Bavarian Minister of Justice, the man who saw to it that the Nazi defendants received lenient minimal sentences during the 1924 trials secured Hitler's early release. During the time he spent there Hitler was treated extremely well; he received visitors in his room and enjoyed unrestricted access to the grounds. It was here, during the latter half of his sentence that he began to dictate *Mein Kampf* (My Struggle) to his fellow prisoners Rudolf Hess and Emil Maurice. On examining this postcard a little more closely we can just make out a large picture of Hitler hanging on the wall to the right, below that a wreath with small Nazi drape attached.

20. Munich, Brown House.

Located at 45 Brienner Strasse and formerly known as the Barlow Palace, this building was acquired by the NSDAP in 1928 using Party funds and contributions from rich industrialists, particularly those of the Rhineland. Following internal alterations to Hitler's own ideas, the 'Brown House' opened as the new headquarters of the NSDAP at the beginning of 1931. The offices of Hitler, Hess, Goebbels and the SA were situated on the second floor; Hitler's office on the left side of the building overlooked the Königsplatz.

21. Munich, Brown House.
Another view of the Brown House, this time photographed from a point near the Königsplatz. On visiting the site today there is nothing to suggest that the building ever existed, no trace remains.

22. Munich, Monument of Remembrance in the Feldherrnhalle.

The Feldherrnhalle (Hall of Heroes) in the centre of Munich stands as a memorial to Germany's past military heroes. It was here on 1 August 1914 before the Feldherrnhalle that Adolf Hitler amidst a large crowd witnessed the German declaration of war. Two days later, on 3 August, Hitler joined the 1st Company, 16th Bavarian Reserve Infantry Regiment, (also known as the List Regiment). Hitler served with distinction during the First World War winning the Iron Cross both First and Second Class; no mean feat for an ordinary soldier.

This postcard shows the bronze memorial plaque erected by the Nazis on the side of the Feldherrnhalle overlooking Residenzstrasse. It was placed there in honour of the sixteen comrades killed in a skirmish with police during the *Putsch* of 9 November 1923; effectively this encounter close to the Feldherrnhalle stopped the revolt in its tracks. Adolf Hitler unveiled this plaque during a remembrance ceremony on 9 November 1933. This important Nazi monument always had two police officers, or in this instance two SS men present as a guard of honour. Passers-by were required to give the Nazi salute.

After the Nazis came to power in 1933 a commemorative march took place through Munich on 9 November each year to honour the memory and sacrifice of those sixteen fallen comrades. The names of those killed during the event are as follows: Felix Allfarth, Andreas Bauriedl, Theodor Casella, Wilhelm Ehrlich, Martin Faust, Anton Hechenberger, Oskar Körner, Karl Kuhn, Carl Laforce, Karl Neubauer, Klaus Maximilian von Pape, Theodor von der Pfordten, Johann Rickmers, Dr Max Erwin von Scheubner-Richter, Lorenz Ritter von Stransky-Griffenfeld, Wilhelm Wolf.

München. Preysing-Palais und Mahnmal gg. Odeonsplatz

23. Munich. Preysing-Palace and Monument towards Odeonsplatz.
It was in this part of Residenzstrasse that the sixteen Nazis died in 1923, and here that the annual commemorative march including Hitler and other leading figures would come to a halt in solemn remembrance of those killed.

24. Munich – Feldherrnhalle – pigeon feeding.
The front of the imposing Feldherrnhalle as viewed from Odeonsplatz. On the left of the structure, as we look into Residenzstrasse, we can just make out the dark shape of the monument to the Nazi dead situated on that side of the Feldherrnhalle.

25. The Feldherrnhalle as photographed in 2004; apart from the obvious removal of the symbols of the regime there appears little to distinguish between this image and postcard number 24.

26. Munich. Führer House at Königsplatz.
Hitler's stylish Munich residence, the building remains unchanged and is located on Arcis Strasse near the junction with Brienner Strasse. Standing before the building today, now a school of music, one can still make out where the fixing points that attached the large eagles to the façade above the porticoes were located. The structures observed on the right of the image with large columns are the Ehrentempeln.

27. The Führer House photographed in 2004 remains unchanged; today it is the *Staatliche Hochschule für Musik* (State High School for Music). The Ehrentempeln, (seen clearly in postcards numbers 28 and 29) constructed as a final resting place for the fallen comrades of 1923, these temples of solemn remembrance for the Nazis, have long since disappeared.

28. Munich. Brown House with Führer House and Ehrentempel.
The Königsplatz, on the left stands the Führer House, the location of Hitler's offices and those of his staff in Munich. To the right of the Führer House and on either side of Brienner Strasse (behind the central lamp-post) stand the Ehrentempeln, (Temples of Honour). The large building observed in the background between the Ehrentempeln is the Brown House. These imposing buildings around the Königsplatz were designed by Prof Paul Ludwig Troost (1878-1934). Troost was Hitler's favourite German architect, following the death of Troost in 1934, this honour passed to Albert Speer.

29. Munich. Brown House with Führer House and Ehrentempel.
The view across the Königsplatz and down Brienner Strasse towards the Obelisk in Karolinenplatz. It was along this stretch of the Brienner Strasse that many Nazi office buildings were located. By late 1939 the Party had over 6,000 people employed in this small area alone, the building on the right was the *Verwaltungsbau der NSDAP* (NSDAP Administration Building). Today the building serves as a museum and associated offices. Beyond the Obelisk and at the other end of Brienner Strasse one finds the Feldherrnhalle. This particular image shows the buildings on either side of the street to be a perfect mirror image of each other, behind the Ehrentempel on the left stands the Brown House. This part of Munich survived heavy Allied bombing during the latter stages of the Second World War with little damage.

30. Munich, Ehrentempel for the Fallen of 9 November 1923.

This postcard shows how the remains of the sixteen Nazi martyrs killed during the unsuccessful 1923 revolt were later housed within the two Ehrentempeln. Each of the Ehrentempeln held eight heavy cast-iron sarcophagi. Central to each sarcophagus lid was the national emblem; a large eagle and swastika. An inscription above the eagle read; '*Der Letzte Appell*' (The Last Roll Call), while the name of the occupant then appeared below the national emblem in each case. The building observed on the right outside the Ehrentempel is the Propyläen, built in 1862, on the left stands the Antikensammlungen.

On the evening of 7 November 1935, and following the exhumation of their remains, the martyrs of the Beer-Hall *Putsch* were brought to the Feldherrnhalle where they spent the night. Early next morning, 8 November, Munich residents were awakened by the noise of a sixteen-gun salute. Later that day, the sarcophagi were borne through the city on carriages to the sound of the Horst Wessel Song being played on loudspeakers. Tens of thousands of spectators and cordons of SA men lined the route. On reaching the Ehrentempeln, and with due ceremony, each sarcophagus was respectfully placed inside one of the two temples. The Führer and leading members of the Nazi hierarchy played key roles throughout the days' solemn proceedings. The Ehrentempeln were instantly 'National shrines to the German people' where the remains of the role-models of Nazi self-sacrifice were to be forever honoured.

The Propyläen and the Antikensammlungen stand in the Königsplatz today. As for the Ehrentempeln; the remains of the occupants of the sixteen sarcophagi were removed and quietly reburied without ceremony in mid 1945. In January 1947 the relatively undamaged Ehrentempeln were demolished by order of the US Army occupation authorities.

31. Munich. House of German Art.

Located on Prinzregentenstrasse near the junction with Königinstrasse, the House of German Art was designed by Hitler's favourite architect Prof Paul Ludwig Troost (1878-1934), together with considerable input from the Führer himself. Troost, a member of the Nazi Party since 1924 had worked on the conversion of the Barlow Palace, later known as the Brown House. Hitler laid the cornerstone for the large neo-classical House of German Art on 15 October 1933. When Troost died in January 1934, Albert Speer was called upon to oversee the completion of the project according to Troost's original plans.

The House of German Art officially opened on 18 July 1937 with an exhibition of work by the best Nazi artists. At the same time an exhibition of what the regime considered 'degenerate art' was on show in the Hofgarten Gallery across the street. This, the first truly representative Third Reich style colonnaded building remains unchanged and continues to perform the function for which it was originally constructed, a centre for the exhibition of art.

32. Munich: House of German Art.

This postcard shows the House of German Art from the opposite side to that viewed in the previous image, postcard number 31. With a commemorative postmark stating; *München – Hauptstadt der Bewegung – Tag der Deutschen Kunst – 16.7.1939* (Munich – Capital of the Movement – Day of German Art – 16 July 1939), this period image reveals something of the hustle and bustle of everyday life in that part of the city. The tall column topped with the statue standing at the opposite end of the Prinzregentenstrasse is the 'Angel of Peace' erected in 1899. This monument stands on the east bank of the River Isar, across the Luitpoldbrücke.

33. The historic meeting on 18 June, 1940 in Munich. Journey through the city.

A motorcade carrying Hitler and Mussolini having passed under the Karlstor makes its way through the city. Cheering crowds waving German and Italian flags line the route saluting the two leaders. France has been defeated. A matter of days later, on 21 June, the Führer would deliver the terms of surrender to the French. On Hitler's instructions, the very railway carriage in which the French had accepted the German surrender in 1918 was transported from its place in a Paris museum and, returned to the exact spot it had occupied twenty-two years earlier in the Forest of Compiègne. The French were then forced to suffer a re-enactment of 1918; this time however, they were not the victors. In performing this action Hitler believed he had reversed the humiliation inflicted on the German nation at the end of the First World War, the much hated Versailles Treaty was finally laid to rest. Three days later, by order of the Führer, the Compiègne site was cleared and the railway carriage brought to Berlin. In early 1945 Hitler ordered the SS to destroy the carriage.

34. The Karlstor today, compared with postcard number 33 it is obvious that many of the surrounding buildings have been renovated or replaced over the years, partly the result of wartime damage and simply the need to modernize. Munich, in keeping with other major cities in today's world moves continually forward.

Berchtesgaden: Fount of Inspiration

Postcards numbers 35 to 45 deal with the town of Berchtesgaden. The area surrounding this beautiful ancient market town is a patchwork of meadow-clad hills and forests rising to bare, rugged, snow-capped Alpine peaks, with mirror-like mountain lakes and fast-flowing rivers. On observing these images one can appreciate and fully understand why Adolf Hitler would choose this region to establish his country retreat. The indescribable rejuvenating essence of the area soothes and claims one's very soul on first contact; then, like some unseen irresistible force, it continually draws the helplessly spellbound individual back unto itself, time, and time again. Such may have been the effect of this region upon Adolf Hitler; that, together with it being reminiscent of his native Austria lying across the nearby border would have proved a combination too strong to resist. Small wonder therefore that the Führer would describe this region as his *Wahlheimat* (chosen homeland).

35. Berchtesgaden.

The charming market town of Berchtesgaden. This early postcard probably dates from the 1920s and shows the town from an angle popular with photographers, in this instance the magnificent Watzmann dominates the background.

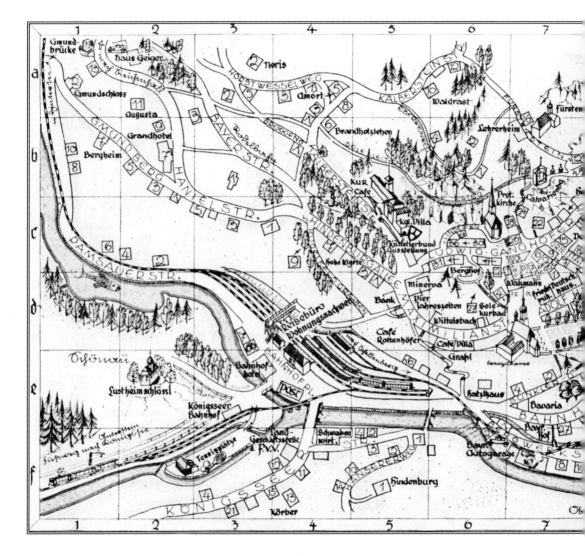

Period map of the town of Berchtesgaden

This 1934 map of the town of Berchtesgaden is exceedingly rare. I stumbled upon it by sheer accident in a second-hand shop in Berchtesgaden in 2009. I could hardly believe my eyes when I noticed it standing in a battered old frame that was literally falling apart; nonetheless the map itself is in superb condition. This printed map, the original of which has been beautifully hand drawn, measures 17 x 38 centimetres (7x15 inches). However, what is of particular interest, is that even at this early stage, we can see that a number of street names have already been changed to reflect the influence and popularity of the new regime.

Map reference A3/4 shows the Horst Wessel Weg, named after Nazi martyr Horst Wessel who was shot in the head by Communists when he answered his door on 14 January in 1930. Wessel, a member of the SA, is best known for writing the *Horst Wessel Lied*, the song became the official Nazi Party anthem. D7/8 shows the Adolf Hitler Str. C13/14 shows the Dietrich Eckart Str., named after Hitler's old friend and mentor. Eckart died in Berchtesgaden on 23 December 1923. The

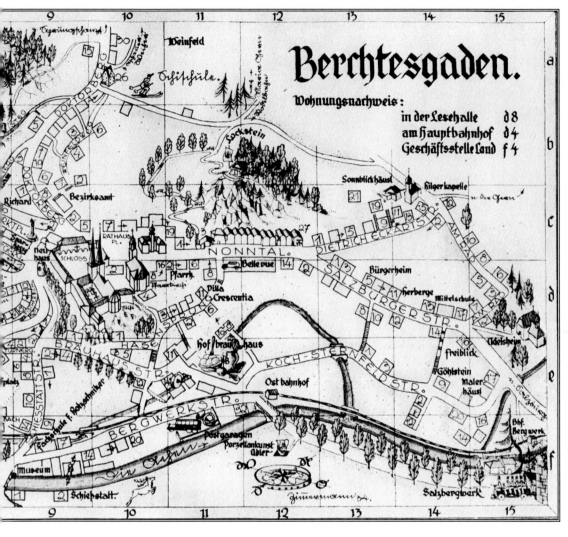

'Sonnblickhäusl' where Eckart died can also be found at map reference C13/14. Eckart is buried in the town Friedhof (Cemetery).

The popular Hotel Geiger, map reference A2, opened in 1874. During the Second World War the Geiger was a rest and recreation centre for officers in the Luftwaffe. Sadly, insolvency led to the closure of the hotel in the 1990s. B2 shows the location of the Grand Hotel. Bought by the Nazis in 1936 and following extensive refurbishment the Grand Hotel re-opened under the new name Hotel Berchtesgadener Hof. Map reference D/E12, an area of open ground between Koch-Sternfeld-Str. and the smaller of the two rivers is where the Nazis held many open air meetings in the early days. E4 shows the location of the train station. The station was rebuilt in 1937 and remains virtually unchanged. The 'Salzbergwerk' (Salt Mines), the source of much of Berchtesgaden's wealth over many centuries are found at map reference F15. The small Nazi flag at map reference B11 pinpoints the location of the Lockstein, a restaurant high above the town. F8 shows the location of the Schießstättsbrücke, the bridge over the Berchtesgadener Ache and the beginning of the Salzbergstraße, the road to the Obersalzberg. Finally, map reference F12/13 reveals the artist's signature, Zimmermann, and the year 34.

43

36. Uncaptioned.
Berchtesgaden in the full grip of winter, this card bears a postmark of 23.1.23; Hitler's first visit to the area in May later that year would leave a lasting impression on the future Chancellor. On his return to the region as Führer in the 1930s, it was Hitler who would leave a lasting impression on Berchtesgaden and the surrounding area.

37. Berchtesgaden today, obviously there has been a degree of development in the area since postcard number 36 was produced, however, both images are comparatively similar in most respects and many features remain unchanged.

38. Berchtesgaden Market Square with Watzmann.
Berchtesgaden's quaint market square, quiet and peaceful. In the background above the rooftops stands the mighty Watzmann. Bearing a postmark dated 12.9.42, the sender tells of their journey from Freilassing to Berchtesgaden by train, how warm the weather is and the wonderfully clear view of the mountains. Freilassing is close to the Austrian border and Salzburg; when travelling to Berchtesgaden by rail one changes trains at Freilassing.

39. The market square in 2004. The fact that this photograph was taken early on an October morning may account for the lack of tourists in this particular instance. Nonetheless, the two images are unmistakably the same market square. Given that over seventy years have elapsed since postcard number 38 was produced the differences between the two images are minimal.

40. Market Square in Berchtesgaden.
Here we view the market square from the opposite side to that seen in postcard number 38. In this instance buildings stand adorned with flags, and swastikas that appear to have been fashioned from the soft ends of pine branches. This image for whatever reason certainly dispels the idea of a town overflowing with Party faithful visiting the area so loved by their Führer. (One must accept that a period of several years may exist between the time of origination of an image and the date of the postmark; therefore any image may represent a different timeframe.)

41. Berchtesgaden with Watzmann.
A peaceful scene showing Berchtesgaden in autumn, chimney smoke drifts skywards and all trees stand bare save the evergreens. With a postmark of 16.9.41, the message on the reverse makes no reference to a war already entering its third year.

42. Berchtesgaden with Hochkalter.
The town as viewed from across the valley with the Hochkalter in the background. Posted on 14.8.41, the sender greets her friends referring to everyday things, the length of her journey, the weather and the stunning view of the Watzmann from her hotel.

43. Berchtesgaden from the Marxenhöhe with Watzmann, Schönfeldspitze and Funtenseetauern.
Berchtesgaden and its magnificent surroundings photographed from the Marxenhöhe. The Marxenhöhe, a hill standing at 829 metres (2,720 feet) is located northeast of Berchtesgaden. In the background stands the unmistakable Watzmann; the distinctive 'pyramid shaped' peak on the extreme left is the Schönfeldspitze at 2,653 metres (8,704 feet). The 'castle-like' building in the centre of the image was the *Distriktskrankenhaus* (District Hospital) built in the mid 1800s. This beautiful building was designed by the famous Munich architect, Professor Gabriel Seidl (1848-1913). Seidl designed many buildings in Munich and grand houses around Berchtesgaden, including Villa Doris and Villa Schoenhäusl. The Berchtesgaden District Hospital was demolished between the wars. An equally impressive building constructed in a similar style now occupies the site where the former hospital once stood on Metzenleitenweg. Written in ink on the reverse are the words; '19 July 1937 Holiday.'

47

44. Berchtesgaden with Watzmann.

This charming scene shows Berchtesgaden in the grip of winter. The twin spires in the centre are those of Stiftskirche (Collegiate Church) while to the right of the spires we see the bell-tower of the Andreaskirche (St Andrew's Church). This postcard was posted on 9 December 1930 to an address in Innsbruck, Austria.

45. Berchtesgaden with Watzmann and Hochkalter.

This postcard was mailed in Marktschellenberg on 21.10.1932. Marktschellenberg, a village approximately six kilometres from Berchtesgaden straddles the road leading from Berchtesgaden to Salzburg. While Hitler had already established his country retreat on the Obersalzberg by the time this card was posted, it was his appointment as Chancellor on 30 January 1933 that heralded the beginning of irreversible changes to this beautiful Alpine region. If one could occupy the position adopted by the photographer of this early 1930s image today, it would reveal many changes; the most obvious being the urbanization of the pasture in the foreground.

Obersalzberg: Spiritual Retreat

Postcards numbers 46 to 51 show the Obersalzberg and surrounding countryside in the early years before the Nazi regime had completely taken over the area. At the time these images were recorded on film, neither the photographers, nor the residents of the homes depicted here, could have possibly imagined the scale of change soon to engulf this peaceful region; change so great it would alter both the landscape and their lives, totally, and forever.

46. Berchtesgaden, Obersalzberg towards the south.
The lower slopes of the Obersalzberg, a patchwork of small farms and rolling pastures, typical of the area prior to the mid 1930s. The town itself can just be seen on the extreme right of the image.

47. Obersalzberg near Berchtesgaden.

Another early scene, the house on the extreme right is Villa Bechstein. This property, built in 1899, was purchased by Edwin Beckstein, a member of the famous piano manufacturing family in February 1927. The house was situated a short distance below Haus Wachenfeld. Helene Bechstein, an ardent Hitler supporter, allowed the Nazi Party to use the property as a guest house. The Goebbels family stayed there many times, as occasionally did Italian leader Benito Mussolini when visiting Hitler on the Obersalzberg. Bormann bought the property in November 1935. Had it not been for the fact that Villa Beckstein was a Nazi Party guesthouse it would not have survived Bormann's destruction of property.

The two buildings in the centre foreground formed the Baumgartlehen. All other buildings in this photograph were the homes and out-buildings of other local farmers. These were demolished in late 1937/early 1938 following Bormann's takeover of the Obersalzberg. Hitler's teahouse at Mooslahnerkopf would be built on the opposite side of the forested area in the centre of this photograph; directly opposite the Baumgartlehen. The pasture-land we see here now forms the bulk of the nine-hole Obersalzberg golf course.

48. Café Restaurant Steiner on the Obersalzberg.
Built in 1883 this stylish property was situated by the roadside a short distance below Haus Wachenfeld. The Steiner was an integral part of the small community of Obersalzberg. Johann and Thekla Kurz bought Gasthof Steiner in 1920. They had a flourishing business; for in addition to being a café and restaurant, a post-office and a bakery were also located on the premises. Flying the flag however did not prevent the owners losing this fine property; like so many in the vicinity of Hitler's residence the Steiner was demolished soon after Bormann bought the property in March 1937.

49. Hindenburg Hill. Obersalzberg with view towards Salzburg.
The central area of this image would later form the heart of the Nazi complex on the Obersalzberg. The building seen highlighted on the right was the home of Dr Richard Seitz. Purchased by Martin Bormann in 1936 and following extensive renovation, this property became the Bormann family home.

Obersalzberg bei Berchtesgaden mit Landhaus Göring. Bayr. Hochland. 9747 Mo

50. Obersalzberg near Berchtesgaden with Landhaus Göring. Bavarian Highlands.

This postcard clearly reveals the elevated position enjoyed by the Göring family home on the Obersalzberg in relation to other buildings in the immediate area. *Landhaus* (country house) Göring is seen standing in open ground on the right. Built in 1934 the property offered commanding views over the entire region, together with a level of privacy beyond that of other residents. The house stood in that part of the Obersalzberg known as Eckerbichl, the most beautiful and sunny spot on the mountain. As we can see the Obersalzberg village still existed when this photograph was taken in late 1934 early 1935.

Bearing a postmark dated 22.8.35; it was around this time that Haus Wachenfeld underwent its greatest transformation, a metamorphosis from which the Berghof would emerge. It was also around this time that Bormann began showing an interest in acquiring the home of Dr Richard Seitz.

51. Obersalzberg near Berchtesgaden, Bavarian Highlands.

The existence of the flag on the hilltop on the right implies that Hitler was already Chancellor at the time this photograph was taken. The flag also pin-points the exact location of the 'Adolf-Hitler-Höhe' (Adolf-Hitler-Hill) on the Obersalzberg, see caption number 58. This peaceful landscape, unchanged for generations, would soon undergo dramatic change as the Nazis began to introduce their ambitious plans for the area. Some of the original buildings are identified as follows; 1. Marienhaüsl, 2. Haus Heß, 3. Haus Hudler, 4. Haus Adler, 5. Haus Göring, 6. Kindersanatorium Dr Seitz, 7. Villa Seitz, 8. Oberwurflehen. With the exception of Haus Göring, all these properties would eventually be demolished following voluntary sale, or compulsory purchase. Bormann's 'enforcer', Gotthard Färber, certainly got results. Reluctant property owners who fell foul of Bormann were encouraged to move out when Färber's men moved in and literally took the roofs off their houses.

Haus Wachenfeld: A Country Home

The following photographs (numbers 52 to 60) have been selected from a series of half sized postcard images by Hoffmann; each series came in a small card packet containing twenty photographs. Hitler's immense popularity at this time dictated the production of these small, more personal images. It is reasonable to assume that such photographs depicting Hitler and other Nazi related subject matter were not only collected by individuals, but were given and received as gifts. Many of these same images are encountered in the usual postcard sizes.

52. View of the Untersberg from Haus Wachenfeld.
While framed in the doorway leading to the balcony on the first floor, Hitler looks out across the valley towards Austria. In the background stands the Untersberg.

53. Our Führer, the great friend of animals.
In feeding these small deer Hitler portrays the gentle image of a man in tune with nature. On Hitler's instructions, the landscape and all wildlife contained within the area of the Obersalzberg were to be preserved. Furthermore, he stated that all construction on the mountain should be unobtrusive in an attempt to maintain a degree of harmony with the natural surroundings.

54. Sun terrace at Haus Wachenfeld.
While bathed in sunshine Haus Wachenfeld's main terrace offered truly spectacular views towards the town of Berchtesgaden, the legendary Untersberg across the valley and, weather permitting, the city of Salzburg in neighbouring Austria.

55. View from the terrace of Haus Wachenfeld towards Berchtesgaden.
The patience of the Party faithful waiting on the road below Haus Wachenfeld is rewarded as the Führer appears on the terrace. Such scenes were quite commonplace through the early years of Hitler's Chancellorship. The small house visible on the left by the roadside is Haus Salzburgblick. This property stood close to where the last SS guardhouse that controlled access to the inner security zone would be built in late 1936 early 1937 (see image 129). Unfortunately such close proximity to the Führer's property meant Martin Bormann ordered Haus Salzburgblick be demolished following the introduction of these increased security measures on the Obersalzberg.

56. A little one's visit on Obersalzberg.
By engaging this endearing child in this attentive way, Hitler projects the image of a caring and approachable leader; a man truly in touch with his people, even with children. Nazi innovation involving the production of these seductive vote-winning images has not been wasted on today's politicians; similarly, they too fully appreciate the appeal and importance of being seen and photographed in the company of such delightful subjects. This particular child, Bernile Nienau, and her relationship with Hitler will be discussed later.

57. View from Haus Wachenfeld towards the Untersberg.
Hitler, posing near the house, gazes thoughtfully across the valley in the direction of his birthplace, Austria. On a clear day the city of Salzburg in Austria was visible from Haus Wachenfeld. This may have been another reason for Hitler's love of the Obersalzberg. In the background we see part of the Untersberg massif. Standing at 1,972 metres (6,470 feet) the Untersberg straddles the German/Austrian border.

58. 'Adolf Hitler Hill' on the Obersalzberg, (1,000 metres above sea level).
Two young women, having reached a point on the Obersalzberg then known as 'Adolf Hitler Hill', give the unmistakable Nazi salute while posing for the camera. A strategically placed flag acts like a magnet attracting people to the spot that was located close to the home of Hermann Göring. In addition to the flag, the location had a stone marker with two plaques attached. The inscription on the larger plaque read, '*Reichskanzler Adolf-Hitler-Höhe 21 März 1933*', this referred to the first opening of the Reichstag under Hitler's Chancellorship. The smaller plaque had a quotation by Bavarian poet and novelist Ludwig Ganghofer; '*Wer Gött lieb hat, lässt er fallen, in's Berchtesgad'ner Land*' (He whom God loves, He drops into Berchtesgadener Land).

59. The Führer on Obersalzberg.
Hitler, in sitting alone on the perimeter wall of the terrace in this way succeeds in communicating the idea of the somewhat solitary, pensive figure; it is he, and he alone who must bear the weight of leadership.

60. The resting Führer with his faithful guard.
Hitler, the ordinary man enjoying life's simple pleasures rests with his faithful companion, his German Shepherd, 'Blonda'. While this image might conjure such interpretation, the fact remains that Hitler had great affection for his dogs and always enjoyed walking on the Obersalzberg. However, these photographs were carefully staged to deliberately present the Führer as a man who enjoyed the great outdoors; a visionary far removed from the banalities of everyday life.

Continuing under the heading 'Haus Wachenfeld: A Country Home', the following postcards, numbers 61 to 120, are the more usually encountered, standard-sized postcard images. These high-quality photographic prints were available at numerous outlets throughout Germany during the Third Reich period; everywhere from newsagents to train stations to souvenir shops and government buildings.

These postcards deal with the unpretentious and traditional Alpine cottage purchased by Adolf Hitler on 17 September 1932; the sale was completed on 26 June 1933. Covering various stages of renovation the following images reveal the improvements Hitler had carried out to the property prior to the almost complete remodelling programme of 1935/36. Thereafter the Führer's country residence would generally be referred to as the 'Berghof'.

61. Haus Wachenfeld Berchtesgaden – Obersalzberg.
This postcard dating from the early 1930s presents the house as it would have appeared to Hitler at the time he purchased the property in 1933. As yet there is no evidence of any renovation work having taken place; the area to the left of the house remains untouched while trees still grow close around the building.

A promotional postmark on the reverse reads; *Skimeisterschaft der Deutschen 8-12 Februar 1934, Berchtesgaden, Bayerische Alpen*. (The German Skiing Championships to be held in Berchtesgaden from 8 -12 February 1934).

Das Hitlerhaus,
bersalzberg bei Berchtesgaden.

62. The Hitler House, Obersalzberg near Berchtesgaden.

Haus Wachenfeld photographed in its original state, peaceful, traditional and possessing great rustic charm; as yet no work has begun. The original path leading to the house can be seen in the foreground. Later, and as the property underwent major renovation, this small footpath would be replaced with a drive giving access to the mountain road on the opposite side of the house. The building glimpsed in the background, upper right, is almost certainly the Unterwurflehen built in 1900. This became home to *SS-Sturmbannführer* (Major) Spahn, Obersalzberg administration officer.

63. Uncaptioned.

This early image sees a rather uncomfortable looking Hitler attempting to relax while on the Obersalzberg. Capable however of making any unwanted visitors feel even more uncomfortable, is his unnerving, everwatchful companion, his black German Shepherd, 'Muck'.

64. Residence of Adolf Hitler on the Obersalzberg near Berchtesgaden.
Haus Wachenfeld photographed from a point just below Hotel zum Türken looking towards the Reiteralpe. The modest pathway leading from the road to the house passes a small enclosed vegetable garden seen in the foreground on the right.

65. Hitler's favourite place to stay in Berchtesgaden.
It is unusual to see Haus Wachenfeld presented from this particular angle. This photograph was taken in the early 1930s. On the extreme left and below Haus Wachenfeld we see part of the Freidinglehen, the farm of Hitler's neighbour, Josef Rasp. Karl Schuster, the owner of Hotel zum Türken was Hitler's closest neighbour; next to Schuster in terms of proximity to Haus Wachenfeld, was the home of Josef Rasp. Martin Bormann, following his decision not to allow private individuals to live inside the Führer's closed-off area, forced Rasp off his farm. Following compulsory purchase in mid 1936 Freidinglehen was demolished soon after. It was the view across the valley towards Austria that never failed to inspire Hitler, continually drawing him back to this magical landscape; this region, having once cast its spell, will not let you go.

66. The Führer in Berchtesgaden.
While accompanied by Hitler Youth Leader, Baldur von Schirach (standing behind Hitler) and Hermann Göring, head of the Luftwaffe (extreme right), the Führer engages his adoring public on the road close to Haus Wachenfeld. In the background we glimpse part of Hotel zum Türken.

67. The house of the Führer.
April 1933 and the renovation of Haus Wachenfeld gets underway. What would become the conservatory (also called the Winter Garden) is visible at an early stage of construction on the left to the front of the house. The whole scene is that of a building site; as such it is surprising this image was ever released, presenting the Führer's residence in a state of disorder.

68. Chancellor Adolf Hitler in Berchtesgaden.

Bearing a postmark of 29.12.33, this image sees Hitler in the company of a small group standing before Haus Wachenfeld. The scene appears non-contrived, informal and relaxed. Apparently surprised, the man on the right draws attention to the presence of the photographer. The man second from the left is Julius Schreck, Hitler's chauffeur and bodyguard. At the time of his death on 16 May 1936, Schreck held the rank of *Brigadeführer* (Brigadier) in the SS. Schreck, who was buried in Munich, was given a state funeral attended by most of the Nazi hierarchy. Adolf Hitler delivered the eulogy.

69. Hitler Youth in front of the Führer's house on the Obersalzberg.

Flag-bearing Hitler Youth congregate on the road near Haus Wachenfeld as an SS man makes his way through the group towards the photographer. Looking at the house itself it is obvious that further alterations are underway; the grassed slope below the conservatory has been removed to accommodate the newly constructed garage, while a temporary workmen's hut on the right has building materials stacked behind it. This image also shows the new drive on this side of the property. The introduction of the new drive provided vehicular access to Haus Wachenfeld making the original small footpath seen in postcard number 62 virtually redundant thereafter.

70. High above the clouds! Reich Chancellor Adolf Hitler's country house 'Wachenfeld' on Obersalzberg (1000m) towards the Reiteralpe.
This postcard reveals yet another stage in the development of Haus Wachenfeld. In this instance it is the small single-storey extension on the left, partially obscured by bushes and the woodpile in front of it. The presence of building material lying on the roof of this latest addition indicates that work is ongoing.

71. Reich Chancellor Adolf Hitler (standing right) on the terrace of his country house Wachenfeld entertaining a little girl from Berchtesgaden (Obersalzberg 1,000m).
Here the conservatory and garage mentioned in caption 69 are observed at close quarters. Tradesmen are working on the property and building materials lie scattered all around. Hitler, in the company of an unidentified man in uniform and a local child, surveys the scene from the terrace above; to the left of this group yet another man captures the moment on film.

72. Adolf Hitler's country house Wachenfeld seen from Alpine Hotel Türken.
Here we view Haus Wachenfeld and the outstretched valley below from the now extended terrace at Hotel zum Türken; again this image clearly demonstrates the close proximity of the two properties. In the end Hitler became irritated by the constant public attention he received from the hotel terrace due to its position. This led to ill feeling between the Führer and the Schuster family who owned the hotel, culminating in the property being confiscated in 1933.

73. View from Alpine Hotel zum Türken to Adolf Hitler's country house Wachenfeld and Reiteralpe Mountains (Obersalzberg 1,000m).
This pleasant and relaxed scene shows guests enjoying the view from the hotel terrace towards Haus Wachenfeld. This image gives a good indication of how near Hotel zum Türken actually was to the Führer's residence. The terrace provided an excellent viewing platform constantly used by those hoping to catch a glimpse of Hitler when he was on the Obersalzberg.

74. Photographed in 2004 and from a similar position to that of the previous postcard number 73, the former site of Haus Wachenfeld appears very overgrown and virtually unrecognizable. Part of the service road which led to the rear of the later constructed Berghof remains visible on the hillside in the lower foreground.

75. A little one's visit on Obersalzberg.

Possessing all the elements of an unexpected photo opportunity, the little girl chosen to be photographed with the Führer appears somewhat bewildered; Hitler on the other hand fully realized the appeal of such images. Politicians do not change! The man standing in the background is Erich Kempka (16.9.1910-24.1.75). Kempka joined the Nazi Party in April 1930. He held the rank of *Obersturmbannführer* (Lieutenant-Colonel) in the SS. Kempka was Hitler's personal chauffeur from 1934 until April 1945. He was captured by US troops in Berchtesgaden on 20 June 1945.

76. Adolf Hitler's dwelling house on Obersalzberg near Berchtesgaden.
Reverse reads: **The high Berchtesgaden health resort Obersalzberg.**
Peaceful and picturesque Haus Wachenfeld as viewed from the main terrace of Hotel zum Türken.
The Obersalzberg and surrounding area had long been considered a health resort due to the purity of the mountain air, particularly for those with breathing ailments or in need of recuperation.

77. Haus Wachenfeld. In expectation of the Führer.
Hundreds of people line the road leading down from Hotel zum Türken towards Haus Wachenfeld in expectation of seeing their Führer. In this particular instance the public have been permitted to make their way halfway up the drive leading to the house. This previously un-encountered and unusual practice makes this a rare image.

78. Reich Chancellor Adolf Hitler in Berchtesgaden.
Hitler, Goebbels and Schreck stand by the drive leading to Haus Wachenfeld. Julius Schreck (1898-1936) joined the Party in 1921; Schreck served time with Hitler in Landsberg prison following the failed *Putsch*. A close comrade of the Führer, Schreck became the first commander of the newly formed SS in 1925 and later assumed the role of personal chauffeur/bodyguard to Hitler. While most accounts of Schreck's death on 16 May 1936 state it to be the result of a motoring accident, others suggest he died of meningitis. The open gates observed behind Goebbels in this instance, were a temporary feature at the property and appear in very few images.

79. Obersalzberg (1,000m) towards Berchtesgaden and Adolf Hitler's country house Wachenfeld.
The Obersalzberg as viewed from a point close to the home of Dr Seitz, (later Bormann's house). In the foreground stands Hotel zum Türken, beyond that Haus Wachenfeld, while Berchtesgaden itself sits peacefully in the valley below. In the foreground on the extreme left is the Marienhäusl, demolished after 1933 to provide part of the site for the kindergarten; above that again on the left is the Bodner farm, also later demolished.

80. We all want to give the Führer our hand.
While accompanied by members of the SS, a fatherly Hitler greets some children selected from the daily gathering on the road near Haus Wachenfeld. The taller girl on the left patiently awaits an opportunity to request the Führer's autograph on the postcard that she carries; quite customary on such occasions. In the background stands Hotel zum Türken.

81. Haus Wachenfeld, country house of the Reich Chancellor in Berchtesgaden.
Photographed from a point uphill and almost behind the property, this image gives an indication of the distance to the mountains opposite and the spectacular views afforded on a clear day.

82. Reich Chancellor Adolf Hitler's Haus Wachenfeld - Obersalzberg.
An image of superb quality reflecting the simple charm of the Führer's mountain home, the one place he continually found peace and refuge from all the complications and pressures associated with statesmanship. Here he could relax and lead the simple life he often yearned for.

83. The Führer on the terrace of Haus Wachenfeld.
A smiling Hitler wearing a traditional Bavarian jacket greets the crowds lining the road below the house with the Nazi salute. Such scenes were commonplace during the early days of Hitler's Chancellorship prior to the creation of the *Führersperrgebiet* (Restricted Area of the Führer) and the introduction of greater security on the Obersalzberg after 1936.

84. A little one's visit on Obersalzberg.

This little girl, Rosa Bernile Nienau from Munich became a favourite on the Obersalzberg. She and her mother, a doctor's widow from Munich, visited the Obersalzberg for the first time in 1932. The following year, 1933, when informed that he and the child shared the same birthday, 20th April, Hitler singled her out from the large crowd gathered below Haus Wachenfeld. Having chatted to the lively and engaging little girl Hitler invited her up to the house. The Führer then walked hand-in-hand with the child back to Haus Wachenfeld. Bernile was treated to strawberries and whipped cream on the terrace on that occasion. Thereafter Hitler often invited Frau Nienau and her charming daughter to visit him on the Obersalzberg. Like Hitler, Bernile's father had won the Iron Cross First Class during the First World War. Heinrich Hoffmann took numerous photographs of Hitler together with Bernile during her visits.

In 1934 an unknown Party busybody with nothing better to do began looking into Bernile's ancestry. When it was discovered that the child's paternal grandmother was Jewish, Martin Bormann was informed. Bormann took it upon himself to tell Frau Nienau that she and her daughter should not to return to the Obersalzberg; they were no longer welcome. As was Bormann's way, he did not inform Hitler of his actions. As time passed Hitler enquired why it was that Bernile no longer came to see him. Bormann, the great manipulator, simply avoided the subject. Bad feeling between Bormann and Heinrich Hoffmann over the publication of a book containing images of Bernile with the Führer resulted in Hoffmann telling Hitler what had occurred. Hitler was furious with those who had denounced his little friend. He told Hoffmann, 'There are some people who have a positive genius for spoiling all my little pleasures!'

Despite knowing that Bernile was 'Vierteljüdin' (quarter Jewish), Hitler continued to correspond with the child. Bernile and her mother resumed their visits to Haus Wachenfeld and this continued until 1938. In May that year the intervention of one of Hitler's adjutants finally brought an end to these visits. Hitler's little friend died in a Munich hospital on 5 October 1943, aged seventeen. She was buried in Munich's Westfriedhof. While undoubtedly endearing images, these Hoffmann photographs of Hitler and Bernile had great propaganda value in the way they were used to present the Führer as fond of children, a man truly in touch with the young. Nevertheless, Hitler's contemporaries, among them members of his own staff, have stated that he was genuinely very fond of children and enjoyed their company.

The reverse of this postcard bears a number of special commemorative postmarks celebrating the 1938 Nürnberg Rally. These annual rallies attended by Hitler and other members of the Nazi hierarchy attracting hundreds of thousands of people. Those present observed marching columns of SA and SS, attended speeches and conferences, and watched military exercises.

85. Thank you very much.

Another of Fräulein Nienau's regular visits to the Obersalzberg provides yet another photo opportunity. Disregarding all others Hitler directs all his attention towards his little visitor. The unfortunate members of the public in the background, many of whom may have travelled some distance to see the Führer, are temporarily ignored. The interaction between Hitler and Bernile would indicate that the child has been given presents by the Führer. Hitler's contemporaries have confirmed that he felt genuine affection for this little girl, a regular visitor to the Obersalzberg until the unnecessary meddling of an interfering Party official into the child's ancestry interrupted her visits for a time.

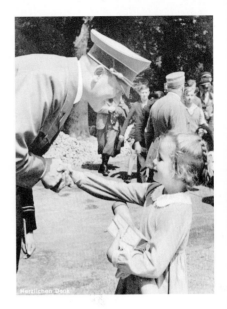

86. A little visitor on Obersalzberg.

The Führer chats with little Bernile during another of the child's visits to Haus Wachenfeld. The older girls in uniform are members of the *Bund Deutscher Mädel* (BDM; League of German Girls) an organization for girls aged ten to twenty-one and organized along similar lines to the Hitler Youth. The BDM also came under the control of *Reichsjugendführer* (Reich Youth Leader) Baldur von Schirach. The *Jungmädel* (JM; Young Girls) a branch of the BDM, was for girls aged ten to fourteen. The *Bund Deutscher Mädel* (BDM; League of German Girls) was for girls aged fourteen to twenty-one. The purpose of the organization was to teach young girls the ways of National Socialism, to prepare them for adulthood, and more importantly, motherhood. Behind Hitler stands his chief adjutant, Lieutenant Wilhelm Brückner of the SA. Brückner held this post from 1934 until 1940.

...iner Besuch auf Obersalzberg

87. A little one's visit on Obersalzberg.

Hitler presents a gift to his little visitor on the terrace at Haus Wachenfeld. Heinrich Hoffmann, the Führer's personal photographer was on hand to capture the moment. Nonetheless, there appears to be genuine warmth in the interaction between Hitler and little Bernile, to a point where neither seems aware of fact that the camera is present. This photograph was clearly taken during the same visit as observed in the previous postcard, number 86.

88. Out of the visiting crowd at Obersalzberg.

Bernile beams as she walks hand-in-hand with the Führer towards the house. The crowds in the background are left to await their return. Her family will be so proud and her friends so jealous when she tells them of her great adventure.

89. Caption reads: Thank you for the birthday invitation.

Bernile kisses the Führer goodbye. The original caption tells us that the child had been invited to spend a short time with Hitler because it was her birthday. Hitler and Bernile shared the same birthday, 20th April. This photograph, whether posed or otherwise, is nonetheless a touching image in that it reveals something of Hitler's close relationship with children. More than that, this photograph shows an intimacy rarely seen in many others; unusually, the child is permitted to hug Hitler, whilst kissing him on the cheek he clearly returns the embrace in response to her innocent affection.

Dank für Geburtstags-Einlac

90. Our Führer's and Chancellor's home on the Obersalzberg.

A figure raises the flag in front of the house. Hundreds of people line the road leading to the property all hoping to see their Führer. Haus Wachenfeld has been renovated and extended; again it would remain as seen here until greatly enlarged in 1935/36 to become the new Berghof. Some of the original farm buildings in the area can be glimpsed through the trees, while on the extreme left is Hotel zum Türken.

91. Haus Wachenfeld.
This photograph was taken from a point on the road where it joined the drive to Haus Wachenfeld. The gates were situated just a few metres from the roadside. This allowed vehicles to stop before the gates but safely off the road itself. The small sign by the fence translates as, Haus Wachenfeld • Entry Forbidden • Guard Dogs!

92. Hitler with the youth in the mountains.
These three images form part of a series of photographs depicting a staged encounter between Hitler and three local children on the Obersalzberg. Countless images showing Hitler interacting with young people were produced in an effort to portray the Führer as the personal friend and guardian of German youth. As time passed, countless thousands of young people came to believe in Hitler as that personal friend and father figure through the encouragement of the many youth organizations set up for that very purpose.

93. Berchtesgaden children congratulate the Führer.
Whether Hitler is giving the apples or receiving the apples is of absolutely no importance. What is important however, is the message behind the image. When we remember that these photographs were taken in the mid 1930s, we must also understand that to see a leading political figure photographed in this way was not just rare, it was astonishing and something unheard of at the time. This was the public face of Nazi propaganda at work. Such innovative and deliberately targeted propaganda broke all the rules. Having never previously been subjected to such highly-developed and subtle propaganda techniques the unsuspecting general public had little understanding of it, and therefore even less defence against it.

94. Visit on the Obersalzberg.
With Hitler in attendance, two of the children already observed in postcards numbers 92 and 93 are presented with gifts by Magda and Joseph Goebbels as their visit to the Obersalzberg comes to an end. Such images have but one purpose; to promote and enhance public perception of the Führer, and in this instance other members of the Nazi hierarchy as caring and approachable whilst appearing genuinely interested in young people.

95. The Führer's faithful guard 'Sirus' at Haus Wachenfeld on Obersalzberg.

Hitler's dog 'Sirus' photographed close to Haus Wachenfeld. Sirus, a Golden Retriever, preceded Blondi, the German Shepherd later gifted to the Führer by Martin Bormann. Hitler was undoubtedly a dog-lover; during the First World War he adopted a terrier he named 'Fuchsl' (Little Fox). The dog, a Jack Russell, had suddenly appeared in the German trench chasing a rat. In time Hitler and Fuchsl became inseparable. Close examination of this photograph leads one to the conclusion that the image of the dog may have been added to original photograph at a later stage; German photographers were extremely skilled in producing composite images.

5228

96. The Führer at Obersalzberg.

Members of the Hitler Youth gather before the gates to Haus Wachenfeld. Each boy eagerly awaits his turn as the Führer autographs the postcards they have brought along. Meanwhile the lad on the right uses his camera to capture their special moment forever.

97. The Führer and his deputy Hess.

Hitler and Hess photographed on the drive near Haus Wachenfeld. While Hitler wears standard uniform his deputy is observed in traditional Bavarian attire. Following the flight of Hess to England in May 1941, his successor Martin Bormann, 'the intriguer', attempted to remove any reminders and all traces of Hess; this extended to anything bearing the image of the former Deputy Führer. Consequently postcards such as this are to be considered quite rare.

98. The Führer with R. Hess at Haus Wachenfeld.

This interesting early postcard shows Hitler and his deputy Hess admiring the view from Haus Wachenfeld towards Berchtesgaden. Both men wear traditional Bavarian dress in what appears to be an informal get together. Rudolf Hess as a subject does not appear frequently in postcards; consequently an image such as this commands a high price.

Der Führer und sein Stellvertreter He

Führer mit R. Hess auf Haus Wachenfeld.

99. Moonlight at Hitler's country house Wachenfeld and Obersalzberg (1,000m).

A beautifully clear night on the Obersalzberg, the full moon casts its magic spell illuminating the entire area to conjure up this fabulous 'fairytale' type scene. This particular postcard is a personal favourite; the photographer's patience has been rewarded and his professionalism has produced an image where the viewer can almost feel the seclusion and the stillness of the night.

100. Haus Wachenfeld, Obersalzberg.

Haus Wachenfeld photographed looking back towards the mountain road. A small group stand talking in front of the garage. Note the assertive posture of the man second from the left wearing a light coloured jacket and dark trousers; characteristically Hitler. If we compare this image (post-construction) with postcard number 67 showing the conservatory during initial construction, we can appreciate the scale of development to have taken place in this particular area.

Haus Wachenfeld, Obersalzberg

101. Hitler's country house Wachenfeld in Berchtesgadener Land (Obersalzberg 1,000m).
The almost daily procession past the Führer's residence was an act of faith for many of the
participants; this truly awesome spectacle began in the late 1920s prior to Hitler being appointed
Chancellor and continued unabated throughout the early years. The frequency of these visits and
the numbers involved were subject to strict control following restrictions introduced after 1936
denying the general public access to the area *en masse*.

102. Heartfelt Best Wishes for the New Year.
A scene of complete tranquillity; Haus Wachenfeld and the surrounding area rests beneath a blanket
of deep snow. The photographer has skilfully used the natural light to produce this particularly
enchanting image. Posted in Berchtesgaden in 1934 part of the message on the reverse reads; 'This
is the home of our dear Führer Adolf Hitler'. The politically motivated postmark states; *Saar-
Abstimmung 13 Januar 1935* (Saar Vote 13 January 1935). This referred to the plebiscite that would
decide the future of the Saar region. The Saar, formerly German territory, an area rich in coal, came
under the administration of the League of Nations in 1919 following the signing of the Versailles
Treaty. In the end, over 90 per cent of the electorate voted in favour of returning to Germany.

103. Hitler's country house Wachenfeld towards Reiteralpe.
Another charming 'chocolate box cover' type study of the residence.
A number of vehicles stand on the parking area by the flagpole, including what appears to be a military staff car.

Sie hat dem FÜHRER die Hand geben dürfen

104. She has been allowed to give the Führer a hand.
These two little girls are so engrossed in their own activity that they seem oblivious to the Führer's presence. Having paused, Hitler observes his little guests as would some proud father during their walk near Haus Wachenfeld.

105. Haus Wachenfeld, country house of the Reich Chancellor in Berchtesgaden.
To say that Hitler's 'little place in the country' offered adequate views of the surrounding area would be something of an understatement to say the least. This postcard allows us to share the magnificent uninterrupted view towards the Untersberg situated opposite the Führer's residence on the Obersalzberg. The Untersberg is steeped in legend; while some say the Emperor Charlemagne sleeps deep beneath the mountain and will return to save Germany in time of need, others state it is the German Holy Roman Emperor Frederick Barbarossa and an army of heroes who slumber awaiting the call. Nonetheless, to have his country home situated overlooking the Untersberg which is part German, part Austrian, must have been a source of deep personal satisfaction for Hitler; from here he could see his native Austria and, weather permitting observe Salzburg and its castle in the distance.

106. Saar children as summer guests of the Führer's sister on Obersalzberg.
The Führer enjoys the company of two little girls from the Saar region who are spending time at Haus Wachenfeld as the guests of his half-sister Angela, his housekeeper from 1928 to 1936. Contemporary accounts indicate that Hitler was genuinely fond of children; nonetheless, what respectable politician would turn down the opportunity to be photographed with these endearing subjects.

107. Haus Wachenfeld the Führer's home on the Obersalzberg.
This image reveals the now completed additional single-storey room already mentioned at an early stage of construction in caption number 70. Both photographs have been taken from almost the exact same point. However comparing the two images reveals a number of subtle changes. Moving left to right, this postcard shows that the small additional room in the foreground has been completed, the chimney on the main roof has been built higher, a screen has been added to the wall around the terrace, work has been done immediately left of the garage doors and a parking area has been created complete with flagpole. It is fair to say that from the time Hitler purchased the property until the 1935/36 redevelopment that produced the new Berghof; Haus Wachenfeld was subject to alterations of varying magnitude on an almost continual basis.

108. Haus Wachenfeld, country house of the Reich Chancellor in Berchtesgaden.
Looking across the garden area towards the original main part of the house, this postcard allows us to appreciate just how much work has been carried out on the property when compared with earlier images showing this side of the residence; for example postcard number 62.

Hoher Göll 2519

109. The Führer in Berchtesgaden.

The Führer attends to paperwork while seated on the terrace of his beloved Haus Wachenfeld. These words, or similar, is how an image such as this might have been captioned at the time this postcard was released. It is probably safe to assume this photograph was taken in late afternoon or early evening. Hitler was not a morning person and seldom rose before midday. Nonetheless the German people were presented with numerous images depicting the Führer working tirelessly for Germany.

110. Haus Wachenfeld on the Obersalzberg.

An aerial view of Haus Wachenfeld and the Obersalzberg region, in this instance appearing somewhat insignificant against the backdrop of the magnificent Hoher Göll.

The sprawl of buildings high on the left in open pasture is Pension Moritz, also called the Platterhof. On studying this image together with postcard number 111, it is evident that the area which later formed the Nazi central zone on the Obersalzberg and accommodated most of the buildings they erected following the takeover, was in fact, quite a small area.

85

Obersalzberg – Original-Fliegeraufn.

111. Obersalzberg – original aerial photo.

This unusual aerial view shows Haus Wachenfeld and that part of the Obersalzberg that later formed the heart of the restricted central area. The house has already undergone considerable redevelopment but would remain as seen here until the grand remodelling programme of 1935/36 from which the new Berghof would emerge. There are people visible on the road and by the gate, but strangely in this instance the vast crowds are conspicuous by their absence. With the exception of Hotel zum Türken, observed just above and to the left of Haus Wachenfeld, all other buildings observed in this photograph would be demolished as the Nazis tightened their grip on the region. The story of Hotel zum Türken is particularly interesting. The first building to be constructed on the site was the Jakobsbichl-Lehen. This was built around 1630. 'Lehens' or 'fiefs' belonged to religious institutions. As such these smallholdings were rented to families and individuals on condition of military service. During his tenancy the unfortunate occupant of the Jakobsbichl-Lehen was required to go off to war against the Turks. On his return this individual acquired the nickname 'the Turk' and eventually the house became known as the 'Türkenhäusl' (Little Turk's House). Karl Schuster, who ran the Purtschellerhaus on the Hoher Göll bought the Türkenhäusl in September 1911 for the sum of 8,000 Gold Marks. Upon being granted one of only two inn licences for the Obersalzberg, Schuster and his wife Maria set about turning their recent acquisition into a successful business. The property was enlarged; however, as would be the case with Haus Wachenfeld, Schuster integrated the original Türkenhäusl into the new larger building. Known as the 'Türken Guesthouse', the property overlooked Haus Wachenfeld.

Karl Schuster was a popular man, for in addition to running a successful guest-house; he was a mountain guide, head of the local fire brigade, and a town councillor. His wife Maria had a reputation as an excellent cook and business woman. Dietrich Eckart, the man who would later introduce Adolf Hitler to the Obersalzberg was a regular guest at the nearby Pension Moritz, later the Platterhof Hotel. Eckart, who knew Schuster personally, also frequented the 'Türkenwirt'. Schuster and Eckart were friends. Despite the economic crisis after the First World War, Schuster again enlarged the Türken Guesthouse. In 1923, during the time that Eckart was living incognito as 'Dr Hoffmann' on the Obersalzberg, Adolf Hitler spoke to an astonished and captivated audience of local people in the Türken.

Hitler and Schuster became neighbours when Hitler began renting Haus Wachenfeld in 1928. In June 1933 Hitler became the new owner of Haus Wachenfeld. Hitler's ever-increasing popularity inevitably led to crowds of people regularly gathering on the terrace of Hotel zum Türken as they watched and waited in the hope of catching a glimpse of the Führer. This 'invasion of privacy' as he saw it began to irritate Hitler. Martin Bormann, probably without Hitler's knowledge, became involved. Bormann demanded that Schuster sell Hotel zum Türken. Schuster refused. Known as a man who spoke his mind, Schuster made the mistake of commenting, '. . . up here one only sees blacks and browns (a reference to the uniform colours of the SS and the SA) and one feels like he is in a prison. This was not the case before the *coup*. Under these circumstances life in France would be better.' This, and other perhaps misguided remarks, would not help Schuster's position.

As the redevelopment of Haus Wachenfeld progressed, Hitler approached Karl Schuster to ask him if he would consider selling a small piece of the bordering land so that he could add a drive permitting vehicular access from the mountain road to the house. Schuster replied, 'No, Herr Reich Chancellor, you may use my land if you wish, but I have six children, whereas you have none; and I don't know how long you will be here for.' Nonetheless an agreement was drawn up and signed permitting Hitler access to Haus Wachenfeld across Schuster's land for a nominal sum. The SA and SS men on the Obersalzberg used Hotel zum Türken as their local watering hole. However, returning home one evening to find this hotel overrun with SA and SS loudly singing their battle songs, Schuster, got into an argument when he refused to serve any more alcohol.

This brief altercation led to Hotel zum Türken being effectively boycotted. Bormann's involvement would ensure Schuster's eventual downfall. Uniformed men stood outside Schuster's property holding placards and turning away potential customers. House guests were left with no choice but to pack up and leave. Even with his business in danger of collapse, Schuster refused to give in. On 19 August 1933 Karl Schuster was placed in 'preventative detention' for four weeks. That same day armed SA men instructed gathering members of the public to vacate the grounds of Hotel zum Türken.

During this period of 'thinking time', Schuster agreed to sell his hotel. On his release Schuster signed the already drawn up sales agreement and left the Obersalzberg. Bormann paid Schuster 165,000 Reichsmarks for the property; a reasonable price. At the last moment, however, Bormann reneged on the sales agreement and withheld 90,000 Reichsmarks of the agreed price. The sale was completed on 20 November 1933. That very day Schuster received a letter from Bormann stating that any outstanding or future action against him would be dropped. The family were given just enough time to pack clothing and personal belongings and leave. Additionally, the Schuster family were forbidden to settle anywhere in the vicinity of Berchtesgaden, or to discuss what had transpired on the Obersalzberg. Karl Schuster invested in a business near Lake Chiemsee, but this proved unsuccessful. Within a year of leaving the Obersalzberg, Schuster died of heart failure on 10 September 1934. Following requisition, Hotel zum Türken was taken over and occupied by Hitler's personal bodyguard, the *SS-Führerleibwache*. Martin Bormann later assigned the building to the *Reichsicherheitsdienst* (RSD; Reich Security Service) who were responsible for Hitler's personal security. As many as forty RSD and SS men were stationed in the hotel.

Again the building was enlarged to meet the new demands. The remodelling, under the direction of architect Alois Degano, began in November 1935 and was completed in July 1936. As the construction of the Berghof came to an end in 1936, a sentry post was built by the roadside in front of Hotel zum Türken together with a security gate that effectively sealed off the road. These measures in conjunction with the guardhouse situated on the road below Haus Wachenfeld (see postcard number 130) increased Hitler's security and further controlled access to the Berghof. Hotel zum Türken was again renovated in 1937 to included living quarters for *SS-Gruppenführer* and *Generalmajor* of Police, Johann Rattenhuber. The cellar was enlarged and detention cells installed. These cells were seldom used; on the rare occasion that they were used it was usually due to some minor drunken misdemeanour by one of the labour force.

The air-raid of 25 April 1945 left Hotel zum Türken badly damaged. Looting by local people and advancing Allied soldiers saw much of the interior fittings and furniture removed. At one point the occupying forces considered demolishing the bomb-damaged remains. The return of Karl Schuster's daughter Therese Partner at the end of 1945 to take up residence in that part of the hotel that remained partially habitable ultimately prevented its demolition. Karl Schuster's widow, Maria, began legal proceedings to reclaim the property in 1948. When it was discovered that Karl Schuster had in fact been a member of the Nazi Party, officials did everything possible to deny the family's claim to the property. To the family's great frustration, the case dragged on until early 1949. Finally in March 1949 a judgement in favour of the Schuster family was reached. The property was returned in December 1949. However, as Karl Schuster had received a sum of money for the property from Martin Bormann the family were required to pay 69,000 Deutsche Mark for what was essentially a ruin.

Hotel zum Türken is unique in that it is the only case of a property on the Obersalzberg that was returned to the original owner after the Second World War. Bormann had seen to it that all privately owned property within what became the inner and middle security zones had been demolished after 1937. The reason Hotel zum Türken survived demolition was due to its location, its proximity to the Berghof, that, and the fact that it was perfectly situated for the work of the *Reichsicherheitsdienst*, otherwise it too would have been demolished. Nonetheless, Karl Schuster's widow Maria, and their daughter Therese, filed a claim to have their property returned. As the family were able prove that their home had been forcefully appropriated against their wishes, and the fact that Karl Schuster had been imprisoned, it was returned. No other family or individual who had owned land or property on the Obersalzberg prior to the Nazi takeover ever had it returned. The circumstances in the case of Hotel zum Türken were quite unique.

While badly damaged the hotel was none the less carefully restored. Following restoration Hotel zum Türken re-opened for business just before Christmas 1950. Therese Partner died in 1971. Her daughter, Ingrid, and her husband Otto Scharfenberg then took over the business. Ingrid Scharfenberg's greatest fear that the state would make every effort to acquire and then demolish her beloved hotel after her death has recently been laid to rest. Having acquired 'historical building' status, Hotel zum Türken is now protected by law.

Opposite top:
112. Guests by the fence on Obersalzberg.
His people have come to the Obersalzberg and their Führer has not disappointed them.
The photographer has chosen his moment well, the delight and excitement on the faces in the crowd is almost contagious and, just as Hitler picks out this young girl for particular attention the camera captures an image full of the 'ah' factor. Photographs depicting a political leader endearing himself to the people don't come any better.

Opposite bottom:
113. Haus Wachenfeld, country home of the Reich Chancellor in Berchtesgaden.
Looking up towards the Führer's residence from the lower slopes of the Obersalzberg. Although obviously extended, the building adheres to typical alpine styling thus allowing a high degree of harmony between structure and landscape.

Zaungäste auf Obersalzber

114. With the Führer People's Chancellor Adolf Hitler on the Obersalzberg.

Enthusiastic crowds salute and greet their Führer as he exchanges a few words with a young woman at the front of this orderly line; the SS are never far away, all the while maintaining order and protecting the Führer. Posted in Dresden on 28.2.34, this postcard then made its way to an address in Stuttgart carrying birthday greetings; an unusual subject matter for a birthday card!

115. Interior of Haus Wachenfeld, country house of the Reich Chancellor.

This interior view of Haus Wachenfeld was photographed in the early days when it was simply the Führer's country home. Unlike the later Berghof this was not a place to entertain and impress foreign dignitaries. Worth noting yet easily missed, is the small figure of a saluting Brownshirt above the lampshade.

116. Interior of Haus Wachenfeld, country house of the Reich Chancellor.

Here we view what is described as the living room. Cosy and unpretentious, this room was located to the right hand side of the main door to the house; it lay behind the small bay window clearly observed in postcard number 82.

117. The Führer takes the favourable voting results on Obersalzberg.

Hitler takes a telephone call informing him of the outcome of the plebiscite on the disputed Saar region held on 13 January 1935. In 1919 and according to the terms of the Treaty of Versailles, the League of Nations took over administration of the area. In 1920, the French took control of the region. With over 90 per cent of the electorate having voted for a return to Germany and the Reich it is small wonder that the Führer appears extremely pleased.

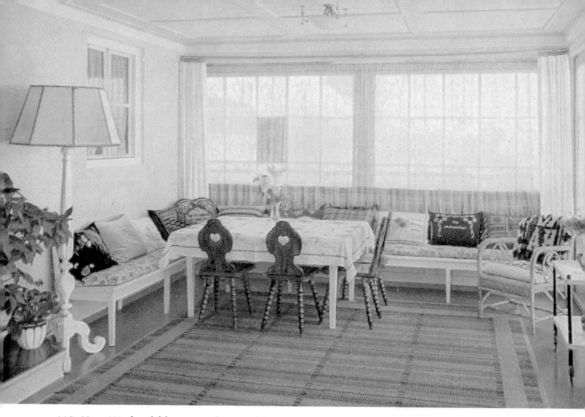

118. Haus Wachenfeld, country house of the Reich Chancellor in Berchtesgaden.
The conservatory (sometimes referred to as the winter garden) appears simply yet comfortably furnished. Close examination of the wicker chair on the right reveals a swastika incorporated into the design just below the armrests, while the cushion on the back of this chair displays the letters 'AH' beneath a partially observed swastika. The steps in the lower left foreground lead back into the room already discussed in postcard number 116.

119. Haus Wachenfeld, country house of the Reich Chancellor in Berchtesgaden.
Here we view the opposite end of the conservatory to that observed in the previous postcard, number 118.
The windows at the end of the room overlooked the drive and the mountain road, while the large window on the left permitted direct access to the main terrace located above the garage.

DER FÜHRER in seinem Heim Haus Wachenfeld

120. The Führer in his home Haus Wachenfeld.

The Führer pictured in the conservatory at Haus Wachenfeld with his dog, Blonda. Hitler loved dogs; he particularly liked German Shepherds. His first dog was a stray, a Jack Russell terrier. Finding the dog in the trenches during the First World War, Hitler adopted the terrier and named him Fuchsl (Little Fox). Hitler was distraught when the dog was later stolen from him. In 1921 Hitler was given a German Shepherd he named Prinz. Prinz was followed by another called Muck. In 1926 he acquired a bitch called Blonda. In 1930 Blonda had pups; Hitler kept one of these naming her Blonda also.

In 1941 Martin Bormann presented Hitler with Blondi. In 1942 Hitler bought Bella, another German Shepherd as company for Blondi. Blondi would have pups in 1945. Of these Hitler selected a male puppy and named it Wolf, his own nickname. Blondi would be with Hitler until 29 April 1945, when on his orders, she was poisoned. As the Russians approached the Reich Chancellery in late April 1945 all the dogs were destroyed. The reverse of this postcard bears a commemorative postmark stating; Berlin: 20 April 1937: *Des Führers Geburtstag* (The Führer's Birthday).

Section Two

Berghof: Secondary Seat
of Government

Visitors to the Berghof

The Führer
and the Surrounding Area

The Munich Agreement

Berghof: Secondary Seat of Government

During his lifetime Adolf Hitler would spend more time on the Obersalzberg than in any other place. From the time he rented Haus Wachenfeld in mid October 1928 until he left the Berghof for the last time on 14 July 1944, Hitler would spend more than one third of that time on his beloved Obersalzberg. By the mid 1930s however, Haus Wachenfeld was increasingly viewed as a home no longer befitting the German Chancellor; this modest Alpine cottage simply did not reflect Hitler's status as Chancellor. The new 'Berghof' that emerged from the 1935/36 rebuilding programme, having absorbed its humble predecessor, offered the Führer a country residence worthy of his position. When not in Berlin, it was at the Berghof that foreign leaders were received and entertained, and later, where important decisions relating to the conduct of the war would be taken.

Hitler, always something of a frustrated architect drew up his own detailed plans for the Berghof; these were then presented to the well-known Munich architect Alois Degano, who in turn was responsible for overseeing the construction of the new residence. The Führer was concerned that the new building might not sit comfortably in its surroundings; his main worry was the potential impact of this much larger building and its possible effect on the landscape. Nonetheless, on seeing the completed Berghof, Hitler expressed total satisfaction with the entire undertaking.

Adolf Hitler described this region as his *'Wahlheimat'*, (his chosen homeland). However, the importance of the Berghof lies not only in the fact that it was Hitler's country residence; additionally it was here that many important political and later military decisions were taken. The question of the annexation of Austria was decided in the Berghof. On 12 April 1938 the Austrian Chancellor, Kurt von Schuschnigg was summoned to the Berghof where he was persuaded that it was in his country's interest to legalize the Nazi Party in Austria and to appoint the pro-Nazi, Dr Arthur Seyß-Inquart Austrian Minister of the Interior. Von Schuschnigg tried to resist the not inconsiderable pressure, but to no avail. Inevitably the *Anschluß* (annexation) was carried out according to Hitler's wishes within a matter of days.

On 15 September 1938, British Prime Minister Neville Chamberlain visited the Berghof to discuss the then escalating crisis surrounding the issue of the Sudetenland in Czechoslovakia. Hitler was determined to deal with the matter of the German-speaking area one way or another. This meeting led directly to the signing of the 'Munich Agreement' two weeks later. The question of the Sudetenland was resolved in Hitler's favour as the Czech government was forced to cede the area to Germany. In March 1939, Hitler, through clever manipulation and pressure brought to bear, attempted to force the ailing President of Czechoslovakia, Dr Emil Hácha to sign the document of the surrender of his country or risk invasion within a matter of hours. Hácha signed. German troops crossed the Czech border the following day; there was no resistance.

In May 1939 Hitler informed his generals that war with Poland was inevitable. To that end he instructed the generals to draw up plans for the invasion of Poland. While at the Berghof in August later that year, Hitler sent a telegram to Stalin outlining his ideas for a 'non-aggression pact' between their two countries. The pact, containing a secret protocol on Poland, was signed in Moscow on 23 August 1939. With Stalin's signature barely dry on the agreement, Hitler summoned his generals to the Berghof where he convinced them that the time to attack had come. The Führer spent the next few days at the Berghof discussing the impending invasion. Germany invaded Poland on 1 September 1939, eight days later.

'Operation Barbarossa' the invasion of the Soviet Union was planned at the Berghof. It has been said that it was the magnificent view of the Untersberg Mountain located across the valley from the Berghof that inspired Hitler to choose the name Barbarossa for the operation. (The story of the Untersberg and the legend of Frederick Barbarossa have already been discussed in caption number 105). The Führer spent months at the Berghof through 1940, during which time he was involved in planning Operation Barbarossa. On 31 July 1940, Hitler informed his generals that he planned to attack Russia early the following year. The Führer signed the final orders for the invasion of the Soviet Union at the desk in his study in the Berghof on 18 December 1940. The German attack on the USSR began on a front extending from the Baltic to the Black Sea on 22 June 1941.

121. The home of our Führer on Obersalzberg.
The steep slope in front of the property rises up towards the garage where minor finishing work is being carried out, then on towards the main house where the area around the large picture window remains unfinished and unpainted. While an unidentified man stands on the terrace, the perimeter fence running along the roadside is clearly visible in the foreground.

122. The Führer in front of his home in Berchtesgaden.

Hitler, standing on the low wall by the perimeter fence in front of the Berghof greets the people. The building on the hillside in the background is Hotel zum Türken. Omnipresent SS men mingle with the smiling crowd who file past saluting their Führer. On the left and situated almost directly opposite the drive to the Berghof stands an SS sentry-box.

Through the late 1920s and early 1930s, the public enjoyed unrestricted access to the Obersalzberg. Obviously, for security reasons, this was a situation that could not continue indefinitely. The creation of the *Führersperrgebiet* (Restricted Area of the Führer) in 1936 saw the introduction of officially organized 'march pasts' where, as this postcard shows, Hitler would often greet the people. These 'march pasts' continued until the outbreak of the Second World War in September 1939.

r tägliche Besuch auf Obersalzberg

123. The daily visit on Obersalzberg.

It has already been stated (caption number 101) that the general public were largely denied access to the Obersalzberg after 1936. However this postcard would appear to contest that statement. Here we see the Berghof completed in 1936 with a large number of people moving along the road below the house.

We can see that the original gates to the property together with the perimeter fence along the roadside have been removed. This indicates that security and access points to the area were located elsewhere and more strictly controlled. Consequently we must assume that this image depicts one of the many 'officially' organized visits to the Obersalzberg for large groups following the reconstruction.

A small group can be seen standing at the end of the drive by the roadside. The figure on the right of this group, wearing dark trousers, is Adolf Hitler. These 'greeting the masses' sessions would sometimes last for hours. In June 1937 a somewhat irritated Hitler eventually complained about the heat and total lack of shade during these sessions. Within days Martin Bormann had procured a mature linden tree from Munich and had it planted within a few metres of where Hitler is seen standing. Having survived the air-raid of 25 April 1945, and the blowing up of the remains of the Berghof in 1952, the linden tree was finally cut down in the mid 1960s. Nonetheless the apparently indestructible linden tree continues to grow as shoots constantly spring up around the stump.

124. The Führer on his walk (In the background Berghof Wachenfeld in front of the Hoher Göll).

It is well documented that Hitler enjoyed long walks on the Obersalzberg. It is said he walked at such a pace that others had trouble keeping up with him at times. The adoration enjoyed by Hitler in these early years was the envy of many political leaders worldwide. He had redressed much of the unfair Versailles Treaty which had been forced upon Germany in 1918; huge unemployment and massive inflation had also been tackled successfully. All this, together with the restoration of the armed forces gave every German the feeling that their nation had regained its place on the world stage. With these achievements in mind, the suggestion has been put forward that, had Adolf Hitler died in mid 1939, he would almost certainly have claimed his place in history as the greatest German statesman who had ever lived – there's food for thought!

Der FÜHRER auf einem Spaziergang (im Hintergrund Berghof Wachenfeld vor dem Hohen Göll)

125. House of the Führer after the 1936 rebuilding.

The impressive new Berghof. However, as with its predecessor Haus Wachenfeld, the Berghof was destined to undergo a number of alterations during its relatively short lifetime. There is a degree of starkness about this image suggesting the possibility that work on the new building had just recently ended. The figures by the roadside appear locked in conversation on the merits of the new residence.

126. Konrad Henlein with the Führer on the Obersalzberg.

Hitler photographed with Konrad Henlein who visited the Berghof in May 1938, during the early stages of the soon to escalate Czech crisis. Partial mobilization took place in Czechoslovakia on 20 May 1938. Born in Maffersdorf in Bohemia on 6 May 1898, Henlein founded the *Sudeten Deutsche Partei* (Sudeten German Party) towards the end of 1933. This organization received substantial secret funding from the Nazis and went on to become the strongest political party in Czechoslovakia. Henlein contrived to see the Sudetenland, that part of Czechoslovakia, formerly Austrian territory bordering Germany, and home to some three million German-speaking people, joined to the Reich.

Konrad Henlein visited the Berghof again on 2 September 1938. At that time there was little doubt that Hitler was determined to solve the Sudeten question by whatever means necessary. The following day, 3 September, the Führer held a military conference with his generals at the Berghof; Hitler informed them that the date for 'Case Green', the attack on Czechoslovakia, was set for 1 October. A hastily arranged 'eleventh hour' four-power conference held in Munich in the last days of September saw France and England abandon Czechoslovakia in an effort to appease Hitler and avoid war; Hitler's planned military invasion of a sacrificed Czechoslovakia was thus thwarted.

Following the conclusion of the Munich Agreement on 30 September 1938, Henlein was appointed *Reichskommissar* (Reich Commissioner) for the Sudetenland. On 1 May 1939, following German occupation of the entire country, Henlein became *Reichsstatthalter* (Reich Governor) of Czechoslovakia with control over civil administration. Captured by the Americans at the end of the Second World War, Konrad Henlein committed suicide on 10 May 1945 while in detention.

127. Haus Wachenfeld, Obersalzberg.
It is difficult to fault Hitler's choice of location for his mountain residence; the Obersalzberg is itself some of nature's finest handiwork. The whole area is surrounded by rugged mountain peaks that rise from wooded uplands with lush pasture and fast flowing rivers that race to the valley where the nearby town of Berchtesgaden is located. With all this in mind and, given the proximity to his native Austria, it is not difficult to see why Hitler was drawn back to this place time and time again.

128. Uncaptioned.
A thoughtful, reticent Hitler sits on the perimeter wall of the terrace at the Berghof. This postcard bears a special postmark celebrating the *Werbeschau der KdF Sammlergruppe* (The Commercial Show for the 'Strength through Joy' organization) in Hannover in April 1941. The 'KdF' (*Kraft durch Freude*) was a recreational organization set up in 1933 as a means to encourage better morale and productivity amongst German workers through various incentive schemes.

101

129. The Führer and Dr Goebbels at Berghof Wachenfeld.
Hitler and Goebbels discuss some topic as they and three comrades stroll away from the house, their progress closely observed by a small group on the terrace. Hitler often walked the relatively short distance to his private teahouse at Mooslahnerkopf with friends in the afternoon; perhaps this was one such occasion. Having survived the bombing of the area in April 1945 the teahouse was torn down in 1951, what remained of the ruin was cleared in 2007. The view towards Salzburg Castle, weather permitting, from the small grassed terrace in front of the teahouse was something Hitler continually found inspirational. The terrace itself remains intact.

130. The Berghof, Obersalzberg.

This was the view from the upper balcony of the Berghof looking towards Berchtesgaden. The photographer has taken up a position in the middle arch on the second floor balcony, a point we can easily identify in postcard number 134. Here the attention to detail, even to the roof timbers can be fully appreciated. The small building in the centre foreground was the last of three manned SS check-points to be passed on the road from Berchtesgaden to the Berghof. The Berghof was situated in the central, most secure zone. The introduction of the *Führersperrgebiet* (Restricted Area of the Führer) in 1936 meant that access to, and through each of these three security zones was strictly controlled thereafter. Entry was then only possible upon presentation of the relevant pass to access each zone in turn as one proceeded up the mountain road. All check-points were manned by men from the Leibstandarte-SS Adolf Hitler (LSSAH). The building beyond the SS guardhouse is Haus Salzburgblick owned by Martin and Anna Zotz. Bormann purchased the property in March 1937, it was demolished soon after.

131. Our Führer's home on Obersalzberg.
The Berghof takes on an even more rural appearance in this particular postcard chiefly due to the row of haystacks standing in the right foreground. It is probably safe to say that this photograph of the Führer's mountain home was taken soon after the 1936 remodelling programme ended; given the early stage of growth of the line of small trees planted along the roadside behind the haystacks. The perimeter fence by the roadside observed in postcard number 121. has been removed. However, what is most unusual is the presence of two flags to the left of the picture window.

132. The Führer's home on Obersalzberg with Watzmann.
An altogether more pleasing study of the Berghof than the previous image, here the growth of established trees and shrubs around the property contribute greatly to the overall look of the residence. An unidentified man stands on the terrace observing the photographer. Whilst obviously the height of summer the Watzmann in the background retains snow on its uppermost peaks.

Berghof Wachenfeld
unseres Führers Heim
inmitten seiner Berchtesgadener Berge

133. Berghof Wachenfeld, the Führer's home in the middle of his Berchtesgaden Mountains.

The term 'Berghof Wachenfeld' used in this caption might seem confusing, however, during construction of the new residence through 1935/36 and on Hitler's instructions, the new building thereafter generally referred to as the Berghof, was sympathetically constructed around Haus Wachenfeld so as to incorporate and preserve the original house to which the Führer was sentimentally attached. This explanation would account for the term 'Berghof Wachenfeld' being applied to the enlarged residence after 1936.

In this instance the Führer's home is viewed from the lower slopes of the Obersalzberg. By including the fence and shrubbery in the foreground the photographer has cleverly added a degree of rustic charm to the image.

134. The Berghof on Obersalzberg.

Comparing this image with postcard number 132, we see that new shutters have been added to the windows of Hitler's study located behind the balcony on the first floor. The large picture window of the Great Hall can be seen below the balcony, if partially obscured by the garage. When required this window could be lowered into the basement by means of a hydraulic system. The smaller part of the building observed on the right and behind the garage is part of the original Haus Wachenfeld which, on Hitler's instructions, had been cleverly incorporated into the new and much larger building in 1935/36.

135. A cheerful fellow hiker with the Führer on the Obersalzberg.

At first glance this image appears to record a spontaneous, unexpected chance meeting between Hitler and an unknown hiker on the Obersalzberg. The stone wall appearing in the background of this photograph would indicate the location as being by the roadside directly below the Berghof. To have been permitted to wander around the Obersalzberg in the mid 1930s, let alone close to the Berghof and accidentally encounter the Führer on the road would have been impossible. The SS man behind Hitler holds an unidentified object in a way as if waiting for the Führer to present it to the young man with whom Hitler is speaking; the evidence tends to indicate a contrived image.

136. Berghof Wachenfeld.

This image, along with postcards numbers 137 and 138, concentrates on that side of the main building which cannot be seen from the drive. Here we get a good view of the main terrace located directly in front of the conservatory. The terrace is clearly provided with more than ample furniture for everyday requirements. A much smaller secondary terrace sits in the foreground. This image, if compared with postcard number 61 (photographed from a similar position) gives an idea of the scale of transformation from early Haus Wachenfeld to Berghof.

137. The Berghof.

This photograph has been taken from a point on the main terrace looking back across the secondary terrace and lawn. These buildings, located on the west side of the main residence acted as an adjutancy accommodating the Führer's military and personal staff when he was residing on the Obersalzberg. As we can see the adjutancy and the Berghof were two separate buildings. The small section of the retaining wall observed between the two buildings is very close to where the heavy iron door through which one gained access to the later constructed Berghof bunker system was installed.

138. Haus Wachenfeld (new building).

These steps lead up from the sloping grounds found directly in front of the Führer's residence; again the main terrace which stood above the garage is located immediately behind the wall seen on the left. The tree-covered slopes of the Obersalzberg continue up behind the property.

139. Dr Goebbels family visit on Obersalzberg.

This scene of informal cordiality has been photographed on the Berghof terrace.
Frau Magda Goebbels (seated far left) together with her husband and two of their children pay a visit to the Obersalzberg. With Hitler in attendance, all appear amused by the interaction between the older of the two children and the other lady, Erna Hoffmann. Heinrich Hoffmann, the Führer's personal photographer and Erna's husband is the man behind the camera in this particular instance. Hitler and Hoffmann met in 1923; the two men became close personal friends.

140. The Berghof (Haus Wachenfeld), Obersalzberg.

Hitler's country retreat in all its glory; the Berghof was not often photographed in this way, that is to say, in a manner that includes the entire structure and the towering background. As we can see the residence sat comfortably in its surroundings. In this instance the photographer has cleverly given us an image that should, given the subject matter, conform to the usual formalities of a 'landscape' shape in 'portrait' form.
In doing so he has captured the beautiful Alpine scenery behind the house to best advantage and crowned it with the awe inspiring, dominating Hoher Göll standing at 2,519 metres (8,264 feet).

141. Obersalzberg. The home of the Führer.

The new Berghof photographed from almost the same point as we have seen Haus Wachenfeld photographed in postcard number 77. In comparing these two images we can determine that both buildings occupy the same site. However, as far as scale, comfort and prestige are concerned they were worlds apart. Haus Wachenfeld, to all intents and purposes, has disappeared having been absorbed into the new building. That point where the drive joins the road is clearly visible.

142. Prime Minister Chamberlain on the Obersalzberg.

Photographed at the Berghof we see left to right; Joachim von Ribbentrop (1893-1946), German Foreign Minister; Neville Chamberlain (1869-1940), British Prime Minister and Adolf Hitler. Behind Hitler stands Dr Paul Schmidt (1899-1970), Hitler's personal interpreter between 1935 and 1945. This rare postcard records Chamberlain's only visit to the Führer's home on the Obersalzberg on 15 September 1938. It was the first time the British Premier had travelled by aeroplane; he had made the journey to meet Hitler in an attempt to solve the Czech crisis which, on the face of it, he had appeared to do. In reality he had merely delayed the inevitable.

**143. Obersalzberg.
The home of the Führer.**
A fine view of the Führer's country retreat as photographed from the roadside prior to the final alterations to the building. The retaining stone wall which ran the entire length of the upper side of the drive is clearly visible; the identical wall in the foreground is situated by the roadside where it remains today.

144. The Führer greets his visitor.
Having taken up a position where the drive joins the road, a smiling Hitler raises his arm in salute.
Uncharacteristically, this particular postcard gives the impression of a completely contrived image produced purely for propaganda purposes.
The reverse bears a special postmark to celebrate the *Anschluss* (joining) of Austria to the Reich on 10 April 1938. For Hitler this was a time filled with emotion and a great personal triumph as his homeland became part of the German Reich.

110

Berghof Wachenfeld mit Watzmann und Hochkalter

145. Berghof Wachenfeld with Watzmann and Hochkalter.

In this instance the photographer has taken up a position near Bormann's house which overlooked Hotel zum Türken (centre) and the Berghof (right). In comparing this image with postcard number 79 we can judge the extent to which both properties have been modernised. On the left are temporary accommodation huts for those working on other buildings situated still further left and out of view, on completion of the work these huts were removed. The highlighted area shows the sentry post (see also caption number 148) built by the roadside in front of Hotel zum Türken in late 1936. While all traces of the security gate that closed the road at this point are gone, the sentry post remains standing.

146. View from Lockstein towards Salzburg with Führer house.

This distinctive postcard presents the Berghof and the surrounding countryside from an unusual angle. In the lower foreground we see part of the Gutshof built in 1938 as a farm to produce food for the complex. Just above that is Villa Bechstein, this became accommodation for visiting VIPs including Goebbels, Hess and Mussolini. Above Villa Bechstein and to the left stands Landhaus (country house) Bormann, formerly the home of Dr Richard Seitz. In the centre we see Hotel zum Türken. Right of that is the Berghof while a little higher, and on the extreme right, stands the Georg Arnhold holiday home, also known as 'Klubheim'; after 1935 'Gästehaus Hoher Göll', the Party guesthouse. Directly below that is the Gutshof *Wirtschaftsgebäude* (economics building).

147. Berghof Obersalzberg.

An excellent overall view of the Berghof, in this instance the large picture window of the Great Hall is shown part open. That part of the building seen above and behind the stone built garage is part of the original house, revealing how 'old' and 'new' were cleverly incorporated into one structure. This photograph depicts the Berghof prior to the final rebuilding of the annex on the left, and the construction of a service road in that area as a means of keeping delivery vehicles off the main drive. Bearing a postmark dated; 16.1.41, three weeks later, on 6 February 1941, Hitler would give command of the newly created *Afrika Korps* to General Erwin Rommel, 'The Desert Fox'.

148. Obersalzberg: View of the Berghof and Berchtesgaden from Bormann House.

Hotel zum Türken and Hitler's Berghof as observed from Martin Bormann's home on the Obersalzberg. The highlighted areas in this image show the aforementioned sentry box in front of a now enlarged Hotel zum Türken (see postcard number 145) and the guard house situated by the roadside below the Berghof (see postcard number 130). Today only the foundations of this former guardhouse remain.

These two guard posts provided both security for, and access to, the central zone, the innermost and most secure zone around the Berghof following the introduction of the *Führersperrgebiet* on the Obersalzberg in late 1936. In the valley below, located between the Berghof and Bormann's home, lies the town of Berchtesgaden. Bormann's home overlooked the Berghof. As such Bormann could see all the comings and goings to the Führer's home firsthand. It is interesting to note that Bormann's children, he had nine children, were provided with a sand-pit seen to the left of the family home; and a swimming-pool, located on the extreme left in the foreground.

s „Wachenfeld" am Obersalzberg (1000 m) gegen Reiteralpe   1023•Phot. H. Huber

149. Haus Wachenfeld on Obersalzberg (1,000m) towards Reiteralpe.
This image confirms the activity of continually carrying out alterations of varying scale around the Berghof. Building materials can be seen by the annex door in the foreground and again on the drive at the foot of the main steps. It is difficult to understand why, when having just completed a building which was enormous compared with the original cottage it should be deemed necessary to enlarge the property further still.

150. The home of the Führer on Obersalzberg with Reiteralpe.
In comparison to the previous postcard number 149, it is obvious that the annex in the foreground has been completely rebuilt and enlarged. It stretches out further than previously from the main building and joins a newly constructed service road. Another floor has been added complete with balcony, new shutters have been fitted to all windows and access to the back of the house has been improved with increased space between the building and the hillside. This is basically how the Berghof would remain until its destruction in 1945. The linden tree that Bormann had planted near the end of the main drive in 1937 in an effort to provide shade for Hitler during the long periods he spent standing there greeting the crowds can be glimpsed on the extreme right of the image.

151. Berghof – Obersalzberg near Berchtesgaden.
Here (although very similar to postcard number 150) we can see how the new service road to the enlarged annex joined the mountain road, while vehicles stand on the original drive near the main entrance. The new service road permitted deliveries to the residence without the risk of disturbing the Führer, or his guests; a possibility when the property had been accessed by a single drive. With many high-level meetings being held at the Berghof, such disturbances would not have been welcomed.

152. Photographed in 2012 are the remains of the service road observed in the previous postcard number 151. On reaching the trees at the end of the service road one still finds the retaining wall that was built next the hillside at the rear of the Berghof, clearly visible in postcard number 150. The site is now very overgrown. Furthermore, the fact that rubble from the demolition of other Nazi buildings on the mountain has been deposited on the site through the post-war years means that ground level today is considerably higher than it was in 1945. However, using the retaining wall as a reference point the determined individual can still work out where Hitler's Berghof stood on the site.

153. Photographed in 2012, this is how the aforementioned service road appears when observed form the former site of the Berghof itself; everything is now very overgrown as nature takes over where man left off. The eternal Hotel zum Türken, having miraculously survived, stands on the hillside a little further up the mountain road.

154. Photographed in 2012 we observe the now almost unrecognizable main drive to the Berghof, this led to the steps below the main entrance to the residence and is located a short distance down the road from the previously discussed service road to the property. The only tangible evidence in this instance is the remains of the original stone built wall next to the hillside on the left; this is clearly visible in postcards numbers 129 and 143. The highlighted area indicates the location of the aforementioned linden tree planted in 1937 and cut down in the 1960s. The tree still produces shoots around the stump giving it a bush-like appearance today.

**155. Obersalzberg, summer 1937.
Girls from Braunau visit the Führer.**
These two young ladies in traditional
dress have travelled from Hitler's
birthplace Braunau am Inn to meet the
Führer at his country home. The SS man
on the right is a member of the Führer's
personal bodyguard, the *Leibstandarte-SS
Adolf Hitler* as indicated on the cuff title
of his uniform.

156. The Berghof.
This image sees the Berghof bathed in
autumn sunshine as the surrounding trees
cast long shadows across the building.
The town of Berchtesgaden itself lies
hidden under a blanket of thick cloud in
the valley below while the Reiteralpe in
the background display the first signs of
approaching winter. Posted on the
Obersalzberg and bearing a postmark
dated 6.10.42, it was around this time
that things began to go badly for German
forces on the eastern front.

116

157. The Berghof on the Obersalzberg with Reiteralpe.

The Berghof photographed on a crisp, bright winter's day. Close inspection of this photograph shows a figure climbing the steps to the entrance of the Berghof. To the left of the tree in the foreground a solitary figure walks up the snow covered drive towards the building. It is possible that these individuals are 'stragglers', members of the group that would accompany Hitler on his almost daily walks to the teahouse at Mooslahnerkopf seen here returning to the Berghof.

Der Berghof am Obersalzberg mit Reiteralpe

Phot. L. Ammon 501

158. The Berghof Obersalzberg, entrance.

The main entrance to the residence as viewed from just inside the door. Beyond the arches on the right was a paved area which in turn led to the flight of steps leading down to the drive. If, as was usual upon arrival at the Berghof, the Führer came out to greet his guest, the individual concerned could easily establish their status in the eyes of the Führer. Should Hitler descend to greet them at the bottom of the steps, they were held in some esteem; if on the other hand he waited at the top of the steps for the visitor to reach him, they were not so highly regarded. The door opposite led to a small projection room adjacent to the Great Hall.

117

Postcards numbers 159 to 165 offer an all round view of the Great Hall (also known as the Conference Room) at the Berghof. This most impressive room was where the Führer entertained foreign leaders, chosen guests and those members of his inner social circle; during the war years it was a venue for important meetings with his military advisors. The Great Hall had a floor area of almost 200 square metres (2,152 square feet). A rich strawberry-coloured carpet covered the floor. For the purposes of maintaining a logical sequence through these images depicting the Great Hall, we will move left to right around the room beginning with postcard number 159.

159. The Berghof Obersalzberg. Part view of the Great Hall.
Many whose names have now been consigned to the history books were led into the Great Hall through this door. Only the finest quality materials were used in the construction of the Berghof. The marble steps led towards the famous picture window at the opposite end of the room. The old masters that hung in the Great Hall were changed regularly. 'Nana', by Anselm Feuerbach (1829-80) was a particular favourite of Hitler's; the painting often appeared on the wall near the fireplace.

160. The Berghof Obersalzberg, Great Hall.
Here we view the seating area around the fine marble fireplace. Hitler, whilst usually seated in one of the chairs in the foreground to the right of the fireplace, would talk long into the early hours with those closest to him. Many and most subjects were discussed during these late-night gatherings, but inevitably at some point the conversation always turned to politics.

161. The Berghof Obersalzberg, Great Hall.
Moving back the photographer has taken in more of the room either side of the fireplace; in doing so this allows an opportunity to observe the wonderful coffer ceiling. The large picture on the right is, 'Venus and Amor' by Italian artist, Paris Bordone (1500-71). Hitler bought the painting from Karl Haberstock in 1936.

162. The Berghof Obersalzberg, Great Hall.
The Great Hall as observed from a point close to the picture window. A bronze bust of Hitler's old friend Dietrich Eckart stands on a pedestal between the two paintings near the opposite corner. It was in these surroundings that many foreign leaders were entertained and flattered by Hitler; and here again where many were intimidated and subjugated.

163. The Berghof Obersalzberg, Great Hall.
Continuing around the room we arrive at the large Untersberg marble-topped conference table situated before the huge picture window located opposite the fireplace. The Great Hall was the venue for many important military conferences between Hitler and his generals. With maps laid out upon the conference table the Führer and his military advisors discussed the situation in the various war zones. The saying 'time flies' takes on a different meaning on examining the clock opposite, adorned as it is with the Nazi eagle. The adjoining room, observed through the doorway on the left, is part of the original Haus Wachenfeld; very few images show the connection between old and new. If, as was often the case, films were to be shown in the evening, the large Gobelin tapestry opposite would be removed and the area of the wall behind it used as a screen upon which to project the films. Occasionally the bowling alley beneath the Great Hall was used as a cinema. A bust of Richard Wagner, Hitler's favourite composer, sits on the sideboard beneath the Gobelin.

164. Berghof Wachenfeld, view of the Untersberg from the Great Hall.

An excellent view of the large picture window in the Great Hall looking out onto the snow-covered Untersberg across the valley.

The picture window had an area of thirty-two square metres (344 square feet) and consisted of ninety individual panes of glass. Standing before this window Adolf Hitler could see his native Austria in the distance. Talking about the window, the Führer once commented, 'Really, I built a house around a window here!' Interestingly, this caption refers to the residence as 'Berghof Wachenfeld', a situation brought about by the act of physically incorporating the original Haus Wachenfeld into the new building, the Berghof.

165. The Berghof Obersalzberg, Great Hall.

The seating area located to the right of the large picture window. This postcard shows the second and largest of the two fabulous Gobelin tapestries, both of which depicted hunting scenes that hung in the Great Hall. On the other side of this wall was the aforementioned projection room. This tapestry could be removed to reveal the apertures through which the films were projected onto the opposite wall. While the Berghof had been decorated and furnished to a very high standard there was nothing particularly ostentatious about what had been achieved.

166. The Berghof Obersalzberg, living room.
This cosy living room, originally part of Haus Wachenfeld, was adjacent to the Great Hall. We can see the connecting doorway between the two rooms in postcard number 163. The large structure on the extreme left, covered in ceramic tiles, is in fact a wood-burning stove; these remain a popular and practical form of heating and traditionally continue to exist in many German properties today.

167. The Berghof Obersalzberg, guest room.
If, as stated in the caption on the reverse, we accept this photograph as representing typical guest accommodation at the Berghof, the image goes some way in dispelling any preconceptions of opulent living at Hitler's country residence. The overall impression is one of simple homely comfort.

168. The Berghof Obersalzberg, winter garden.
This study of the winter garden at the newly constructed Berghof shows it to be quite different to its predecessor at Haus Wachenfeld (observed in postcards numbers 118 and 119). The large window on the left looked out across the valley towards the Untersberg while also permitting direct access to the main terrace located above the garage. The large picture on the wall depicts the Führer House and Ehrentempeln in Munich's Königsplatz (see caption number 28).

169. The Berghof Obersalzberg, winter garden.
This image shows the opposite end of the conservatory that overlooked the secondary terrace already observed in postcard number 136. Again, as with other rooms in the residence where there was no great need for formality, furnishings are richly patterned and inviting. The large painting on the left appears to be the work of Italian artist, Giovanni Pannini (1691-1765). Pannini produced many studies of classical Roman ruins.

170. The Berghof Obersalzberg, dining room.

The dining room used by the Führer and his guests. Hitler always sat in the middle on the right, facing the window overlooking the Untersberg. Eva Braun sat on his left. Rare and expensive cembra pine has been used as wall panelling, in today's terms it would cost a vast amount to install. The Führer, a strict vegetarian after 1931 did not smoke and strongly disapproved of drunkenness. Hitler was a teetotaller. Occasionally he might have a glass of wine or champagne when attending official functions; in general Hitler preferred herbal drinks.

171. The Berghof Obersalzberg, dining room.

Another view of the Führer's dining room, this time photographed from the opposite side to that seen in the previous postcard number 170. This image reveals the area of the bay window and the furniture contained there. While as one would expect the fixtures and fittings in the Führer's country residence were of the highest quality, in general terms there appears to have been nothing ostentatious about the Berghof in any real sense.

172. The Berghof Obersalzberg, guest room.
This particular postcard has been encountered with a caption stating it to be Eva Braun's room; however in most instances it is simply described as a guest room. Whatever the case, it provided every comfort for a pleasant stay.

173. Berghof Wachenfeld, study of the Führer.
A splendid view of Hitler's study situated on the first floor above the Great Hall. The large windows opened onto a long balcony (seen clearly in postcard number 132) allowing the Führer privacy to enjoy the fabulous uninterrupted views across the valley. Hitler's desk is located before the middle window; the portrait hanging to the left of this window is certainly Hitler's mother, while the other, to the right of the desk and partially obscured by the lamp, is his father.

174. Berghof Wachenfeld, study of the Führer.

Here we observe that part of the study opposite the windows. The Führer's desk is on the left. The fitted bookcases at the other end of the room appear well filled and probably include a copy of *Mein Kampf*. Hitler had always been a voracious reader, he maintained a vast library. The mood of the study is one of intimacy and stylish comfort. This particular postcard bears an 'Obersalzberg' postmark dated 1.7.37 from where it has made its way to an address in Münster.

175. The Führer in his study on Obersalzberg.

Hitler, wearing a light coloured double-breasted suit looks solemnly towards the camera whilst seated at his desk in the Berghof. Hoffmann, the Führer's photographer, has obviously managed to persuade Hitler to sit at his desk purely to make this image more interesting and complete; the total lack of paperwork on the desk makes this abundantly clear. The telephone on the Führer's desk was extension 501 via the Obersalzberg telephone exchange.

Visitors to the Berghof

The following is a list of just some of the visitors to Hitler's residence on the Obersalzberg. The fact that these individuals were received at the Berghof indicates the level of status the area had achieved under the Nazis. This list, while not comprehensive, shows the year that each individual made their first visit to the Berghof. Furthermore, the visitors' names appear in order of their arrival through each respective year. Naturally many of these people would visit the Obersalzberg more than once.

1936   Jósef Lipski, Polish Ambassador. Admiral Miklós Horthy, Hungarian Regent. David Lloyd George, British Liberal Party leader and former British Prime Minister. Count Galeazzo Ciano, Italian Foreign Minister, and Mussolini's son-in-law.

1937   Dr H. H. Kung, Chinese Finance Minister. Prince Aga Khan, leader of the Ismaili Muslims. Duke (formerly King Edward VIII) and Duchess of Windsor. Lord Halifax, British Foreign Minister.

1938   Kurt von Schuschnigg, Austrian Chancellor. Guido Schmidt, Austrian Secretary of State for Foreign Affairs. Konrad Henlein, leader of the *Sudeten Deutsche Partei* (Sudeten German Party). Italo Balbo, Italian Minister of Aviation. Neville Chamberlain, British   Prime Minister. André François-Poncet, French Ambassador. Umberto, Crown Prince of Italy. General Hiroshi Oshima, Japanese Ambassador. Count Jacques Davignon, Belgian Ambassador. Shigeenori Togo, Japanese Ambassador. Rauf Fico, Albanian Ambassador. Lü-Y-Wen, Manchurian Ambassador. Roberto Desprandel, Dominican Republic Ambassador. Carol III, King of Romania. Michael, Crown Prince of Romania. Oswald Pirow, South African Defence and Economics Minister.

1939   Colonel Józef Beck, Polish Foreign Minister. Monsignor Cesare Orsenigo, Papal Nuncio. Khalid al Hud, Special Envoy of the king of Saudi Arabia. Monsignor Józef Tiso, Slovakian State President. Adelbert Tuka, Slovakian Prime Minister. Count István Csáky, Hungarian Foreign Minister. Sir Nevile Henderson, British Ambassador.

1940   Paul, Prince Regent of the kingdom of Yugoslavia. Mihai Manoilescu,   Romanian Foreign Minister. Ion Gigurtu, Romanian Prime Minister. Bogdan Filov, Bulgarian Prime Minister. Ivan Vladimir Popoff, Bulgarian Foreign Minister. Alexander Mach, Slovakian Interior Minister. Marie-José, Crown Princess of Italy. Boris III, King of Bulgaria. Ramón Serrano Suñer, Spanish Foreign Minister. Leopold III, King of Belgium. Aleksandar Cincar-Markovic, Yugoslavian Foreign Minister. Helene, Queen Mother of Romania

1941   General Ion Antonescu, Romanian Prime Minister. Benito Mussolini, Italian Fascist Leader. Károly Bartha, Hungarian Defence Minister. Dragiša Cvetkovic, Yugoslavian Prime Minister. Admiral Jean-François Darlan, acting French Prime Minister (Vichy France). Dino Alfieri, Royal Italian Ambassador. John Cudahy, US Ambassador to Belgium. Ante Pavelić, Croatian Head of State.

1943   Italo Gariboldi, Supreme Commander Italian 8th Army. Vidkun Quisling, Norwegian Prime Minister. Pierre Laval, French Prime Minister (Puppet government under Germany, 1942-44). Knut Hamsun, winner of Novel Prize for Literature and Nazi sympathizer.

In addition to the Berghof, and following the *Anschluss* with Austria in April 1938, Hitler also used Klessheim Castle located 4 kilometres (2.5 miles) west of Salzburg as a venue for talks with foreign diplomats. After 1941 however, the number of visits made to the Obersalzberg by foreign representatives became less as the need for diplomacy steadily diminished. Thereafter Klessheim Castle was the main venue for diplomatic encounters until mid 1944.

     Nonetheless, Hitler continued to receive his military commanders and other Party leaders at the Berghof during that time. In general terms, from mid 1944 until the end of the Second World War, it was only these individuals and members of Hitler's 'inner social circle' who spent much time on the Obersalzberg; where daily life continued in an almost uninterrupted, and for the most part, 'normal' fashion.

The Führer
and the Surrounding Area

The following postcards, numbers 176 to 200, observe Hitler both on the Obersalzberg and in the surrounding area. The Führer is depicted in numerous situations, whether in the company of associates, alone, or interacting with some of the nameless thousands who descended upon the region in the hope of encountering him. Each of these had their own reasons for making the journey, sometimes hundreds of miles; motives ranging from total devotion to simple curiosity.

176. The Führer with his most loyal supporters in Bad Elster, 22 June, 1930.
Included in this small group of leading Nazis are, from left to right; Heinrich Himmler (1900-45), head of the SS and chief of Gestapo. Behind Himmler stands Martin Mutschmann (1879-1947), Gauleiter of Saxony. The man standing in the doorway is Karl Weinrich (1887-1973), Gauleiter of Kurhessen. Beside Himmler stands Dr Wilhelm Frick (1877-1946), Reich Minister for the Interior. Adolf Hitler. Immediately behind Hitler stands Dr Joseph Goebbels (1897-1945), Minister for Propaganda. Julius Schaub (1898-1967), adjutant to Hitler. General Franz Ritter von Epp (1868-1947), Governor of Bavaria and Reich Leader of the NSDAP. On the extreme right stands Hermann Göring (1893-1946), chief of the Luftwaffe and Reich President. Bad Elster is a small town situated in southern Saxony close to the Czech border. This photograph was probably taken at the time of the provincial elections held in the region in June 1930, which resulted in the Nazis becoming the second strongest party in Saxony. Such early images depicting the main Nazi leadership together in this way, are quite rare.

r kleine Autogrammjäger

177. The little autograph hunter.
A young admirer requests the Führer's autograph. As Hitler prepares to sign the ubiquitous postcard which was customary on such occasions, he appears to observe the lad with some affection; the boy's attention however remains fixed on the postcard itself. This endearing scene depicts the approachable and caring leader who gives of himself without hesitation.

178. The Führer in the Predigtstuhl Mountain Hotel near Berchtesgaden.
Hitler relaxes on the terrace of the Predigtstuhl Hotel located on the outskirts of Bad Reichenhall. A popular spa town and health resort since the late 1800s, Bad Reichenhall lies about 17.5 kilometres (11 miles) northwest of Berchtesgaden. Access to the hotel is via the famous Predigtstuhl Bahn (cable car). The first in Germany it opened on 1 July 1928 and takes less than ten minutes to reach the hotel situated at a height of 1,583 metres (5,193 feet) on top of the Predigtstuhl Mountain. The views over Bad Reichenhall and the surrounding area from the hotel terrace are breathtaking. The building was taken over by the US after 1945 but has since been returned to German hands.

Die kleine Autogrammjägerin

179. The little autograph hunter.

A caring Hitler shares an intimate moment with a proud mother and daughter. The little girl been fortunate enough to receive the Führer's autograph; something she will always remember. This encounter, as with the previous postcard number 178 has been photographed on the occasion of Hitler's visit to the Predigtstuhl Hotel. Interestingly, the Atlas Fountain by the famous Third Reich sculptor Josef Thorak that once graced the inner courtyard of Hotel Platterhof on the Obersalzberg now stands in the Kurpark in the centre of Bad Reichenhall. The fountain, now called the Solebrunnen, was removed from the Platterhof during the renovation of the hotel in 1950 and brought to Bad Reichenhall.

180. World Health Resort Bad Reichenhall. View from the Predigtstuhl to the Mountain Hotel.

The photographer looks back on the Predigtstuhl Hotel from a point a little further up the mountain. The terrace where we saw Hitler seated in postcard number 178 is located along the left side of the building as we see it. In this instance the magnificent backdrop is provided by the Hochstaufen at 1,771 metres (5,810 feet). The Hochstaufen stands at the eastern end of the Chiemgauer massif.

181. Bad Reichenhall. Holidays on the Predigtstuhl.

The Predigtstuhl and its hotel photographed in winter. The two figures in the foreground appear to be wearing military uniform. They may be off-duty *Gebirgstruppen* (Mountain Troops) enjoying some recreational skiing while at the same time polishing their skills. An enormous *Gebirgs-Artillerie-Kaserne* (Mountain Artillery Troops Barracks), the Ritter-von-Tutschek-Kaserne was built in Bad Reichenhall between 1934 and 1936. This barracks is used by the German Bundeswehr today. Another barracks, *Gebirgsjäger Kaserne* (Mountain Troops Barracks) the Mackensen-Kaserne was built nearby. The latter was home to 3rd Battalion *Gebirgsjägerregiment* 100. While unused, the reverse of this postcard has a large and unusual 'Kriegsmarine Feldpost' postmark rubber-stamped on it.

At the beginning of May 1945 twelve French Waffen-SS men, volunteers of the 33rd Waffen-Grenadier-Division der SS (Französische Nr 1) – *Charlemagne*, surrendered to US troops in Bad Reichenhall. They were held with other POWs in the former *Gebirgsjäger* barracks close to the town. Bad Reichenhall was occupied by the 2nd Free French Armoured Division under General Jacques Leclerc on 6 May 1945. On hearing this and fearing reprisals, the twelve French SS men tried to escape. The escapees were captured by Leclerc's men at Karlstein, a wooded area on the outskirts of the town. Arriving on the scene Leclerc accused the prisoners of being traitors in German uniform. One of the prisoners dared to comment on the fact that Leclerc himself was wearing American uniform. Leclerc's 2nd Free French Armoured Division was in fact supplied and equipped by the US and wore modified American uniforms. The prisoners were shot for their insolence. Leclerc ordered that the bodies be left where they lay. US forces buried the bodies three days later. Leclerc was never charged or brought to account.

182. The Reich Chancellor Adolf Hitler in his beloved mountains.
While out on one of his numerous walks in the area Hitler stops in passing to talk to this small boy. In the background is Geli Raubal, the daughter of Hitler's half-sister Angela, his housekeeper at Haus Wachenfeld. Geli committed suicide in Hitler's Munich flat (while Hitler himself was travelling to Hamburg for a meeting with SA leaders) on the night of 17/18 September 1931, amid rumours of their having had an affair, though this has never been proved. Following the untimely death of his niece Hitler remained inconsolable for many weeks. Geli Raubal's appearance in this photograph makes this a rare and interesting image; furthermore it confirms the time of origination as pre-September 1931. The very existence of this early postcard confirms Hitler's popularity, more than that, it confirms Nazi propaganda's endless efforts to promote and maintain an image of the man in the forefront of the public consciousness.

Phot. F. G. Zeitz. Nr. 458

183. The People's Chancellor, Adolf Hitler, in Berchtesgaden.

The Führer, having just been presented with flowers by this local girl passes them rather smartly to his SA adjutant, Wilhelm Brückner; the young lady meanwhile appears somewhat awe stricken by the whole experience. This postcard bears a postmark dated 26.8.34; Hitler had recently declared himself 'Head of the German State' following the death, on 2 August of President von Hindenburg (1847-1934).

184. Her wish is fulfilled.

A young lady, who bears a striking resemblance to the girl seen in the previous postcard number 183, poses with the Führer. She carries a postcard of Hitler which will be duly autographed. At the time this was equivalent to being photographed with your favourite film or pop star, such was the popularity and adoration enjoyed by Hitler; true celebrity status.

185. A quiet hour in the Berchtesgaden area.

Hitler poses thoughtfully for the camera amid tranquil surroundings near Berchtesgaden. The postmark on the reverse states; *München 19.10.38 Hauptstadt der Bewegung* (Capital of the Movement), Munich is thus celebrated as the foundation city of the NSDAP.

186. A Berchtesgaden boy greets the Führer.

Members of the SA and SS accompany the Führer on walkabout as he is greeted by a local child selected from the crowd. As a smiling Hitler takes the boy's hand the photographer captures a vote-winning image that sets the standard for modern political campaigning. While photographed in the early 1930s, this image is proof of the direct relationship between early Nazi campaigning methods and modern electioneering techniques that have been adopted directly from Nazi innovation. The Nazis pioneered many of today's basic electioneering principles; advanced ideas that are still used very successfully by numerous politicians worldwide.

Ein Berchtesgadener Bua begrüßt den Führer.

Hintersee bei Berchtesgaden

187. The Führer at Hintersee near Berchtesgaden.

Yet another charming image from the continuing programme for the winning of hearts and minds. Hitler chats with two local children while visiting the Hintersee not far from Berchtesgaden. Following an unbelievable stroke of luck and by sheer coincidence, I discovered that the small boy seen photographed with Hitler still lived in the region. Here was an opportunity not to be missed; having acquired a telephone number I made contact with this gentleman and, having explained my interest, he kindly agreed to a meeting later that same week.

The bus journey from Berchtesgaden to Hintersee takes about forty-five minutes, passing through some of the most wonderful Alpine scenery on the way. On arrival at Hintersee I made my way to Bartels Alpenhof, the address I had been given for our two o'clock meeting. Bartels Alpenhof is a long established family business where, on making enquiries, I was led to the large kitchen where I was introduced to the subject of my attention. Gerhard Bartels, now over eighty years old, is a charming man who continues to work in the hotel as he has done for almost seventy years. We spent the next hour talking in a quiet part of the hotel where Gerhard, who gave generously of his time, recalled what he remembered from the occasion of being photographed with Hitler in the summer of 1937.

Born in January 1932, Gerhard clearly remembers being told on the day; that he must wear clean clothes, he must not get dirty, he was being photographed. 'I was not allowed to play with the others; I might get my clothes dirty' recalls Gerhard, 'I didn't like that, I just wanted to be out with the other children', at the time he could not understand what all the fuss was about. The little girl who appears in the photograph was Gerhard's cousin, Anni, born in July 1931, (unfortunately Anni is no longer alive). Anni's father, Isidor 'Dori' Weiß, (Gerhard's uncle) had been Hitler's sergeant for a time during the First World War. The two men had remained in contact with Hitler visiting his old comrade at the Hintersee almost every summer where Dori Weiß owned Hotel Post.

It was through this personal contact that Gerhard and Anni were selected to be photographed

135

with the Führer on that occasion. During the photographic session which took place at the nearby Hotel Post; Gerhard remembers Hitler asked, 'What kind of cake do you like to eat?' Gerhard replied, 'Apple cake'. At the end of the photographic session, Gerhard, when finally released from all restrictions and running off to play was asked; 'What did the Führer say to you?' To which he replied, 'I don't remember; it wasn't important!' During the course of our conversation it emerged that the apple cake in question has yet to materialize.

On speaking to Gerhard Bartels more recently, we inevitably touched upon the subject of his childhood once more. During the course of these conversations the following information was gathered.

Gerhard Bartels attended school in Bad Reichenhall, some 24 kilometres (15 miles) from Hintersee. He remembers the morning of the air-raid on 25 April 1945. This would be his last day at school for some time. He told me how as the air-raid sirens began to wail, that the teachers led all the children down into the cellar beneath the school. Gerhard explained that as children they came to view air-raids as fun. At that time the air-raid sirens sounded as many as thirty or forty times a day, but often as not this was due to Allied aircraft flying high above the town *en route* to other targets. However, 25 April 1945 would be different; that day the town of Bad Reichenhall was the intended target. Gerhard remembers sitting in the cellar with dust falling everywhere. He could hear the girls crying for their mothers. When they eventually emerged from the cellar the school caretaker's wife brought them in and made pancakes for everyone before they were sent home. The roof and upper floor of the school had been destroyed. We collected our books and began to walk home. We boys were thinking; 'Great, no more school!' The bombing caused a lot of damage in Bad Reichenhall, particularly in the town centre and at the train station. Over 200 people were killed, while the large army barracks on the outskirts of the town survived untouched.

Two of us were walking along the road by the Saalachsee when a German Army Kübelwagen came along. The car stopped and the two soldiers gave us a lift to Schneizlreuth where we got out. As we continued along the Deutsche Alpenstraße towards Hintersee we were given another lift by a soldier on a motorcycle. We both climbed into the sidecar and he brought us as far as Hindenburglinde. We thanked him and continued on foot from there. Smoke generating equipment had been installed throughout the area to cloud the valley from view in the event of an air-raid. This equipment had been turned on when the Obersalzberg had been bombed earlier that morning; this resulted in a strong vinegar-like smell and fog everywhere. Gerhard continued, 'I was upset because this meant the end to one of my favourite hobbies. One evening a week I attended classes where we built model aeroplanes and learned about flying. I wanted to join the *Nationalsozialistisches Flieger-Korps* (NSFK; National Socialist Fliers' Corps). I wanted to be a pilot and fly Me 109s.'

Situated close to the Hintersee, Bartels Alpenhof looks out on the magnificent Hochkalter standing at 2,607 metres (8,553 feet). Following the bombing of the Obersalzberg on 25 April 1945, and on Hitler's orders, Alpenhof was taken over by Martin Bormann's brother, Albert. Albert Bormann was head of Berchtesgaden's Reich Chancellery. Many former employees of Obersalzberg, together with numerous SS officers and Hitler's private secretary, Christa Schröder then began living at Alpenhof. Gerhard recalls how the ladies would sit and chat with his mother. The hotel had in effect become the last headquarters of the Third Reich. Gerhard remembers some ten cars arriving from the Obersalzberg carrying both people and supplies. The cellar was used to store such delights as chocolate, nougat, and numerous sacks of coffee, all from the Obersalzberg. Such things were unavailable at the time. On 30 April Gerhard remembers seeing a high-ranking SS officer sitting at a table in the hotel. Suddenly an SS man came in and standing before the officer the soldier said, '*Der Führer ist Todt*' (The Führer is dead). As the news spread, some of the ladies began crying; the men began drinking cognac. On 8 May 1945, reports reached Alpenhof bringing news of the imminent arrival of the Americans. These reports saw most of the men recently arrived from the Obersalzberg, make every attempt to evade capture. Many simply disappeared into the surrounding countryside, while others used an old, and for the most part, forgotten mountain trail leading across the border into nearby Austria. However the women and children remained behind at Alpenhof.

Gerhard clearly remembers finding one of Hitler's fabulous Mercedes 770 motor cars parked in the barn behind the house. He told me how it was that he and his friend Eugen Bühler, the son of Hitler's gardener on the Obersalzberg who were among those then living at Alpenhof, found Hitler's Mercedes. 'We found it a couple of days after these people came to Alpenhof; before the Americans came.' Climbing into the vehicle the two boys found cases of Martell cognac and packs of sugar-cubes stored in the back of the car. Well, boys will be boys; they proceeded to drink cognac and eat sugar to a point where they were both sick. Despite the fact that the car had been carefully hidden under hay in the barn, the vehicle disappeared soon after; only to miraculously reappear in America sometime later. Two Polish POWs in the area informed the Americans of the car's location.

The Americans were the first to arrive at Hintersee; they came in vehicles similar to our German half-tracks. Then the French arrived. They didn't stay long, maybe two or three days; just long enough for them to do some looting. The American 101st spent the whole summer at Hintersee; they were there until September 1945. They were OK really. They took over Alpenhof. That meant that the women and children from the Obersalzberg were moved into another house nearby. Conditions were cramped there; they lived two and three to a room. The Yanks treated us lads well enough; they took us around with them in their Jeeps. Gerhard recalls a cook with the 101st who used the kitchen in Alpenhof to make over a hundred pancakes for breakfast every morning. If one of the soldiers shot a mountain goat they made hamburgers. The cook would make huge amounts of hot chocolate for the men. Sometimes he would let us take some away in cans. 'They had things like maple syrup and peanut butter for the pancakes. We had never seen peanut butter before, but we liked it', recalls Gerhard.

Gerhard went on to tell me about his friend Eugen Bühler. Eugen's father had had an important job on the Obersalzberg. He had overseen the growing of all the vegetables required by those residing on the mountainside. That included those required for the Führer's table. Hitler became a vegetarian soon after the death of his niece Geli Raubal in September 1931. The vegetables were grown in huge greenhouses that stood a little further up the road from Hotel zum Türken. Vegetables grown on the Obersalzberg would be harvested and delivered by aircraft to wherever the Führer happened to be. Hitler's former gardener arrived at Hintersee with many seed plants he had salvaged before leaving the Obersalzberg. The two boys helped Eugen's father to prepare a wonderful vegetable garden at Hintersee. This included erecting a high fence to keep local deer in the area from destroying the plants and vegetables. They used an ox to plough the ground before planting. The two boys worked in the garden through the summer; weeding and so on. Eugen and his father stayed at Hintersee until September 1945 when they returned to Stuttgart.

Dr Fritz Todt (1891-1942) owned a house at Hintersee. Todt bought the Altes Zollhaus (Old Customs House) on Hirschbichlstraße in 1939. Fritz Todt, as Inspector General of German Road Construction and leader of the Organization Todt was responsible for constructing the German Autobahn system between 1933 and 1938. Todt is also credited with constructing the Deutsche Alpenstraße (German Alpine Road) in 1935. Described as the most beautiful mountain road in Europe, the Deutsche Alpenstraße covers 450 kilometres (280 miles) running from the Bodensee in the west to Berchtesgaden/Königssee in the east. From 1940 to 1942 Todt was Reich Minister for Armament and Munitions. In 1941 Organization Todt was tasked with constructing the Atlantic Wall, a line of fortifications along the French coast designed to defend against an Allied invasion of the Continent. Following Todt's untimely death in 1942 he was succeeded by Albert Speer. Gerhard Bartels' mother encountered Fritz Todt on a number of occasions when he was staying at Hintersee.

To have unexpectedly encountered Gerhard Bartels in such a way was quite remarkable; it is best described as one of those experiences that defies explanation. For having agreed to see me, for his hospitality, and for being so generous with both his time and his memories, I remain most grateful. Since that first meeting I have visited Gerhard Bartels and his family at Hintersee many times. My wife and I spent Christmas at Alpenhof some years ago and enjoyed our stay immensely. I have taken small groups to Alpenhof on tour where, to their absolute delight, Gerhard has made time to join us at the table to enthral them with his memories.

188. Our Führer in Hotel Post at the Hintersee with War Comrades.
The Führer greets some of his old comrades from the First World War during a visit to the Hintersee. The man in the centre is Isidor 'Dori' Weiß (06.05.1864-17.11.1928), as already mentioned Weiß owned Hotel Post; he had been Hitler's sergeant for a time during the First World War. The two men had remained on friendly terms and Hitler often ate at the hotel when he visited the area through the years prior to the death of his old sergeant in 1928. Isidor Weiß is buried in the small churchyard in Ramsau.

nser FÜHRER im Hotel Post am Hintersee mit einem Kriegskameraden

Unser Führer
am Hintersee
mit Göring,
Brückner u.
s. Schwester.

189. Our Führer at Hintersee with Göring, Brückner and his sister.

This photograph shows Hitler and his entourage on yet another visit to the Hintersee. Hitler is accompanied by Göring (centre) and his adjutant Wilhelm Brückner, who is almost completely hidden by the lady on the left. However, what is unique and quite remarkable about this particular image is the fact that this lady is Adolf Hitler's sister, Paula. As previously mentioned, Paula Hitler, at her brother's request, adopted the family name Wolf to avoid any unnecessary public attention. It has been said that Hitler was somewhat distant and aloof in his relationships with close family members. This single and quite unique image certainly challenges that argument in so far as his relationship with his only surviving full sibling is concerned. Paula, the last child of Alois and Klara Hitler was born on 21 January 1896. She described her childhood relationship with her brother as a mixture of almost continuous bickering and great affection. Paula stated that 'Adi', as he was known to the family, constantly challenged his father's wishes; that this led to harshness with Adolf being beaten almost daily.

She remembered her brother's special interest in history, geography, architecture, painting and music. He particularly liked the music of Richard Wagner and Franz Liszt, but also theatre and the opera. Paula had little contact with her brother after 1908. Then, in 1921, they met in Vienna where Paula was working as a secretary. She thought her brother had perished during the First World War, and was delighted to see him again after so long. She said that they spent several happy days together during that first reunion. As Hitler achieved notoriety and it became known that she was his sister, Paula was dismissed from her secretarial post. That was when she began using the name Wolf. Paula moved to Munich where she related her situation to her brother. Hitler told her that he would provide for her. In addition to a regular allowance, Paula received a gift of 3,000 Marks every Christmas.

Missing Vienna, Paula returned to the city. She only ever visited Berchtesgaden at her brother's invitation. These invitations came once or twice a year when Paula would spend perhaps two weeks in Berchtesgaden. She never visited the Berghof and met Eva Braun only once. Paula stated that she enjoyed these rare opportunities to spend time with her brother. The Führer's sister never attended any official functions or major events, although Hitler sent her a ticket for the *Reichsparteitag* (National Party Days) in Nürnberg every year; she never attended, it was not her way. Paula never joined the Nazi Party. She said her brother never broached the subject, but she said that had he asked her to join, she would have, to please him.

In 1941, Paula, with Adolf's help, purchased a small house in Weiten in the Wachau, north of the town of Melk. In April 1945 two SS men arrived at the house. They told Paula they had been sent to bring her to Berchtesgaden. She quickly packed some personal belongings and left with them. Paula was brought to Hotel Berchtesgadener Hof. Within days, and with the Americans approaching the town, Paula was then taken to the Dietrich Eckarthutte at Hinterbrand. She stayed there until December 1945. Apart from one small suitcase she brought from the Berchtesgadener Hof, everything else she left in the hotel was lost. Paula Wolf moved into lodgings in the Alpenwirtschaft Vorderbrand owned by Franz Beer. The Beer family treated Paula very well; she repaid their kindness by helping out in the kitchen. Coincidentally, this was the inn frequented by Dietrich Eckart in 1923, see caption 249. Paula Wolf eventually returned to Vienna. In 1952 she moved into a two-room apartment in Berchtesgaden where she lived a quiet, peaceful, and for the most part anonymous life until her death on 1 June 1960. I could hardly believe my eyes when I first saw this postcard; I simply had to have it, regardless of cost!

190. The grave of Paula Hitler as it appeared when photographed in early 2007. Her final resting place is in the Bergfriedhof on the outskirts of Berchtesgaden. As we can see the grave is very well cared for and covered in flowers. In late 2007 a new plaque bearing a different name was placed over the original marker bearing Paula Hitler's name. This means the plot is very difficult to find. This is not uncommon practice; it simply means that someone else owned the plot, perhaps former friends of Paula Hitler who allowed her to be laid to rest there. Accordingly, when the owner next requires the plot and a new burial takes place, a new plaque bearing the name of the recently deceased is fixed to the existing marker as has happened here. Nonetheless, Paula Hitler is still buried here.

191. Uncaptioned.

Whether Hitler's decision or that of the photographer, an attempt is made to get just one more photograph with the still immaculately dressed Gerhard Bartels who appears in postcard number 187. However it is plainly obvious that young Gerhard has had quite enough; he draws away from the Führer, who in turn keeps hold of the boy lest he run off. Consequently, and with this in mind, it is difficult to understand why an image which clearly fails in its objective to depict the warm interaction between Hitler and the young was ever passed for publication. We can safely assume that this would have been the last photograph taken of Hitler and little Gerhard on the day; further attempts would have necessitated tying the youngster to a chair to keep him from his playmates.

192. German Youth greet the Führer.

While displaying great discipline by standing to attention and patiently awaiting the Führer's greeting, the older boys cannot hide the excitement on their faces; Hitler meanwhile, engages the smallest of this little group of ardent followers. This photograph was taken on the same occasion as postcards numbers 187 and 191, this can be determined in two ways; firstly, Hitler is seen wearing the same suit in all cases; secondly, the building in the background together with the furniture seen in postcards numbers 187 and 192 are one and the same.

Deutsche Jugend begrüßt den FÜHRER

193. Our Reich Chancellor Hitler on his morning outing in his Berchtesgadener Land.

The informal composition of this particular image suggests the idea that Hitler and the other members of the group are unaware they are being photographed. This is an early image, produced during the first year of Hitler's chancellorship in 1933. The photograph bears absolutely no resemblance to other, well-orchestrated and totally professional propaganda images produced during the period. It is difficult to understand the reasoning behind allowing the production of what is, for want of a better term, a 'dysfunctional' image. As revealed on earlier pages and prior to Hitler being appointed Chancellor, we know that the Nazi Party were more than capable of producing quality propaganda images, so why release an image such as this into the public domain? Again close examination of the photograph seems to indicate that this image is a montage; a photographic marriage between the foreground and the background. German photographers were very skilled in such techniques.

The photograph was taken close to the Hochlenzer, a restaurant situated at 896 metres (2,939 feet) overlooking Berchtesgaden. Hitler made numerous visits to the Hochlenzer during the periods he spent on the Obersalzberg. One can still walk the same route through the forest to the restaurant. There is a marked path, the 'Lindeweg', beginning by the roadside close to the Documentation Centre parking area on the Obersalzberg. Follow the signs for the Hochlenzer along Lindeweg, in doing so one passed the remains of the former Theatre Hall (see postcard number 245) on the right hand side below the forest path. This particularly enjoyable walk takes less than hour. The superb panoramic view from the Hochlenzer terrace more than compensates for the effort.

The reverse of this postcard bears a postmark dated 5.10.33. A second promotional postmark reads, *Skimeisterschaft der Deutschen, 8-12 Februar 1934, Berchtesgaden, Bayerischen Alpen*, the German Skiing Championships to be held in Berchtesgaden in February 1934.

194. A little one's visit.
While enjoying some refreshment the Führer graciously receives a little girl who is obviously another autograph hunter. Hitler appears to hold the ubiquitous postcard in a way so as to tease the child; nonetheless, she will receive her memento, duly signed, before returning to her family who are probably just out of camera shot.

195. Reich Chancellor Adolf Hitler and Reich Youth Leader Baldur von Schirach.
Hitler, appearing confident and composed, now carries the aura of authority with ease. He is a man who welcomes and understands the adoration of his people and their need of him. Standing behind Hitler is Baldur von Schirach, the man responsible for the education of German youth in the ways of National Socialism; he sows the seed that will flower in obedience to the Führer's will.

Der FÜHRER auf dem Königs

196. The Führer on the Königssee.

The beautiful Königssee (King's Lake) near Berchtesgaden has been a popular tourist attraction for many years. Here we see Hitler sitting in the stern of one of the many pleasure craft that travel the lake. These boats are electrically powered so as to eliminate the risk of pollution to the clear waters. The lake is the cleanest in Germany. Being some eight kilometres (five miles) long and 1,200 metres (¾ mile) wide the Königssee has been compared to a Norwegian fjord. At almost 200 metres (650 feet) the Königssee is very deep. The Führer's expression and demeanour suggest his mind may be occupied elsewhere.

197. The Führer at Obersee-Königssee.

To reach the spot where Hitler is observed in this postcard is a journey of approximately one and a half hours from Berchtesgaden. The bus trip from Berchtesgaden (Train Station) to the Königssee takes just under fifteen minutes. The boat trip to Saletalm at the opposite end of the lake itself takes about fifty minutes, leaving a fifteen minute walk along the path to the Obersee. On reaching the Obersee one finds the instantly recognizable large rock before which the Führer is standing. With scenery that is undoubtedly some of the best in the region this trip is well worth the effort.

Unser Führer am Obersee-Königssee

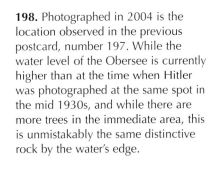

198. Photographed in 2004 is the location observed in the previous postcard, number 197. While the water level of the Obersee is currently higher than at the time when Hitler was photographed at the same spot in the mid 1930s, and while there are more trees in the immediate area, this is unmistakably the same distinctive rock by the water's edge.

Der Kanzler am Obersee
bei Berchtesgaden

199. The Chancellor at the Obersee near Berchtesgaden.
A wistful, uniformed Hitler sits on a rock located only a few metres from the spot observed in postcard number 197 during another visit to the Obersee. As with certain other postcards, this image has been encountered where it includes another individual on the rock behind the Führer. However on this occasion, as is most commonly the case, the Führer sits alone.

200. Photographed in 2004 is the location observed in the previous postcard number 199. Having spent some time examining the rock formations along the edge of the Obersee and, allowing for the considerable growth of trees in the immediate area during the interim, this particular rock emerges as that most likely used by the Führer as his resting place.

The Munich Agreement

While perhaps not directly relevant to the subject matter of this book, the Munich Agreement held more importance for Hitler than might be considered at a glance. Firstly, there was the fact that the negotiations were held and concluded in Munich, the city where the Führer's political career as a beer-hall agitator had begun, and almost ended. Secondly, it allowed Hitler to dictate the terms of the agreement to Germany's old adversaries and the dictators of the Versailles Treaty; France and England.

The Munich Agreement was probably the Führer's greatest, single diplomatic success; if a bitter-sweet victory for Hitler on a personal level. Through skilful manipulation of all parties concerned he had achieved exactly what he had set out to do, and yet, he had been denied the one thing he really wanted; the military conquest of Czechoslovakia. Hermann Göring, to his credit, did everything possible to facilitate and bring about the conference. His efforts should not be disregarded or underestimated. Had Göring not taken the lead in this regard, 'Case Green', the German plan for the attack on Czechoslovakia would have gone ahead on 1 October 1938 at the risk of a European war. The Führer stated that the return of the Sudetenland, formerly Austrian territory ceded after the First World War and home to some three million ethnic Germans, would bring about an end to Germany's territorial demands in Europe. Britain and France were inclined to believe him. British Prime Minster Chamberlain, in particular, worked extremely hard to persuade the Czech government to accept Hitler's demands. In the end the Czechs had to comply.

The following postcards are a fascinating visual record of the event that took place in the Führer House (already observed in postcard number 26) on Munich's Königsplatz on 29/30 September 1938. In the final analysis, the Munich Agreement permitted German forces unhindered entry and occupation of the Sudetenland in Czechoslovakia; this was carried out peacefully and as scheduled the following day, 1 October 1938. Hitler had seen the weakness of the British and the French for himself during the negotiations in Munich; the results of these observations would soon be felt throughout Europe, and beyond. Having acquired the Sudetenland, a somewhat frustrated Hitler would have to wait almost another six months before bringing about circumstances whereby German forces could occupy the remainder of Czechoslovakia to create the Protectorate of Bohemia and Moravia.

201. The Führer and Prime Minister Chamberlain.
Hitler and Chamberlain pose for the photographer; while neither individual looks particularly comfortable, the British Prime Minister, through circumstances chiefly due to his choice in clothes appears to represent something from a bygone age. A seemingly impassive Hitler assumes a more formal pose. This meeting took place in Rheinhotel Dreesen at Bad Godesberg on 22/23 September 1938 where the two leaders met to discuss the deepening Sudeten crisis, then near breaking point. An earlier meeting between the two men at the Berghof on 15 September ended in failure to reach agreement. The Führer appeared immovable in his demands for the proposed annexation of the Sudetenland in Czechoslovakia.

On this occasion Hitler stayed in the Dreesen, a hotel he knew well; he stayed there numerous times through the 1930s. He visited the hotel for the first time on 28 November 1926. The Führer had stayed in the hotel on the night of 29/30 June 1934, the night of the Röhm Purge; the so-called 'Night of the Long Knives.' Chamberlain was accommodated in Hotel Petershof located on top of the Petersberg on the opposite bank of the River Rhein. As it turned out this meeting was merely a precursor to the Munich Agreement concluded a week later.

202. 29.9.38 Kufstein.
Two statesmen and friends greet each other.

Hitler and Mussolini exchange warm greetings as the Italian leader alights from his train at Kufstein on the Austrian-German border. He was *en route* to Munich to take part in the negotiations which were essentially the beginning of the end for Czechoslovakia. Hitler boarded the train at Kufstein where the two leaders spent the remainder of the journey in discussions about the meeting scheduled to begin later that afternoon. It was Mussolini who had suggested the four power conference with the intention of reaching peaceful agreement to the Czech crisis. Again, it was Mussolini who produced the documents suggesting the order of business for the conference. In reality these proposals had been drawn up by the Germans only the day before, but it was believed a better result would be achieved if they were introduced to the meeting by the Italian leader as his own ideas.

203. Uncaptioned.

It is hardly surprising to find this postcard uncaptioned; one must remember it was produced at a time when both men had achieved such eminence on the European political stage that they were considered instantly recognizable. This superb Hoffmann image sees Benito Mussolini, Fascist leader of Italy, standing next to his friend and ally Adolf Hitler, Nazi leader of Germany.

The photograph was probably taken at some point during the conference held in the Führer House in Munich in September 1938, the meeting concluded with the signing of the 'Munich Agreement'. Through the latter half of the 1920s Hitler had viewed Mussolini's success in Italy with a mixture of envy and admiration; a decade later, it was Mussolini who stood in awe and admiration of Hitler as the Führer's deeds surpassed his own achievements. Thereafter Mussolini played a subordinate role in a relationship dominated by Hitler.

Benito Amilcare Andrea Mussolini was born in Dovia di Predappio in the province of Forlì on 29 July 1883. In 1902, following a short time as a school teacher he travelled to Switzerland where, among other things, he worked as a translator. Returning to Italy in 1905 he spent a year in the army. On Italy's entering the First World War in 1915, Mussolini volunteered and served until wounded during military exercises in 1917. After the war his political views seem to have changed on more than one occasion; having starting out a staunch socialist, Mussolini later embraced the extreme nationalism he was to maintain for the rest of his life.

Mussolini and Hitler share certain similarities, not least of which were the ways both men were to achieve political success; their appeal to the masses and the methods used to promote their political ideas as a cure for the severe economic crises and instability ravaging their respective countries at the time. Mussolini, as with Hitler in Germany, won the support of a cross section of the population through his oratory and the accompanying ferocious street battles. By 1921 Mussolini's *Fascio di Combattimento* (Union of Combat), better known as the Fascists, had achieved substantial political success with over 30 seats in the Italian parliament. Mussolini and his Blackshirts marched on Rome in October 1922 forcing the resignation of the Italian Premier, Luigi Facta. King Victor Emmanuel III appointed Mussolini Italian Prime Minister soon after. Within two years, Mussolini, Il Duce (the Leader) had silenced all opposition.

In the wake of more military setbacks than successes, with the threat of Allied invasion and his support at home disappearing, Mussolini was summoned and dismissed by King Victor Emmanuel on 25 July 1943. Having endured detention at various locations following his dismissal, Mussolini attempted an escape to Switzerland, the attempt failed when the small group were captured by Italian partisans. Benito Mussolini, his comrades and his mistress Clara Petacci who was travelling with him were executed on 28 April 1945; their bodies were displayed in a grotesque and most undignified way in a public square in Milan.

The news of Mussolini's death and the gruesome way his body had been put on public display, shocked Hitler; this, as much as any other reason accounts for the Führer's decision that he would not to be captured alive. As the Red Army encircled Berlin in 1945, Hitler feared that his remains, if discovered, might also be put on exhibition; perhaps even in Moscow by his ideological enemy Stalin. The Führer ordered that in the event of his death his remains be disposed of by fire. Following his suicide on 30 April 1945, this order was obediently carried out. SS Major Otto Günsche (Hitler's adjutant) assisted by SS Major Erich Kempka (Hitler's chauffeur) and SS Major Heinz Linge (Hitler's valet) carried out the Führer's last order.

204. The Führer signs the Munich Agreement.

Adolf Hitler adds his signature to the Munich Agreement as his personal aide and adjutant, *SS-Obergruppenführer* (Lieutenant-General) Julius Schaub (second from right) looks on. Just one of a number of personal adjutants, Schaub held this position from 1940 until 1945. On 22 April 1945, Schaub, on Hitler's orders, travelled to the Berghof where, as instructed, he destroyed all the Führer's personal documents and paperwork. On the extreme right Joachim von Ribbentrop, German Foreign Minister observes the moment. Following lengthy discussions and final agreement, the paperwork was signed in Hitler's office in the Führerbau (Führer Building) in the Königsplatz in Munich (see postcard number 26) at around 2.30a.m. on the morning of 30 September 1938. Standing in the background Göring and Mussolini appear locked in conversation on events.

205. Prime Minister Chamberlain signs the Munich Agreement.

Neville Chamberlain carefully adds his signature to the Agreement under the watchful eye of Mussolini who leans on the chair behind the British Premier. The reverse of this postcard carries a commemorative postmark reading; 'Sudetenland durch Adolf Hitler frei, Okt. 1938' (The Sudetenland is free through Adolf Hitler, Oct. 1938). While the Agreement was concluded on 30 September; it was the following day 1 October 1938, that German forces crossed the Czech border to peacefully occupy the Sudetenland. The local German-speaking population welcomed the German troops showering them with flowers as they marched through the streets

206. Prime Minister Daladier signs the Munich Agreement.

Édouard Daladier, the French leader, adds his signature to the Agreement which effectively sealed the fate of the independent state of Czechoslovakia. Ribbentrop, (Hitler's Minister for Foreign Affairs) on the extreme right leans on the desk observing the moment while Dr Schmidt, Hitler's interpreter, is seen on the left. Two commemorative Nazi postmarks celebrating the event appear on the reverse of this postcard.

207. Head of Government Mussolini signs the Munich Agreement.

The Italian leader adds his signature to the Agreement. Dr Paul Schmidt who had acted as official interpreter throughout the conference observes the moment, blotter in hand.

208. Historic four power conference in Munich 29.9.38.

The leaders of the four powers and signatories of the Munich Agreement on 30.9.38; standing left to right are Chamberlain (Britain), Daladier (France), Hitler (Germany) and Mussolini (Italy). On the extreme right stands the Italian Foreign Minister, Count Galeazzo Ciano (Mussolini's son-in-law). In the background standing left to right are; Dr Paul Schmidt, Hitler's interpreter; Sir Horace Wilson, Chamberlain's adviser and emissary to Hitler; Joachim von Ribbentrop, Hitler's Foreign Minister; Ernst von Weizsäcker, German Secretary of State at the Foreign Office, and Alexis Léger, General Secretary of the French Foreign Office.

209. Visit of Prime Minister Chamberlain to the private residence of the Führer on 30.9.38.

The British Premier visits the Führer in his Munich apartment on Prinzregentenplatz on the morning of 30 September 1938, prior to his return to England later that afternoon. During the meeting Chamberlain produced a statement he had drafted advocating that their two countries should never again go to war with one another. Hitler agreed, and both leaders added their signatures to the document. Chamberlain then presented Hitler with a copy of their personal agreement. On reaching London later that day the British Prime Minister triumphantly held this same piece of paper aloft announcing; 'peace with honour' and 'peace for our time'.

Section Three

Hotel Platterhof

Göring's Obersalzberg Home

Other Buildings on the
Obersalzberg

Tunnel and Bunker System

The Destruction of the
Obersalzberg

The Kehlsteinhaus (Eagle's Nest)

Hotel Berchtesgadener Hof

Nazi Buildings around
Berchtesgaden

Hotel Platterhof

The Platterhof, originally a farm called the 'Steinhauslehen' was acquired in 1877 by Mauritia 'Moritz' Mayer. This single-minded, enterprising lady set about turning the property into a guesthouse, renaming it 'Pension Moritz'. This led to a considerable increase in the number of visitors to the area; but it was not until 1888, when the railway arrived in Berchtesgaden that the region was really thrown open to tourism. The area had a reputation as an 'air cure resort' attracting people for the quality of the mountain air and beautiful scenery. Mauritia Mayer died on 1 March 1897. However her sister Antonie continued running the business until 1919. The property then changed hands. On 26 July 1919 two doctors from Berlin, Ernst and Eugen Josef bought the business. In 1921 they installed one Bruno Büchner, a former engineer and pilot to run the guesthouse on a concessionary basis. Büchner and his wife purchased the property in July 1928. On making his first visit to the area in 1923, Adolf Hitler readily found accommodation at Pension Moritz where his friend Dietrich Eckart was a regular patron.

Martin Bormann, 'Lord of the Obersalzberg' purchased the guesthouse in March 1937, by which time it had already been renamed Gasthaus 'Der Platterhof'. Between 1939 and 1941 the Platterhof underwent reconstruction on a massive scale. However, once again, and on Hitler's instructions, as with Haus Wachenfeld the old building was 'incorporated' into the new one, thus preserving as much of the original guesthouse as possible. Boasting absolute luxury the new *Volkshotel* (People's Hotel) opened on 1 September 1941. This was to be a 'national people's hotel', built to accommodate the ordinary people during their pilgrimage to the Obersalzberg. The initial concept, that any German citizen could spend a night in the 150-bed hotel for the sum of just 1 Mark, proved transitory. In reality, Bormann's wish to ever-increase the privacy and seclusion of the Führer on the mountain meant that the new hotel quickly became a place to accommodate high-ranking officers, members of the Nazi hierarchy and visiting dignitaries. The life of '*Volkshotel* Platterhof' was short-lived; the hotel, having received guests for a mere eighteen months was given over to operate as a military hospital due to the deteriorating war situation and remained as such until the end of the Second World War.

During the bombing of the area in April 1945 the Platterhof complex suffered considerable damage, particularly the employee's accommodation block; the main hotel itself survived the attack relatively well. The Platterhof then lay unused for a number of years. Nonetheless, the hotel was destined to survive the demolition of all former Nazi buildings on the Obersalzberg carried out in 1952. The restored Platterhof, having been renamed 'General Walker Hotel' re-opened for business in 1953. Bormann's former '*Volkshotel*' served as a recreational facility for US forces until 1996 when the entire area was returned to the Bavarian State. Amid much controversy the hotel was demolished in 2000.

Following research of the Obersalzberg archives and on examining some of the older parts of the former Platterhof in 1999, a beam from the original Steinhauslehen bearing the date 1671 was uncovered. The existence of this beam confirmed that the

Nazis had indeed preserved the original Steinhauslehen when they constructed the new Platterhof between 1939 and 1941. The very presence of this ancient beam, under German law for the preservation and protection of historic sites, should have prevented demolition the following year. However the idea of preserving the former Nazi *Volkshotel* on the Obersalzberg was obviously something the authorities felt uncomfortable with and demolition went ahead regardless. The former site of the Platterhof is now a car-park serving the nearby recently constructed Documentation Centre, while the adjacent bus terminal caters for those wishing to visit the Kehlsteinhaus (Eagle's Nest).

Postcards numbers 210 to 214 depict Pension Moritz in the early days when it was still a simple guesthouse offering relaxation amid beautiful surroundings. Postcards numbers 215 to 228 depict the later Platterhof as rebuilt under Martin Bormann's direct influence.

210. Hotel and Guesthouse Moritz, 1,000m. Obersalzberg-Berchtesgaden.
An early view of Pension Moritz prior to any major development of the property. Few postcards show the cowsheds on the right; these were later demolished. The town of Berchtesgaden sits in the valley on the right, the background is provided by the Reiteralpe while on the left stand the Hochkalter mountains.

211. Platterhof on the Obersalzberg with Untersberg.
The mighty Untersberg forms the backdrop to this charming Alpine scene where the caption clearly indicates the new of the hotel. On the right above the building stands a flagpole, unusually in this instance topped with a swastika; its very presence implies this image is probably post 1933.

212. 'The Platterhof' Guesthouse, Obersalzberg above Berchtesgaden.
This postcard shows the view towards the Reiteralpe from one of the guestrooms in the Platterhof prior to Bormann's purchasing the property in 1937 and the subsequent clearing of many of the trees in the foreground.

213. Mountain restaurant 'Platterhof' with the Untersberg.
In comparing this image with postcard number 211 we can appreciate the changes that have taken place at the Platterhof. There is a degree of starkness about this photograph, brought about chiefly by the creation of the parking areas around the building where previously there were trees and pasture. Much of the early rustic charm has already been lost through this quite limited development. This photograph shows the Platterhof in 1937 shortly after the Nazis had acquired the property, but prior to the rebuilding. The building in the centre is Haus Hoher Göll constructed in 1882. Mauritia Mayer built the house to operate as a dependence of Pension Moritz. Martin Bormann bought Haus Hoher Göll in October 1935.

214. Mountain restaurant Platterhof with the Untersberg.
The Platterhof is now in a position to receive visitors arriving by bus, thanks to the large parking area which has been created at the expense of the landscape. With business increased, additional accommodation has been provided in the new building visible through the trees on the extreme right. In the background the Untersberg massif stands sprinkled with snow.

215. The Platterhof on the Obersalzberg.
The fabulous new Platterhof Hotel, having cost much more than was originally estimated during its two-year construction, opened on 1 September 1941. Using only the finest quality materials available, the new Platterhof had been conceived as a 'people's hotel' to accommodate the Party faithful. In reality it became a showpiece to accommodate visiting dignitaries.

216. The Hotel Platterhof.
Looking at this image and comparing it to post card number 211 we can see that the new hotel is located in the same area as the much smaller Platterhof of earlier times. The building furthest away in the background on the left is 'Klubheim', (also clearly visible in postcard number 213) now rebuilt and renamed 'Gästehaus Hoher Göll'. This new guesthouse provided accommodation for Hitler's Chiefs of Staff and high-ranking Party members visiting the area. Martin Bormann's main office was also located in the building. The small building on the extreme left, the Terrassenhalle, became the 'Skyline Room', a US Army restaurant prior to the closing of the later General Walker Hotel in 1995. This is the only part of the former Platterhof to remain standing.

217. Photographed in 2004 and from a similar position to that adopted by the photographer of the previous postcard, number 216, the changes in the area appear quite staggering. A large parking area has been created where the hotel complex once stood. The former Terrassenhalle on the left is the only thing to link these two images. This last piece of the once fashionable Platterhof is now a restaurant, the *Berggasthof* Oberalzberg.

218. Platterhof, terrace view.
The Hochkalter mountains (left) and the Reiteralpe (right) as viewed from the Platterhof terrace. Photographed from a point found in postcard number 215 being just inside the archway located on the extreme left where the few steps next to the short wall lead to this particular arch.

219. Approach to the Platterhof.

The Reiteralpe provide the background in this instance where the hotel has been photographed from the opposite side to that shown in postcard number 215.
The large building on the right housed the reception area. The building observed on the left by the stationary buses was a post office and souvenir shop. Guests generally travelled the relatively short distance, about twenty minutes driving time, between the hotel and Berchtesgaden's large and impressive new train station (rebuilt in 1937) by bus.
The single-storey building in the foreground is part of the *Bergschenke* (Mountain Inn).

220. Platterhof towards Reiteralpe.

This photograph has been taken from a position where the photographer has moved much further back in relation to the previous image number 219. Here we view virtually the entire complex from the east. The flagpole, observed here to the left of the main building is a good point of reference to draw comparisons between the two images, appearing as it does in the previous postcard.

221. Platterhof with Watzmann and Hochkalter.
Magnificent Alpine scenery forms the backdrop to this fine view of the entire hotel complex. The large buildings in the foreground were the garages and staff accommodation blocks. The rooftops seen in the bottom of the photograph are part of the SS barracks. In this instance, the photographer has taken up a position on the hillside above the greenhouses (see postcard number 243).

222. The Platterhof reception hall.
Reception at the Platterhof was spacious and furnished in traditional Bavarian style; numerous room keys hang behind the main desk while newspapers are provided on the table to the left. The large portrait of Hitler at the opposite end of the room goes almost unnoticed at this distance. Information on the reverse of this postcard reads; The Platterhof, Obersalzberg above Berchtesgaden. Telephone: Berchtesgaden 2921.

223. Large dining room in the Platterhof.

Elegant surroundings with tables set a discreet distance apart. The six large columns supporting the ceiling of the dining room were formed of Untersberg marble. As already stated only the finest quality materials were used in construction; this was reflected throughout the hotel even to the smallest detail.

224. Coffee hall in the Platterhof.

The coffee hall. This particular part of the hotel operated as a completely separate enterprise having been established to provide the visiting Party faithful with refreshment during their 'pilgrimage' to the Führer's home and the Obersalzberg. The hotel logo is visible on the tableware.

225. Coffee hall in the Platterhof.

The coffee hall again. This time we observe the rich tapestries hanging on the wall opposite the windows seen in the previous postcard, number 224. Again the large window frames in the coffee hall were formed of fine Untersberg marble.

226. Platterhof, the Mountain Inn.

The Platterhof's *'Bergschenke'* (Mountain Inn) provided refreshment for those groups visiting the Obersalzberg through the later 'officially organized' trips to the region. Following the aforementioned restrictions introduced in late 1936 (denying the general public access to the Obersalzberg in the previously uncontrolled huge numbers), these officially sanctioned tours then offered the public virtually their only opportunity to visit the Nazi complex. A large picture of the Führer hangs on the wall on the right.

227. Platterhof, the Mountain Inn.
The Mountain Inn photographed from a point diagonally opposite to that of the previous image and looking back towards the main entrance. The 'Bergschenke' became a popular watering hole with the SS guards on the Obersalzberg.

228. The Platterhof, the Wooden Room.
This particular postcard confirms the level of expenditure lavished on the building. The cembra pine used throughout this room is of the type already discussed in caption number 170, referring to the dining room at the Berghof. To install this particular panelling today would be extremely expensive.

Göring's Obersalzberg Home

The following section, postcards numbers 229 to 241 deals with the country home of Hermann Göring and his family on the Obersalzberg. The Göring home, unlike Hitler's residence nearby was not extensively photographed; consequently postcards depicting Göring's property are limited and quite scarce.

The house itself was situated in the same region of the Obersalzberg as the Bormann family home. That said its location probably offered Göring more privacy than any other resident living on the mountain. It has been stated that the property occupied one of the most beautiful parts of the Obersalzberg. Hermann Göring, unlike his neighbour Martin Bormann, enjoyed a high level of popularity with the people of Berchtesgaden due to his decent attitude towards them.

229. General Field Marshal Hermann Göring with wife and little daughter.
A nicely posed family photograph where Göring and his wife Emmy gaze adoringly at their only child, Edda. Hermann Göring married his second wife, the actress Emmy Sonnemann on 10 April 1935, amid great ceremony in Berlin; Adolf Hitler acted as best man. Göring's first wife, Carin von Kantzow, the daughter of a Swedish nobleman, died of tuberculosis on 17 October 1931, leaving her husband devastated.

Generalfeldmarschall Hermann Göring mit Gattin und Töchterchen

230. Göring's mountain home on Obersalzberg (1,000m).
While giving the impression of having been photographed surreptitiously, this charming image offers a glimpse of the residence through the branches of nearby evergreens.

231. The christening in the Göring home.
This fabulous image sees proud parents Emmy and Hermann Göring on the occasion of the christening of their little daughter Edda. The christening was held at Carinhall, Göring's country estate in the Schorfheide Forest northeast of Berlin on 4 November 1938. Reich Bishop Ludwig Müller performed the ceremony. Hitler, at Göring's request, accepted the role of godfather to the child.

232. Hermann Göring's home on Obersalzberg 1,000m above sea level.
This photograph depicts the Göring home at a stage close to completion. Inspection of the foreground reveals building materials and evidence of minor finishing work still in progress.

233. The General Field Marshal and his little daughter.
Göring the proud father poses for the camera with his daughter Edda.
The child, whom Göring adored, was born in Berlin on 2 June 1938. Interestingly the reverse of this postcard bears a postmark dated; 10.7.40, the day the Luftwaffe began their attacks on England.

234. Hermann Göring house on Obersalzberg.
This image shows the property from the opposite side to that seen in postcard number 232. Taken together they offer a good all round view of the house. The abundance of wild Alpine flowers in the foreground contributes greatly to the overall charm of the image.

235. The home of our General Field Marshal Hermann Göring on Obersalzberg.
In this instance Göring's Obersalzberg home is photographed looking towards Salzburg in neighbouring Austria. The property was typically Upper Bavarian in style; its location, although only minutes on foot from the Berghof and the heart of the complex, afforded seclusion.

Frau Emmy Gör... ...rem Töchterchen Edda

236. Frau Emmy Göring with her little daughter Edda.
This superb studio study of Göring's wife and child is unusual in that it is not the work of Heinrich Hoffmann, the Party photographer. Produced for mass consumption such images were used to promote the importance of family bonds and unity throughout the Reich. Emmy Göring moved to Munich after the war where she lived with her daughter until her death on 8 June 1973. Edda Göring followed in her mother's footsteps to become an actress. She makes no apologies for her father Hermann Göring, whom she believes was wrongly judged by the Allies after the Second World War. Edda, who never married, lives in Munich. She attends numerous veterans' reunions and spends considerable time raising funds for their welfare.

237. Hermann Göring's country house near Berchtesgaden.
As previously stated Göring's home occupied one of the finest locations on the Obersalzberg, this postcard would appear to confirm that viewpoint. The footpath seen to the left of the house led towards the Berghof. Göring had the house extended in 1941. This was carried out tastefully and in keeping with the style of the existing property. An outdoor swimming pool was later constructed in front of the house. Official duties permitting, Göring would often spend several days at a time on the Obersalzberg. His wife Emmy on the other hand would spend months at a time on the mountainside.

238. Interior of Göring's country house. Obersalzberg near Berchtesgaden.
The living room, while fashionably furnished offered a level of comfort and intimacy not readily found inside Göring's other homes; 'Carinhall' for example, the Field Marshal's fabulous country estate northeast of Berlin was a huge, lavishly furnished palace when compared to his modest home on the Obersalzberg.

239. Interior of Göring's country house. Obersalzberg near Berchtesgaden.
Hermann Göring's study at his home on the Obersalzberg appears comfortable and unpretentious. Pictures of Göring's first wife, Carin von Kantzow who died in October 1931 appear on the opposite wall above the bookcases. A photograph of Hitler sits on the desk. Carin's death left Göring emotionally crushed. He later had her remains brought to Carinhall; the estate he named in her honour.

240. Interior of Göring's country house. Obersalzberg near Berchtesgaden.
A view of the cosy seating area at the opposite end of the study. The small figure of a horse on the desk also appears in the previous postcard number 239. Accordingly, it forms a link between the two images, thus aiding the viewer to follow the layout of the study more easily.

241. Interior of Göring's country house. Obersalzberg near Berchtesgaden.
The simple and traditionally furnished dining room appears functional and very homely. The plates and tankards on the shelves around the walls is something typically Bavarian. In contrast to his public persona as a *bon vivant* with a *penchant* for wearing flamboyant uniforms, these images of Göring's Obersalzberg home are totally at odds with everything about Carinhall, his sumptuous country estate. These images suggest a preference for the understated; something bordering on a rustic simplicity.

Other Buildings on the Obersalzberg

While Hitler's private residence on the Obersalzberg was undoubtedly the main attraction for all visitors to the mountain throughout the period the Third Reich; this included the many photographers whose work produced innumerable postcards, the fact remains that certain other buildings in the immediate area appear to have been neglected, photographically so to speak.

The home of Martin Bormann for example, the man who perhaps wielded the most authority on the Obersalzberg, compared to what we have already seen, might just as well have not existed. An explanation for the lack of postcards in this particular instance may be found in the character of Bormann himself, for it is said that he disliked being photographed. As a result images of Bormann are scarce. Where photographs of Bormann do exist, he is usually to be found lurking in the background. Again it is known that Martin Bormann was guarded in his private life. Furthermore, we know that *Reichsleiter* (Reich Leader) Bormann issued orders that his Obersalzberg home should not be photographed, thus guaranteeing his privacy on the mountainside. Given Bormann's reputation, only a foolish or a particularly brave and dedicated photographer would ignore such instructions; if discovered the penalty might be harsh.

The Kampfhäusl (Fighter's Hut) was a small wooden cottage near the Platterhof. On his release from Landsberg Prison in December 1924 Hitler returned to the Obersalzberg. Soon after his arrival he began renting this log cabin from Bruno Büchner, owner of the Platterhof. It was here in 1925, on the mountain he would eventually call home, that Adolf Hitler proceeded to write the second part of his book *Mein Kampf*. Hitler dedicated this part of the book to his old friend Dietrich Eckart. Following the Nazi takeover of the Obersalzberg this rather humble cottage achieved 'shrine' status and became known as the Kampfhäusl. The cabin survived the 1945 bombing of the area with only minor damage. The Kampfhäusl was demolished in 1952; however, the stone foundations can still be found in the woods across the road above the Documentation Centre lower-level car-park.

The Unterwurflehen, this was the house occupied by *SS-Sturmbannführer* (Major) Spahn, Obersalzberg administration officer. The house stood below Bormann's home, it was located on the hillside almost directly opposite the main drive of the Berghof. Period photographs of the Unterwurflehen are virtually non-existent. This house, built in 1900, was acquired by Bormann in February 1937. The building suffered damage during the 1945 air-raid, what remained was later demolished. Parts of the foundations of the Unterwurflehen can still be found today.

The Kindergarten (see postcard number 1) was constructed close to Hotel zum Türken. This served the children of the SS officers stationed on the Obersalzberg and those of the many employees living on the mountainside. During the air-raid in 1945 the kindergarten was completely destroyed. A model house for architectural planning (see postcard number 1) situated close to the aforementioned kindergarten, housed models of the buildings to be constructed on the Obersalzberg and those planned for cities throughout the Reich.

Göring's adjutancy, a short distance from his own home, was occupied by his adjutant General Karl Heinrich Bodenschatz, his staff, and their families. Undamaged during the Allied air-raid the former adjutancy stands virtually unchanged. A small complex consisting of four accommodation blocks was constructed at Hintereck close to Göring's adjutancy. Designed for multi-family occupancy they provided accommodation for Obersalzberg employees and administration personnel. One of these blocks suffered a direct hit during the bombing of the area on 25 April 1945. The three remaining blocks are now state owned and rented as apartments to local families.

The Jugendpflegeheim (Youth Care Home), this hostel-type building stood on the opposite side of the road to the Platterhof, close to where the Karl von Lindeweg trail begins. Constructed in 1939 to help accommodate some of the *Hitlerjugend* (HJ; Hitler Youth) and *Bund Deutscher Mädel* (BDM; League of German Girls) coming to the area, this large wooden building saw little use in its intended role as these youth groups stopped coming to the Obersalzberg once the Second World War began. During the war the Jugendpflegeheim was a 'war-home-industry' centre. A well-constructed and extensive basement beneath the hostel housed bathrooms, kitchens and several storage rooms. The building was badly damaged during the bombing of the area in April 1945; the site was cleared later that same year. While today the site is very overgrown and quite difficult to locate, the aforementioned basement still exists below ground.

The Klaushöhe Settlement was situated outside the heart of the Nazi complex close to the start of the Rossfeld road, one of Germany's highest Alpine roads. This road, another of Bormann's ambitious ideas was not completed until the 1950s. Klaushöhe, a settlement consisting of thirty-two apartment houses, each large enough to accommodate two or three families was constructed in 1939. This settlement was home to married SS officers serving on the Obersalzberg and their families. Despite the fact that this small community of some ninety families was situated outside the main target area, a number of buildings were destroyed during the air-raid. Apart from the demolition of these bomb-damaged ruins after the war, the Nazi constructed Klaushöhe Settlement remains intact. Today the houses are state owned and just like those at Hintereck provide rented accommodation for local families.

The Buchenhöhe Settlement was the largest settlement constructed on the Obersalzberg outside the central zone. The construction of the Buchenhöhe Settlement began in 1940. This larger settlement consisted of forty multi-family dwellings; each house could accommodate two to four families. In addition to the living accommodation, shops, a kindergarten, a school, an inn, a gymnasium and an open-air swimming-pool were also constructed. The location of the Buchenhöhe Settlement in the shadow of the towering Hoher Göll meant that new roads had to be constructed, rivers diverted and all manner of obstacles created by the difficult terrain overcome. When completed Buchenhöhe provided housing for government employees, including administration staff and maintenance personnel. Buchenhöhe also suffered damage during the Allied air-raid. The settlement survives as an interesting example of Third Reich architecture in the region.

The greenhouses that produced the vegetables for all the tables of the Obersalzberg together with fresh flowers for the homes of the Nazi hierarchy were located close to the roadside opposite the Obersalzberg administration building (see postcard number 1). These huge greenhouses were constructed on two levels; each measured 110 metres (360 feet) long by 26 metres (85 feet) wide. As already mentioned (caption number 187), Eugen Bühler was Hitler's gardener on the Obersalzberg. The greenhouses were totally destroyed during the air-raid. Today the retaining wall next the hillside is all that remains to identify where the greenhouses once stood. The area is now a car-park.

The Koksbunker (Coal Bunker), a large building capable of holding up to 10,000 cubic metres (over 3,500 tons) of coal was constructed in 1940. This bunker stored the fuel for the entire Obersalzberg. The Koksbunker stands in the trees on the opposite side of the road to the former employees' accommodation houses at Hintereck, not far from Göring's former adjutancy. Coal was deposited into the bunker from the upper road, where the roof of the bunker was at road level. Fuel was taken from the bunkers by smaller trucks on the lower road where, having reversed into the bunker on the lower level, the coal was deposited through shafts in the ceilings into the waiting trucks. Despite the fact that the Koksbunker was set on fire by the SS prior to their leaving the area in early May 1945 in an effort to deny the advancing Allies anything of use, the Koksbunker is remarkably well preserved. It is said that the bunker was still burning in October 1945.

Bormann's Gutshof (Manor Farm) see postcard number 146. Martin Bormann had once been an agriculturist. This interest in farming would lead to the construction of an experimental 'model farm' on the Obersalzberg in 1938. The bulk of the former Gutshof complex remains intact. Bormann's farm was built in the vicinity of Albert Speer's home. The complex occupied the lower slopes on the opposite side of the main mountain road. The buildings featured many innovations making the farm the most modern and efficient in all Germany. Should the experiment prove a success, the model would be adopted as a template for farms throughout the Reich.

Unfortunately, a combination of high altitude and poor soil meant that attempts to grow crops proved unsuccessful. Nonetheless, the Gutshof managed to produce enough cider, dairy products, eggs and meat for most of the Obersalzberg residents. The breeding of cattle and pigs proved a more successful side of the operation. Despite the fact that the Gutshof was the most modern agricultural complex in Germany, the aforementioned factors led to its complete failure on an economic level. In the end Bormann utilized the Gutshof to pursue his own hobbies, raising Haflinger horses and bee-keeping for the most part. The land connected to the farm amounted to about 80 hectares (200 acres).

Bormann's Gutshof survived the bombing of the area in April 1945 virtually unscathed. The complex was taken over by the Americans after the Second World War. The former Gutshof then became a sports lodge complete with restaurant and golf course. In winter time skiing takes place in the area. The original administration/staff accommodation building, a very large farmhouse and an integral part of the complex, while still structurally sound and perfectly serviceable, was demolished in 2007.

242. Dr Seitz children's convalescent home, Obersalzberg near Berchtesgaden.
Villa Seitz, the home of Dr Richard Seitz was located on the hillside opposite Hotel zum Türken. The house was built in 1922. Occupying an elevated position the residence overlooked both the hotel and Haus Wachenfeld. Martin Bormann, having purchased the property in January 1937 then set about having it remodelled and enlarged as the family home. The interior was exquisitely furnished and provided all modern comforts. The house suffered a direct hit during the air-raid in April 1945; today no trace of the building remains.

243. The complete SS barracks, Obersalzberg.

The SS barracks was situated a short distance from the Berghof, lying just beyond the crest of the hill behind the Führer's home. Construction of this complex of several large buildings comprising; living quarters, kitchens, administration offices, garages, and training and sports halls got underway in April 1937. Initially some 300 troops were accommodated in the barracks. Later, during the Second World War, between five and six hundred men were accommodated there.

An underground rifle range was located beneath the large parade ground in the centre. The buildings seen here suffered extensive damage during the Allied air-raid in April 1945. Following demolition, the former parade ground was turned into a football field serving those who patronized the later restored Platterhof, then renamed the General Walker.

The house observed in the background on the right and above the barracks is Landhaus (country house) Bormann following the renovations, just below that, further right and almost completely obscured by trees are the greenhouses; these provided fresh vegetables for those living on the mountain, including Hitler. A huge 138-room Intercontinental Hotel has recently been constructed on the hill above the spot where the greenhouses once stood.

Postcards depicting the SS complex are rare due to the usual restrictions applying to the photographing of military installations. To photograph the SS barracks on the Obersalzberg would have required permission from the highest level, and, where granted, would have been subject to strict limitations for obvious security reasons. Photographs of Martin Bormann's home are equally rare; *Reichsleiter* (Reich Leader) Bormann issued orders stating that the house was not to be photographed.

244. Obersalzberg near Berchtesgaden Georg Arnhold Klubheim, Bavarian Highlands.
A better view of the property already observed in postcards numbers 213; before reconstruction (as is the case in this instance) and number 216 following reconstruction in 1935, thereafter known as 'Gästehaus Hoher Göll' the intended Party guesthouse. While a number of visiting dignitaries did stay there, the building was mainly used as administrative offices by Martin Bormann's staff. This, the original house was built in 1882 as part of Pension Moritz.

The building survived the 1945 bombing of the area relatively well; nonetheless looting played a large part in the demise of the interior through the post-war years. The former guest house having been largely demolished in the late 1990s was reborn to open as the new 'Dokumentation Obersalzberg' on 20 October 1999; the centre provides a permanent exhibition of the history of the mountain region under the Nazis.

245. Theatre Hall on the Obersalzberg.
This postcard provides an excellent view of the façade of the then recently finished Theatre Hall on the Obersalzberg. A lone soldier stands guard on the steps near the entrance while evidence of building materials in the foreground suggest that work on the building is now virtually complete. The front of the Theatre Hall is festooned with garlands of flowers.

heaterhalle Obersalzberg mit Watzmann

246. Theatre Hall Obersalzberg with Watzmann.

Few images depict the Theatre Hall on the Obersalzberg. Martin Bormann, on Hitler's instructions, ordered construction of the building in 1937. On completion the Theatre Hall could accommodate an audience of up to 2,000 people. Many of the labourers working on the various projects on the Obersalzberg were permitted to attend performances in the Theatre Hall; entertainment consisted of the showing of newsreels and films in addition to the usual floor shows. The large Theatre Hall proved the perfect venue for propaganda events and the official meetings that were held there several times a year.

This rare postcard shows the building which, apart from the foundations and supporting columns was constructed entirely of timber. In this particular instance, and for some unknown reason, there is an individual standing on the roof of the building next to the chimney, thus we are better able to fully appreciate the scale of the structure. In the winter of 1943 the roof of the Theatre Hall collapsed under the immense weight of accumulated snow that had fallen in the region; less than one hour previously a large audience had attended an evening performance in the building. The Theatre Hall was reconstructed soon after. Having survived the 1945 air-raid intact the Theatre Hall was torn down later that same year.

247. Uncaptioned

Images of Hitler's teahouse situated at Mooslahnerkopf below the Berghof are rare indeed. When he was residing on the Obersalzberg, the Führer, always accompanied by selected guests, friends and close associates, visited this private teahouse then about twenty minutes walk distant almost every day. Indeed the daily afternoon walk to the teahouse became something of a ritual. Martin Bormann initiated construction of the building in 1936. The teahouse was designed by architect Roderick Fick. Fick would go on to design the Kehlsteinhaus (Eagle's Nest), Hitler's second teahouse. Undoubtedly the Berghof and the Mooslahnerkopf teahouse were Hitler's favourite places on the Obersalzberg. The teahouse survived the bombing of the area in April 1945 unscathed; however, the building was torn down in the early 1950s due to its association with Hitler. In 2007 the remaining ruins of the former teahouse were cleared to a point where little now remains. However, the original specially constructed 'overlook' close to the building where Hitler was often photographed with its stunning views across the valley towards Salzburg is still there. Photograph courtesy Verlag Plenk, Berchtesgaden.

248. Antenberg Community Camp with Hochkalter and Reiteralpe.

The Hochkalter (left) and Reiteralpe (right) provide the magnificent backdrop to this rare and interesting image that shows part of the barracks of one of the labour camps built to accommodate some of the thousands of construction workers who toiled to build most of the Obersalzberg complex. Situated close to the previously mentioned Theatre Hall, Antenberg was one of the main camps on the mountain. Some 700 workers lived in the Antenberg camp. Looking at the image we can see that the buildings and grounds appear functional and well maintained. At the height of construction in the area some 6,000 workers were housed in fourteen such labour camps.

A large, albeit basic air-raid shelter was built into the Antenberg hill to provide protection for these labourers. This shelter even extended beneath the nearby Theatre Hall. Basic or not, the shelter certainly did its job in providing essential protection for the Antenberg camp workers when the Obersalzberg was finally bombed on the morning of 25 April 1945. The entrance to the air-raid shelter can still be found. Remains and foundations of many of the buildings that made up the Antenberg camp are still visible.

Gemeinschaftslager Antenberg m. Hochkalter u. Reiteralpe.

249. Walk on the Obersalzberg.

This caption for whatever reason is somewhat inaccurate, in that the property viewed here then known as the Dietrich Eckart Lodge (or Göllhäusl) is located approximately 2 kilometres (over 1 mile) from the Obersalzberg. The Göllhäusl was built in 1903 as a holiday home by a Bavarian aristocrat, Countess Caroline zu Ortenburg. The Countess and invited friends would spend part of the summer in the house every year. Countess Caroline zu Ortenburg died in 1920. The property was sold soon after her death but remained largely unused. Dietrich Eckart moved into the Göllhäusl in 1923. Eckart often dined at Alpengasthof Vorderbrand, a mountain inn located by the roadside below the house. It is said that he met Hitler there several times through 1923. The Göllhäusl was enlarged by the *Reichsbund Deutscher Beamter* (Civil Service League) in 1927/28 and renamed 'Dietrich Eckart Lodge' in memory of Eckart's stay there.

Between 1937 and 1942 the enlarged and modernized house was used by *Reichspost* employees as a holiday centre accommodating up to as many as twenty-five people at a time. In 1942 the Nazi Party made the Dietrich Eckart Lodge an annex of the Platterhof Hotel. The house is situated at the end of Scharitzkehlstraße at Hinterbrand. This image shows Adolf Hitler (right) and Hermann Göring (left) in conversation with Minister of War and Commander in Chief of the Armed Forces, General Werner von Blomberg. This charming image certainly reveals the outstanding natural beauty of the area.

250. Dietrich Eckart cottage 1118 metres.

This postcard affords a view of the rear of the Dietrich Eckart house, looking towards the Watzmann. Eckart, one of the founding members of the *Deutscher Arbeiterpartei* (DAP; German Workers' Party) the forerunners of the *Nationalsocialistische Deutscher Arbeiterpartei* (NSDAP; National Socialist German Workers' Party) is said to have exercised great influence over Adolf Hitler in the early days; during the period when Hitler was formulating his own political ideas. Dietrich Eckart died in Berchtesgaden on 23 December 1923 of a heart attack. He is buried in the Alter Friedhof in Berchtesgaden. Also buried in the same cemetery are; Professor Ludwig Hohlwein (1874-1949) a prominent artist and the designer of numerous visually striking poster images during the Third Reich, and Dr Hans-Heinrich Lammers (1879-1962) Head of the Reich Chancellery from 1933-45.

251. The former Dietrich Eckart house as it appeared when photographed in late 2011. As we can see the building has been renovated through the intervening years. It was here, while the cottage was still known as the Göllhaüsl that Eckart came seeking a place to hide from the Weimar government in 1923. The authorities were interested in questioning Eckart about the anti-Semitic nature of his publications. Had he been discovered, Eckart would have been arrested. It was Dietrich Eckart who introduced Adolf Hitler to the region. The Dietrich Eckart Lodge was taken over by the US AFRC (Armed Forces Recreation Centre) after the Second World War and used as a ski-lodge for members of the US Forces and their families. In 1950 the building was renamed 'Hinterbrand Lodge'. The former Dietrich Eckart house has since been used as a training establishment and in more recent years as a summer camp facility by Overseas Dependent Schools. The house is closed to the general public.

252. I was fortunate to have been permitted to take this photograph of the living room in the former Dietrich Eckart Lodge in 2010. The traditional tiled '*Kachelofen*' (Porcelain Stove) is the main feature in the living room. This stove and the wood panelling were in place when Eckart stayed in the house.

253. Albert Speer's former home on the Obersalzberg as photographed in 2012. The house, known as Waltenbergerheim was built in 1903. Martin Bormann bought the property on 10 September 1937. In 1938 Adolf Hitler offered the house once owned by painter Georg Waltenberger to Albert Speer. Speer and his family spent considerable time on the Obersalzberg. The Führer's favourite architect would build a large architectural studio close to his home in 1938. Hitler and Speer were on particularly friendly terms. The two men spent many hours together pouring over plans and drawings in Speer's studio. Speer's former home and studio are located on Antenbergweg, almost directly opposite the Gutshof, some distance below the Berghof in what then would have been the 'middle' security zone. Both buildings survived the bombing of the area in April 1945 and remain virtually unchanged. The former Speer home is now privately owned while his studio is currently an annex of the new Intercontinental Hotel. Period photographs of Speer's home on the Obersalzberg are virtually non-existent. From 1947 until 1995 Speer's former studio was known as 'Evergreen Lodge' and used to accommodate senior US officers vacationing in the area. The studio was sold as part of the land purchase agreement to the owners of the Intercontinental Hotel on the Obersalzberg.

254. Albert Speer's former *Atelier* (studio) as it appeared when photographed in 2012. On turning onto Antenbergweg, Speer's studio stands by a bend in the road roughly halfway between the turn off and his former home located further up the hill. It was here that Hitler and Speer often reviewed architectural plans and models.

255. The studio as viewed from a little further up the mountain road. As one would expect the studio is very well constructed. Speer, in adhering to typical Alpine styling, designed a building that sits comfortably in its natural surroundings.

Tunnel and Bunker System

It would be impossible to complete this book without discussing the ambitious subterranean plans the Nazi's endeavoured to carry out on the Obersalzberg. While we may be impressed with the scale of planning and building work carried out on the surface; what was conceived for below ground is almost beyond imagination. The scale and volume of tunnels and bunkers built to protect those residing on the Obersalzberg is quite staggering. Work on this underground labyrinth began as early as 1940 when Hermann Göring initiated the building of an air-raid shelter beneath his Obersalzberg home. Göring wanted to ensure adequate protection for his family in the event of an Allied air-raid; not to mention having a secure place to store part of his vast art and antiques collection. When completed, Göring's bunker (H on map) had over a dozen luxurious rooms and connected with his nearby adjutancy.

As the tide of war began to turn against Germany, Heinrich Himmler, *Reichsführer-SS*, in 1943 issued orders for the 'enlargement of' and 'addition to' those already existing anti-aircraft installations in the area. The enormous task of constructing the tunnel/bunker system beneath the Obersalzberg finally got underway in August 1943. From the outset the plans stipulated that there should be easy access to the bunker system from each of the homes of the Nazi hierarchy situated on the mountainside. The work was overseen by a team made up of both SS and civilian architects, engineers and geologists. A workforce of over 3,000 men was employed on the project. Two-thirds of these were Czechs and Italians. While there were cases of forced labour on projects carried out around Berchtesgaden; those employed on the Obersalzberg were paid workers, and reasonably well treated. However as time passed more foreign workers were brought in. To ensure that work never stopped, labourers worked in shifts round the clock. The conditions below ground were terrible, and as the war dragged on the daily food ration was little better than meagre. Bormann would make unannounced surprise visits to the worksites to check that schedules were being adhered to; anyone thought to be slacking faced punishment.

Entertainment for the Obersalzberg workers with enough energy left at the end of the working day consisted of films and shows put on in the Theatre Hall. Additional 'entertainment' was provided in a brothel at Unterau. Martin Bormann, concerned by the large number of foreign workers in the area, was anxious to ensure that local German women were not subjected to the unwelcome attentions of these workers. In an effort to prevent this, a brothel, solely for the use of foreign workers, was established in 1937. The 'P-Baracke' (P-Barracks) as it was called, was constructed on the Gartenauer Insel near Unterau; about 6 kilometres (4 miles) from the Obersalzberg. By 1938 some twenty girls, mainly French and Italian, were working in the 'P-Barracks'. These girls were subjected to regular medical checks. The former brothel building was finally torn down in 1977.

The tunnels on the Obersalzberg were to be equipped with numerous safety measures. In addition to basic necessities such as electric power, drainage and water supplies; systems for ventilation, heating and dehumidification were also installed. Additionally, effective measures to counter the introduction of poisonous gas into the

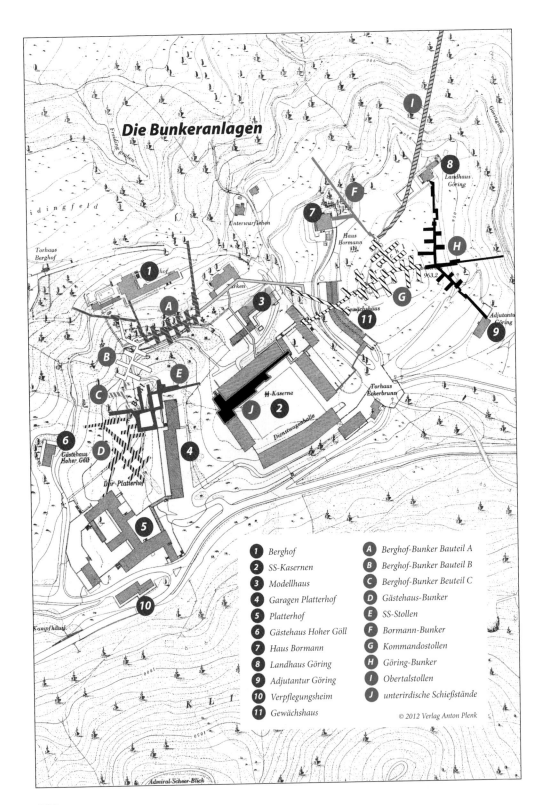

Die Bunkeranlagen

1 Berghof
2 SS-Kasernen
3 Modellhaus
4 Garagen Platterhof
5 Platterhof
6 Gästehaus Hoher Göll
7 Haus Bormann
8 Landhaus Göring
9 Adjutantur Göring
10 Verpflegungsheim
11 Gewächshaus

A Berghof-Bunker Bauteil A
B Berghof-Bunker Bauteil B
C Berghof-Bunker Beuteil C
D Gästehaus-Bunker
E SS-Stollen
F Bormann-Bunker
G Kommandostollen
H Göring-Bunker
I Obertalstollen
J unterirdische Schießstände

© 2012 Verlag Anton Plenk

ventilation system were included. In the event of the external power supply being interrupted, diesel submarine engines had been installed in the tunnels to provide independent power; to that end, large underground tanks were built to store the necessary fuel. Furthermore, Bormann ordered that all thirty access points must be protected by machine-gun positions. These machine-gun posts were sited so as to give the defenders every advantage. The bulk of the tunnels were constructed on two levels. The upper levels were for everyday activity, while the lower levels accommodated miles of electric and communications cables, ducting for ventilation and heating, assorted pipe-work and storage areas stocked with food supplies and ammunition.

In September 1944 Martin Bormann announced plans to enlarge the already vast tunnel/bunker system yet further, and deeper. However, Albert Speer, Hitler's Minister of Armaments and War Production had the final say on how and where vital resources of steel and cement were allocated. Speer vetoed Bormann's request. Nonetheless, by the time the Obersalzberg was bombed on 25 April 1945 an unbelievable 6 kilometres (4 miles) of tunnels and bunkers had been constructed beneath the mountain. Some of these tunnels were in an unfinished state, having been merely excavated, while others had been completed to, in some cases, luxurious standards. The labourers were still at work on the morning of the air-raid. Fortunately, thanks to the tunnels there were few casualties; those who took refuge in the tunnels survived. The tunnels were extremely well constructed and withstood the air-raid with no structural damage caused. The tunnel walls are 1.45 metres (5 feet) thick; being made up of several layers of brick, concrete, water-draining gravel and a waterproof membrane called Oppanol. A synthetic material, Oppanol proved perfect in preventing water penetration in the bunkers. There are places in uncompleted sections of the tunnels where pieces of Oppanol are exposed. The material retains its strength and flexibility, and remains watertight.

The tunnels and bunkers on the Obersalzberg are closed to the public, with two exceptions, part of the system constructed beneath Hotel Platterhof (now accessed via

The Bunkers

This excellent up-to-date map shows the various sections of tunnels and bunkers that were constructed beneath the Obersalzberg during the Third Reich period. With the exception of Hermann Göring's independent bunker, this being the earliest constructed in 1940, everything else was excavated and constructed between August 1943 and April 1945, a mere twenty months. On studying the map it seems almost inconceivable that so much could have been achieved in so little time; some 6 kilometres, almost 4 miles of, for the most part, completed tunnels and bunkers. This map is the property of Verlag Anton Plenk, Berchtesgaden. It is used with their permission and by prior agreement.

Key to numbers:		Key to letters:	
1	Berghof	A	Berghof-Bunker Section A
2	SS-Barracks	B	Berghof-Bunker Section B
3	Model House	C	Berghof-Bunker Section C
4	Platterhof Garages	D	Guest House Bunker
5	Platterhof	E	SS-Gallery
6	Guesthouse Hoher Göll	F	Bormann-Bunker
7	House Bormann	G	Command Gallery
8	House Göring	H	Göring-Bunker
9	Göring's Adjutancy	I	Obertal Gallery
10	Youth Care Home	J	Underground Shooting Range
11	Greenhouses			

To the left of Bormann's home (number 7 on the map) we see the Unterwurflehen, the house occupied by *SS-Sturmbannführer* (Major) Spahn, Obersalzberg administration officer.

the Documentation Centre) and part of the system beneath Hotel zum Türken. The section that can be visited beneath the now disappeared Hotel Platterhof can be seen at two stages of development, these are finished sections, and sections abandoned during excavation. The tunnels accessed via Hotel zum Türken however, once the headquarters of the *Reichsicherheitsdienst* (RSD; Reich Security Service) while less extensive, were completed. These tunnels connected to Hitler's personal bunker beneath the nearby Berghof. The section beneath Hotel zum Türken never fails to impress. Visitors are generally surprised by the depth of the tunnels, not to mention the formidable defensive machine-gun positions. While the tunnels have been stripped bare (this is also the case even in those sections that have been closed to the public for decades) visitors come away with a better understanding of the scale of what had been constructed below the Obersalzberg. However, we should remember those sealed sections that are not open to the public remain structurally sound. The fact that these sealed sections' drainage systems have not been maintained since 1945 means that there is a level of water in some tunnels and bunkers, nonetheless, that aside, they remain as they were when they were sealed many years ago.

A number of distinct facilities would emerge from this underground labyrinth on the Obersalzberg. While many underground facilities located outside the central zone where the leadership had their homes were constructed as rudimentary air-raid shelters, those constructed on a grander scale are worthy of further discussion. The Berghof bunker complex for example (A, B and C on map) had been constructed to accommodate a large number of occupants. For in addition to Hitler and Eva Braun, these included, Dr Theodor Morell, Hitler's personal physician, and as many as forty other people; Hitler's personal staff, servants and so on. The accommodation in the Berghof bunker was quite luxurious. It was fully furnished, with panelled walls and rugs on the floors, there were bathrooms, kitchens, living quarters for the staff, storage rooms, even a private surgery where minor operations could be carried out. An extensive communications system connected this with all other bunkers on the mountainside, and of course the outside world. The Berghof bunker entrance was but a few steps from the back door of the house. On passing through an iron door built into the retaining wall behind the property, sixty-five steps led down into the bunker complex. It seems that nothing had been overlooked.

The other main underground complexes on the Obersalzberg include Bormann's bunker complex (F on map). This was accessed via the cellar of Bormann's home and was large enough to accommodate his own large family and a number of staff. The aforementioned Göring bunker complex (H on map) was the first complex to be built on the Obersalzberg. However it remained unconnected to the later constructed underground system. The long term animosity that existed between Bormann and Göring meant that Bormann would not allow Göring's already existing bunker to connect with those then being built.

The High Command bunker complex (G on map) was the beating heart of the entire Obersalzberg underground system. This particularly large bunker housed an elaborate communications system permitting direct contact with Berlin. While all military activity in the various war-zones was followed and plotted on three large glass walls in a large room located 25 metres (80 feet) below the surface. This, together with the most up-to-date radar equipment and a continuous flow of information being received and analysed from observers posted around the region, ensured that those on the Obersalzberg were aware of any Allied air activity within a 30 kilometre (20 mile) radius. Additionally, all anti-aircraft defence was controlled from this bunker capable of accommodating over forty people. The High Command bunker was built deep beneath the hillside opposite Hotel zum Türken.

The SS bunker complex (E on map), a large part of which remained undiscovered until 2001, was built on two levels. While never fully completed, it is estimated that this complex could have accommodated some 350 individuals. When completed, these particularly deep tunnels beneath the SS barracks would have provided access to every machine-gun position throughout the entire underground system. In 2001, some ten enormous, previously unknown subterranean halls were discovered on a much deeper level to those already known beneath the SS barracks. These were in fact so deep as to suggest they were being constructed with the idea that they could withstand a nuclear attack. The area marked J on the map shows the location of the underground shooting range at the SS barracks.

The Platterhof bunker complex (D on map), already partly discussed, was entered via the basement of the hotel. Towards the end of the Second World War wounded German soldiers were being cared for at the Platterhof and in the bunker beneath. These tunnels were never fully completed. This bunker housed two large diesel submarine engines intended to provide electric power throughout the underground complex in the event of a failure in the external supply, or if that supply were deliberately cut off. With this in mind, large tanks capable of storing many thousands of litres of fuel were constructed in a room adjacent to the engines. As Martin Bormann's offices were located in Gästehaus Hoher Göll (currently the Documentation Centre) Bormann utilized parts of the Platterhof bunker complex to store important files and papers. As work on the complex progressed it was decided to include a lift to connect the Platterhof bunker with Hitler's Berghof bunker some 30 metres (100 feet) deeper. To that end an uncompleted elevator shaft can be found at one end of one of the tunnels in the Platterhof complex. The Platterhof bunker was shared between hotel staff and Bormann's staff working in Gästehaus Hoher Göll, the location of *Reichsleiter* Bormann's administrative offices.

The Nazis were even planning an incredibly deep subterranean road (I on map). Work on this road got underway with the excavation of a 1.1 kilometre (2/3 mile) long tunnel being blasted and drilled through solid rock beginning at Obertal. The tunnel is still accessible and remains as it was left when it was abandoned at an excavated stage. It is estimated that the Obertal tunnel lies just over 100 metres (some 338 feet) below the Berghof bunker system. Had work on the Obertal road ever been completed, those in the bunkers above would have accessed the road below, and the waiting vehicles, by lift; a shaft for the installation of a lift had already been blasted. A similar tunnel, at the same depth, was under construction close to the Gutshof on the other side of the Obersalzberg. On studying the relatively clearly defined directions of these two tunnels it soon becomes clear that they were intended to meet as work progressed. On completion this underground highway would have provided vehicular access to, and escape from Obersalzberg in opposite directions; from Obertal towards Salzburg, and from the Gutshof towards Berchtesgaden.

The Allies knew that the Nazi's were constructing underground facilities on the

Obersalzberg. However they were fully unaware of the scale of these most ambitious plans. Nonetheless, the Allies were concerned that the Nazi leadership might make a last stand on the Obersalzberg in the final days of the Second World War. In reality, apart from Hermann Göring, the majority of the leadership were in Berlin. However, on the morning of Wednesday 25 April 1945, some 375 Allied aircraft dropped a total of 1,232 tons of bombs on the relatively small area of the Obersalzberg in two waves over a 1½ hour period. Some 3,000 to 3,500 people had been going about their usual business on the mountainside that morning. The vast majority of these were labourers, together with the regular staff from the various buildings dotted around the complex. On hearing the air-raid warning these people quickly made their way into the tunnels. Despite the Allies' use of a number of 12,000-lb (5,443 Kg) 'Tallboy' deep-penetration bombs specifically designed to penetrate and destroy underground facilities, the tunnels and bunkers on the Obersalzberg survived the air-raid intact and undamaged. All who took refuge in the tunnels survived. Of those unable to reach the safety of the underground facilities in time, it is said that twenty-two were killed. The damage caused to the buildings on the surface as a result of the bombing was extensive.

On reaching the Obersalzberg on 5 May 1945 the Americans found that many of the structures both above and below ground had already been looted by local people. Nonetheless, the American and the French soldiers who arrived on the mountain soon after them also plundered the former homes of the Nazi hierarchy before order was eventually restored. Exploration of the cellars of the ruined homes revealed vast supplies of alcohol, cigars and other luxuries unavailable at the time. The bunkers were well stocked with large quantities of food supplies; enough to keep a large number of people fed for several months.

The following recent photographs show some of the emergency exits that served sections of the extensive bunker system built deep beneath the Obersalzberg.

256. One of the emergency exits to the Berghof bunker system. This reinforced concrete exit with its heavy iron door is located in the hillside below the where the Berghof once stood, not far from where the last SS checkpoint was located.

257. Another emergency exit to the Berghof bunker system is found below the road opposite Hotel zum Türken. In this instance the iron door is located a few metres inside the entrance. This exit was shared with the tunnels and bunkers beneath Hotel zum Türken.

258. This emergency exit served Hermann Göring's independent bunker system. Built into the hillside, it is located halfway along a forest trail that begins close to where the Göring family home once stood and that of his former adjutancy. This is not the original door; this door was installed after the Second World War. If visiting the Intercontinental Hotel on the Obersalzberg, Göring's former adjutancy is the large building on the right below the drive.

259. This almost completely hidden emergency exit served both the High Command bunker and Bormann's bunker. While bricked up and sealed after the Second World War, some enterprising individual, or individuals, have broken through at some point. Years of neglect and soil erosion have almost completely covered the entrance. However, apart from a level of water in the tunnel that cannot drain away due the remaining brickwork and debris packed high in front of the entrance, the tunnel itself appears structurally sound. This exit can be found in the hillside opposite Hotel zum Türken, not far from where the greenhouses once stood.

260. Another exit serving the Command bunker that is more easily found. This emergency exit is located by the roadside opposite Hotel zum Türken. Some years ago I was fortunate enough to be taken inside the Command bunker using this very entrance. The original door was much larger; the door we see here was installed after the war. However, on entering the tunnel and closing the door behind us we were in total darkness. It was a warm summer's day and the cool temperature in the tunnels was pleasant to begin with, but after just a few minutes it felt very cold, and damp. The tunnels and rooms of the Command bunker remain structurally sound and apart from a little water lying on the floors they were dry. However it is the overall scale of the bunker that takes your breath away.

Making our way through the tunnel we passed rooms of varying sizes off to each side. At one point, out of curiosity, I turned back and switched my torch off; there was absolutely no trace of light, just total blackness. Venturing further into the complex it crossed my mind that should our torches fail for any reason we would have great difficulty finding our way out. One particular room near the centre of the Command bunker with a domed ceiling was so large that I found myself just standing there looking up, wondering why? At one point we came to a flight of stone steps, these I was told had led to the cellar of Bormann's home high above.

We passed the only piece of original equipment to remain in the bunker, part of the communications system, an old switchboard, now slowly rusting away. There were rooms with tiled walls and floors, for the most part the wall tiles had fallen off and lay scattered across the floors. I was struck by the silence; apart from the sound of our own movements, it was eerily quiet. My eyes struggled to adjust to the light as we stepped back out in to the warm sunshine. My visit to the Command bunker was over, but what a treat, sadly one that will never be repeated.

261. The Obertal tunnel entrance as photographed in 2012. The tunnel (I on map) lies off an unmarked forest trail on the lower slopes of the Obersalzberg, northeast of the former Nazi complex. Local knowledge of the area is essential to locate the tunnel. Naturally there are no period photographs showing the tunnel under construction, other than those privately taken. As work on all the tunnels and bunkers on the Obersalzberg was carried out during the Second World War, it is reasonable to assume that strict security measures would have been in place and secrecy maintained. However, in an effort to avoid discovery through Allied aerial reconnaissance of the area, all spoil was removed by fleets of lorries under cover of darkness. Having been taken away, the excavated rock was crushed and used to provide material for road-building and suchlike.

262. This photograph was taken a few metres inside the entrance. Walking through the tunnel one still finds remains of the wooden sleepers that once held the track upon which small wagons carried the excavated material from the tunnel face back to the entrance. Pieces of wood and metal that once held electric cables in place remain attached to the walls. Had work on this ambitious project been completed, a new road would have been constructed connecting the tunnel with the already existing road in the valley below.

263. Built neatly into the hillside, this small store-room is located and a little way past the Obertal tunnel entrance. It was constructed to store the explosives required for blasting work.

The Destruction of the Obersalzberg

The bombing of the Obersalzberg on 25 April 1945, a mere twelve days prior to the actual surrender of all German forces on 7 May, now appears inconsequential, even unnecessary. The objective of such an attack is far from clear, it certainly had little bearing on events elsewhere; the German surrender would have taken place regardless, and the effect on public morale at that point in time would have been negligible to say the least.

Nonetheless, on that morning, 359 Avro Lancaster bombers and 16 De Havilland Mosquitos attacked the Obersalzberg to drop over 1,230 tons of bombs on the Nazi mountain complex. Despite the considerable measures taken to conceal the buildings on the Obersalzberg from Allied aerial reconnaissance, including camouflage paint applied to the buildings and wire netting with artificial grass and foliage attached covering the buildings, all structures within the inner security zone suffered damage during the air-raid. While a few buildings emerged unscathed, many were badly damaged, and several were completely destroyed.

Hermann Göring, his wife Emmy and their daughter Edda were on the Obersalzberg on the morning of the air-raid; as was Martin Bormann's wife Gerda and her nine children. There were over 3,000 people on the Obersalzberg on the morning of the bombing. These included staff from the various residences and those who worked in the administration buildings together with a number of SS and RSD, not forgetting some 3,000 labourers.

Nevertheless, it is plainly obvious that the Nazi complex on the Obersalzberg would be subject to a process of eradication at some point for political and ideological reasons; consequently there is little tangible evidence of Hitler's southern headquarters on the mountain today. Alternatively, given the incredible number of visitors who now descend upon the area, had some the buildings on the Obersalzberg been spared, they might have been used for educational purposes.

In this regard the Kehlsteinhaus (Eagle's Nest) provides the perfect example. During the period that the Eagle's Nest is open each year, from early/mid May until mid/late October, depending on weather conditions, Hitler's second teahouse alone receives over 300,000 visitors. These figures are taken from the sale of bus tickets and do not include the unrecorded numbers of those who undertake the long hike up the mountain to the building. The numbers of visitors to the Obersalzberg increases year on year.

264. Hitler's Berghof Obersalzberg.
The bomb damaged remains of the Berghof following the air-raid on the morning of 25 April 1945. Every building situated on the Obersalzberg suffered during the attack; while some escaped with superficial damage, most were destroyed. The Berghof itself as we can see was badly damaged; looting also took its toll soon after the bombing. Hitler's former country residence remained in this state for several years. In 1952 it was decided to demolish the Berghof and the remaining ruins of all other Nazi buildings in the area so as to leave nothing that might act as a focal point for any future advocates of Nazi ideology.

265. Berchtesgaden land, holiday country on the Obersalzberg.
Somehow this caption seems unconnected to the image; in a way as though it should apply to the description of an entirely different scene. However, this image certainly gives a clear indication of the devastation inflicted on the area in April 1945. In the centre we see what remains of Bormann's home. On the left we see the damaged Platterhof, on the right stands the Berghof. The overall impression is one of complete desolation extending far beyond the bomb-damaged structures to the very landscape itself. The highlighted area on the right reveals the aforementioned seemingly indestructible linden tree that, having recovered, still grows close to a point where the Berghof drive meets the mountain road.

266. Berchtesgaden, Obersalzberg. SS barracks and Platterhof.
In the foreground lie the completely destroyed and partly overgrown SS barracks. Behind that we see the badly damaged employees' accommodation block of Hotel Platterhof, later torn down. The lesser damaged main hotel building itself is furthest away. This was later restored only to be demolished in 2000 for reasons that still evade satisfactory explanation.

267. Hermann Göring house.
The former Göring family home on the Obersalzberg following the bombing of 25 April 1945. While the front of the house suffered considerable damage, the rear of the property, that part constructed as an extension in 1941 remained largely in tact. Again, as with all other buildings located on the Obersalzberg looting took place on a grand scale; much of it carried out even prior to the arrival of Allied forces several days after the bombing.

268. Obersalzberg – The Berghof.

The Berghof photographed circa 1950. The snow-covered Hochkalter in the background lend something of a curious stark beauty to this image. There is clear evidence of bomb craters on the hillside behind the property. The main drive with its linden tree appears undamaged. Today the main drive is terribly overgrown and virtually unrecognizable; however the service road on the left is still there. Following the bombing of the Obersalzberg on 25 April 1945, the last remaining SS in the area were ordered to set incendiaries in the building prior to their departure so that nothing should remain for the invaders. This was done on 4 May. American troops occupied the Obersalzberg the next day, 5 May. Between 25 April and 5 May the former Nazi leaders' homes on the Obersalzberg were looted almost without interruption, firstly by local people, then after 5 May chiefly by US and French military personnel. French soldiers in particular wrought havoc in the homes of the local population. Undisciplined French troops were responsible for raping and looting throughout the area.

269. The blowing up of the Berghof ruins on 30.4.1952.
This postcard captures the very moment when the remains of Hitler's Berghof were blown up on Wednesday, 30 April 1952, at 17.05 that afternoon. The bulk of the former site was later cleared. The retaining wall next to the hillside on the left is about all that remains today. The whole site is now very overgrown. Bormann's linden tree planted in 1937 is again highlighted near the end of the drive. Following US occupation the Obersalzberg would be a restricted off-limits area until May 1949 when the area was once again opened to the public.

The Kehlsteinhaus (Eagle's Nest)

The Kehlsteinhaus is absolutely unique; it is a marvellous achievement for its architect Roderich Fick, and the engineers and construction workers of the 1930s. The building should not be mistaken, as is often the case, for Hitler's teahouse; it would have taken over two hours, all uphill, to reach the Kehlsteinhaus on foot from the Berghof — a long way for a cup of tea. The Führer's private teahouse, which he visited almost daily when at the Berghof, as already stated, was located below the Berghof at Mooslahnerkopf, then less than thirty minutes walk distant; today it takes about forty-five minutes due to present restrictions lengthening the route. The Kehlsteinhaus has on occasion been referred to as the D-Haus, (House for Diplomats) as a number of VIPs were entertained there during the Third Reich period. If splitting hairs on the subject, one might describe the Kehlsteinhaus more accurately as Hitler's 'second teahouse'.

Perched as it is on a rocky outcrop on top of the Kehlstein Mountain at 1,834 metres (6,017 feet), the panoramic views on a clear day are truly magnificent. Martin Bormann initiated the idea of the building, it would be something special to present to the Führer and in doing so he might gain further favour with Hitler. Discussions on the project began in April 1937. However, such was the urgency expressed by *Reichsleiter* (Reich Leader) Bormann, that building work began before the end of the year. We must remember, that prior to this undertaking, the Kehlstein Mountain was untouched, in a virginal state, no roads or buildings existed there. Thus this entire undertaking and everyone involved in it were starting from scratch.

The project had to be completed in time for Hitler's 50th birthday on 20 April 1939. Incredibly the work finished ahead of schedule at the end of 1938. Given the difficulties involved the achievement almost defies belief. Under the direction of Dr Fritz Todt, a new road was blasted out of the mountainside, this exceeded 6.5 kilometres (4 miles) when completed. The road has only one true hairpin bend. All materials had to be moved to site over the most difficult of terrain. During the winter progress was particularly slow and teams worked round the clock using searchlights during the hours of darkness. As for the road; the original plan was that the road should continue all the way up to the building. However, on reaching a point above the tree-line, it soon became clear that this last section of road would be clearly visible from the valley below. This would counter everything that had been done to deliberately blend the road into the mountainside on the lower slopes. From the outset the idea had been to incorporate the road into the mountainside as unobtrusively as possible.

This last section of road presented a major problem. When the idea of constructing a tunnel and installing a lift as an alternative to continuing the road was suggested, Bormann, on being informed that the difference in costs was marginal, approved the tunnel/lift option. A tunnel would lead from a parking area located at the end of the mountain road below the house. A lift at the end of the tunnel would then carry visitors up to the building. This hand-finished, marble block-lined tunnel, constructed through solid rock, is almost 124 metres (406 feet) long. At the end of the tunnel one enters a large circular waiting room with walls and domed ceiling constructed of large Rupholdinger marble blocks; here one finds the lift. As for the lift, it is spectacular, for it is more like something one would expect to find in a top hotel rather in the heart of a mountain. The highly polished brass walls in the lift reflect light in such a way so as to make the interior appear even larger. This lift climbs the remaining 124 metres to arrive inside the Kehlsteinhaus in just over forty seconds. While during the 1930s and 40s the lift might carry perhaps ten people at a time, today as many as forty-six passengers are squeezed into this, the original lift.

As to the construction of the building itself, the high altitude, the weather and the particularly cramped working conditions on the mountaintop called for ingenuity. Having constructed a double-skinned wooden framework according to the plan of the building, this, when approved, was filled with cement. When the cement had set and the wooden planks were removed, this left what amounted to a prefabricated shell of the structure. The outer walls of the concrete shell were then clad in precisely pre-cut granite blocks, each bearing a unique number relating to the detailed blueprints. Thus each block had a preordained place in the scheme of the building before it even left the quarry. This method of construction meant that building work proceeded quickly. Again the limestone blocks for the interior of the reception/conference room arrived in a similar pre-cut fashion.

A cable system covering a distance of 1,270 metres (4,166 feet) with a difference in elevation of 670 metres (2,200 feet) was installed. This temporary cableway carried building materials from a point accessible by road in the valley below to the summit. On completion, the Kehlsteinhaus consisted of; a reception/conference room, a dining room, the 'Scharitzkehlstüberl' (referred to as Eva Braun's room), Hitler's study, a guardroom, a kitchen, a full basement and the usual facilities. Only the most experienced engineers and craftsmen had been employed on the project and only the finest quality materials used in construction. We must remember that there are no bedrooms in the Kehlsteinhaus. Bedrooms never featured in the original plans, no-one ever spent the night in the building. From the outset the Kehlsteinhaus was conceived as a gift from the Nazi Party to Adolf Hitler, somewhere to visit during good weather, occasionally with visiting VIPs.

The estimated cost of this most extravagant of birthday presents was some 34 million Reichsmarks. At the time that figure would equate to around 10 million US Dollars; 140 million US Dollars in today's terms. When completed it is believed that over 3,500 workers had taken part in the task. While the workers were well paid and also received generous allowances, the work was fraught with danger. Despite strenuous efforts to educate the workers about the dangers of working at high altitude and in such conditions, ten labourers lost their lives during the construction period. Five workers died as the result of a landslide on 10 August 1937. A driver died when his lorry left the road and plunged 200 metres (some 660 feet) down the mountain. Another worker died when he fell down the lift-shaft during construction. Another unfortunate fellow, refusing to pay a bet he'd lost, was stabbed to death in one of the labour camps.

Hitler's first visit to the Kehlsteinhaus was on 16 September 1938; the NSDAP officially presented it to him on the occasion of his 50th birthday on 20 April the following year. The Führer made fourteen official visits to the Kehlsteinhaus between

1938 and 1940. Notwithstanding a small number of private undocumented visits with Eva Braun and members of his inner circle, Hitler's last official visit took place on 17 October 1940. Nonetheless it was in this fabulous building that foreign heads of state were entertained. All came away much impressed by this triumph of German ingenuity and engineering. On 18 October 1938, the French Ambassador, André François-Poncet visited the Kehlsteinhaus, while later commenting on the experience he used the term 'Eagle's Nest' in his description of the event, in doing so he coined a new name for the building, a name that has been used ever since. Bormann, Goebbels, Himmler, Ribbentrop and Speer are but a few of the Party hierarchy to have visited the Eagle's Nest. On 3 June 1944, Eva Braun organized for the wedding reception of her sister Gretel, to SS General Hans Georg Otto Hermann Fegelein to be held in the Kehlsteinhaus. Owing to the war situation the Führer did not attend.

Due to its location, being some distance from the Obersalzberg complex, the Kehlsteinhaus survived the air attack of April 1945 unscathed. The Kehlsteinhaus would have proved a difficult target in any event. Firstly, there is its location; perched on a rocky outcrop. Secondly, it is a small target. Thirdly, the granite-clad outside of the building ensures it blends in very well with the natural rock of the mountain. Furthermore, a light snowfall in the area days before the air-raid would also help to disguise the Eagle's Nest. However, having survived the air-raid, the building was marked for destruction in 1952 alongside all remaining Nazi structures in the area at that time. But for the intervention of *Landrat* (District President) Karl Theodor Jacob, the Kehlsteinhaus would have been blown up. Returned to the Bavarian State in 1952 this historic building now serves as a mountain restaurant and remains a major tourist attraction in the area.

270. Berchtesgaden – The Kehlsteinhaus 1840 metres above sea level.
This study of the magnificent Kehlsteinhaus probably dates from the early 1950s; little changed, it remains today almost exactly as it appeared to Adolf Hitler on the occasion of his first visit on 16 September 1938. Eva Braun visited the Kehlsteinhaus frequently, often accompanied by her sister Margarethe, known as 'Gretel', her old school friend Herta Schneider, Margerethe Speer and Gerda Bormann together with their respective children.

271. Hitler's Eagle's Nest (1,832 metres).
This postcard, again photographed in the 1950s, shows the entrance tunnel that leads to the large lift. What we see of the Kehlsteinhaus high above, is that part of the building that was the conference room, now a restaurant offering fabulous panoramic views of the entire region. The large cartouche above the tunnel entrance bears the inscription *'Erbaut 1938'* (Built 1938).

272. Hitler's Eagle's Nest (1,832 metres) Bavarian Alps.
The path leading from the Kehlsteinhaus towards the position adopted by the photographer carries on along the ridge of the mountain to arrive at the Mannlköpfe at 1,958 metres (6,423 feet). This particular postcard offers a good overall view of the building, its location on the Kehlstein and, weather permitting, as is the case here, uninterrupted views of the surrounding mountains, in this instance towards the Lattengebirge.

Continuing under the heading 'The Kehlsteinhaus (Eagle's Nest)', the following images, with the exception of postcard number 275, are a unique contemporary collection of privately taken photographs of the Kehlsteinhaus. To date, with the exception of postcard number 275, I have not found any postcards depicting the interior of the building other than post-war examples.

Imagine my delight when unexpectedly stumbling upon this group of unusual photographs. Mercifully the standard payment of 'an arm and a leg' was not required in this particular instance. As one would expect, these privately taken photographs are uncaptioned. In addition to covering the interior of the Kehlsteinhaus these wonderful images reveal other interesting aspects of this unique and fascinating building.

273. The dining room reveals the finest quality sand-blasted oak panelling together with a superb coffered ceiling. The long table could seat up to thirty guests. The large oak buffet seen on the right was the only piece of original furniture to remain in the building after 1945. The reason for this was that the piece had been assembled in the building and could not be removed without breaking it up; it simply would not fit in the lift. Otherwise it would most definitely have been taken. The buffet was finally removed in 2010 to be placed in a Munich museum.

274. The circular reception hall/conference room in the Kehlsteinhaus was spacious and tastefully furnished. The interior walls are formed of thick limestone blocks. The outer façade consisted of granite blocks quarried near Hauzenberg, Lower Bavaria. It is said that the red Italian marble fireplace was gifted to Hitler by Benito Mussolini. The luxurious thick carpet in the conference room was a gift from the Japanese Emperor Hirohito (1901-89). The carpet was cut into pieces by GIs as souvenirs!

275. Hall in the Kehlsteinhaus.
Another view of the reception hall, the steps in the centre of the image lead back up into the dining room. The impressive marble fireplace is undoubtedly the main focal point in the reception/conference room. The fine tapestry above the mantelshelf was made in the early 1600s. This was one of two tapestries ordered in late September 1938. Described as depicting 'richly costumed figures in a country hunting scene' this tapestry alone cost 32,000 Reichsmarks. The oak beams in the ceiling were installed on Bormann's instructions following an off-the-cuff remark by Hitler. These visually pleasing timbers support nothing whatsoever; they are there simply because they are pleasing to the eye. This is just one example of the lengths to which Bormann would go in order to please his Führer.

276. Often referred as Eva Braun's room, the Scharitzkehlstüberl off the conference hall was finished in rare and expensive cembra pine panelling (as used in the Berghof dining room). The original windows could be lowered to provide breathtaking views towards the Hoher Göll and the Königssee. The original wall lights are still in place today. The large tapestry on the right, dating from the early 16th century described as 'richly costumed figures in scenery' cost 24,000 Reichsmarks.

277. The Führer's Study located behind the dining room in the Kehlsteinhaus was actually never used by Hitler.

278. The guard room as used by the SS between 1938 and 1945. Inspection tours of the security fences in the area were regularly carried out from here. Today the former guard room performs a more peaceful role as an additional dining room.

279. The then up-to-date and fully-equipped kitchen stands ready for use. At the time of completion towards the end of 1938 the kitchen was the most modern in all Germany, boasting all electrical appliances. However, the facility was only ever used to prepare hot drinks or to reheat food that had been prepared on the Obersalzberg then brought up the mountain in thermal containers.

280. These large brass door handles in the form of two lions holding a ball in their front paws were designed by Professor Bernhard Bleeker. They were fixed to the outer doors at the tunnel entrance. The original handles were taken by the Americans at the end of the Second World War. One is now in the possession of the Eisenhower family; the other is in the hands of a private collector. Later replica replacement door handles have also been removed. Both the inner and outer doors are made of copper and brass.

281. A view of the 124 metre long, marble-lined entrance tunnel looking back towards the inner doors as discussed in the previous caption number 280. Surprisingly, the original light fittings seen here are still in the tunnel. When visiting the Kehlsteinhaus it was customary for high-ranking Nazi officials to be driven to the end of the tunnel. They then exited the vehicle and walked through the waiting room to the lift. With no space to turn the vehicles around, the unfortunate drivers were required to reverse all the way back down the tunnel to the outside parking area. The waiting room is located close to where the photographer is standing in this particular instance. The tunnel was originally heated. Vents close to the floor pumped warm air into the tunnel from the adjacent service tunnel mentioned in caption number 284.

282. The entrance to the large lift with highly polished solid brass interior and leather seating as observed from the aforementioned waiting room, which itself has a superb domed ceiling formed of large marble blocks.

283. Looking down the 124 metre deep lift-shaft. The shaft was constructed by blasting through the rock of the mountain. Using low impact charges to avoid excessive damage and reduce the risk of cave-in, teams at the bottom of the shaft blasted and worked their way up to meet with teams blasting down from above. Records state they only one centimetre off centre when the two shafts finally linked up. As already mentioned one of the workers lost his life when he accidentally fell down the lift-shaft during construction.

284. This service tunnel, running parallel to the main entrance tunnel, accommodated all necessary electrical wiring and pipe-work for hot air systems servicing both the entrance tunnel and lift-shaft. In an effort to comply with the original concept surrounding this monumental project; that all construction carried out should be as unobtrusive as possible, all electric cables running up the mountainside were installed below ground.

285. This large eight-cylinder MAN diesel submarine engine was installed in a specially constructed underground engine-room in 1938. Built in Bremerhaven, its purpose was to supply power in the event of a breakdown in the normal power supply to the Kehlsteinhaus. The engine is fully operational and remains ready to perform its original function should the need arise. The engine-room is located inside the mountain. It stands at the end of a tunnel behind a small metal door set into the cliff not far from the main tunnel entrance in the parking area. The original 'shadow-board' on the wall in the engine-room still displays all the original tools for working on the engine.

Hotel Berchtesgadener Hof

The Grand Hotel Auguste Victoria opened for business in 1898. With magnificent mountain views the establishment instantly proved a favourite with visiting members of the royal family and the aristocracy. The Nazi Party bought the hotel in 1936 and immediately set about completely renovating the building. No expense was spared during the costly renovation. Following extensive refurbishment the hotel re-opened having been renamed Hotel Berchtesgadener Hof. The new hotel was under the administration of *Reichsamtsleiter* (Reich Office Leader) Gotthard Färber, Special Representative for House and Land Affairs of the NSDAP. Färber, who also ran the Hotel Deutscher Hof in Nürnberg, had previously been employed by Martin Bormann as an enforcer; persuading landowners on the Obersalzberg to sell their homes and farms when the Party took the decision to acquire the entire mountainside.

Numerous foreign dignitaries were accommodated in the Grand Hotel/Hotel Berchtesgadener Hof when visiting the area to meet with Hitler at the Berghof on the Obersalzberg. Those who stayed at the hotel include; the Duke (formerly King Edward VIII) and Duchess of Windsor; Neville Chamberlain, British Prime Minister; David Lloyd George, former British Prime Minister and leader of the British Liberal Party. In addition to accommodating numerous foreign dignitaries the hotel accommodated many prominent figures of the Third Reich, these include; Albert Bormann (Martin Bormann's brother and head of Hitler's second Reich Chancellery in Berchtesgaden), Eva Braun, prior to moving into the Berghof, Dr Joseph Goebbels, Hitler's Minister for Public Enlightenment and Propaganda; Heinrich Himmler, *Reichsführer-SS*; General Wilhelm Keitel, Commander in Chief of the German Army; Admiral Erich Raeder, Commander in Chief of the German Navy; Joachim von Ribbentrop, Hitler's Foreign Minister; General Erwin Rommel, Commander of the Africa Corps, and last but not least, Hitler's own sister, Paula. Paula Hitler lived there incognito as Paula Wolf. Interestingly, 'Wolf' was a name Hitler had used in the early days to keep his whereabouts unknown to the authorities.

The end of the Second World War saw Hotel Berchtesgadener Hof taken over by the US Army. Again the hotel was used to receive visiting dignitaries, later it became one of the US Armed Forces Recreation Facilities. The Berchtesgadener Hof finally closed with the departure of the US Army in 1995. Sadly, this famous hotel then stood empty until 2006 when it was demolished to make way for a new 'Haus der Berge'. While staying in Hotel zum Türken in 2006 I was fortunate to meet a lady who was in the area to photograph and document Hotel Berchtesgadener Hof prior to its being demolished. This lady invited me to join her in a clandestine visit to the hotel one evening. Despite the security fencing and the presence of security personnel we gained entry to the building. I have to say I don't believe the guards were actually all that interested in our presence. Had we been observed exiting the building carrying away fixtures and fittings it might have been a different matter! Notwithstanding that the police station overlooked the hotel. The demolition team had finished work for the day and we explored the entire interior unnoticed and unchallenged.

We could see where the teams had begun to rip out the original oak wall-panelling, the coffered ceilings, the floors, etc. Large pieces of beautiful marble lay strewn around the reception area and on the staircase. Most of the internal fixtures and fittings were already gone. It was sad to see what had once been a luxurious building humbled in such a way. As we explored we wondered how and why the decision to demolish the Berchtesgadener Hof could had been taken. It was quite obvious that the building had been in good order prior to the demolition teams moving in. We concluded that the decision had been politically motivated. However I must say that it was a real treat to have been able to see inside this iconic building prior to its destruction. I visited the hotel on at least three occasions during my stay.

286. This photograph taken in 2006 and prior to demolition shows the main entrance to the hotel on Hanielstrasse. The removal of the interior fixtures and fittings was already well underway by that time.

287. Hotel 'Berchtesgadener Hof' Berchtesgaden – Dining Room.
This postcard reveals something of the fine oak panelling in the dining room of the hotel. When I explored the interior in 2006 much of the panelling we see here had already been removed. The former dining room was in a sorry state at that time.

288. Hotel 'Berchtesgadener Hof' Berchtesgaden – Reception Hall.
On the reverse of this postcard someone has written; B'gaden on 15 Sept. 1942. The following day, 16 September 1942, the battle for Stalingrad began. Again fine oak-panelling covers the walls and ceiling. As we can see the spacious reception hall was very tastefully furnished.

289. Hotel 'Berchtesgadener Hof' Berchtesgaden – Breakfast Room.
The windows of the breakfast room overlooking Hanielstrasse were located on the same side of the building as the main entrance. The oak-panelled ceiling in the dining room was still in place when I visited the hotel in 2006, but most of the internal fittings were already gone.

290. Hotel 'Berchtesgadener Hof' Berchtesgaden – Wine Room with Bar.
The wine room was located on the lower ground floor at the back of the hotel with views toward the Watzmann, the wine room overlooked Gmundberg the road behind the hotel. In this instance expensive cembra pine has been used to cover the walls and ceiling.

291. Hotel 'Berchtesgadener Hof' Berchtesgaden – Wine Room and Bar.
This postcard shows the bar located in the aforementioned wine room. The chairs and bar stools were covered in red leather. The distinctive tiles on the front of the bar and on the walls in the background were still there when I visited the building in 2006.

292. Hotel 'Berchtesgadener Hof' Berchtesgaden – View from the great hall to the Watzmann.
A view of the magnificent Watzmann as seen through one of three sets of double doors in the great hall that opened onto the terrace. Standing at 2,713 metres (8,901 feet) the Watzmann is one of Germany's highest mountains.

219

**293. Hotel 'Berchtesgadener Hof'
Berchtesgaden – View of the terrace.**
A view of part of the back of the
hotel together with the terrace and
the three sets of doors leading to the
great hall mentioned in the previous
caption. The hill observed in the
background lies close to the
Obersalzberg.

**294. Hotel 'Berchtesgadener Hof'
Berchtesgaden – Terrace towards the
Hoher Göll.**
This postcard shows the
aforementioned terrace together with
some of the balconies of those
rooms located on the floors above.
The tables and umbrellas on the
terrace are laid out with typical
efficiency and attention to detail.
The mountain in the background is
the Hoher Göll standing at 2,522
metres (8,274 feet).

295. Hotel 'Berchtesgadener Hof' Berchtesgaden – View towards the south.
The back of the entire building as viewed from the south. Again to the right of the image we can see the terrace with its distinctive umbrellas. The arches seen below the terrace led into the kitchens. On visiting the building in 2006 much of the kitchen equipment was still in place.

296. This photograph taken in 2010 shows the garages of the Berchtesgadener Hof Hotel located a little way down Gmundberg behind where the main hotel building once stood. These were the only original buildings of the former hotel complex still standing in 2010. However, in 2011 demolition work began here also. The former garages with driver's accommodation located above offended no-one. They had been used as storage facilities by local residents for many years. The upper floor, formerly the driver's accommodation part of the building seen on the right had been removed by Christmas 2011.

By November 2012 this upper floor had been rebuilt in a modern style to reflect the new and almost completed Haus der Berge (House of the Mountains) now built on the site of the former Hotel Berchtesgadener Hof. The two-storey building in the background on the left remained virtually untouched. Perhaps it can survive. As to the new Haus der Berge, local opinion implies that these cold, uninviting, and for the most part featureless modern buildings do not sit well on the outskirts of a small 1,000-year-old Alpine market town.

Nazi Buildings around Berchtesgaden

One might be forgiven for believing that construction in the region during the Nazi period was confined to the area of the Obersalzberg alone, but this is not so. Other buildings were constructed in and around the town of Berchtesgaden itself. When completed, these structures performed various functions including administration, accommodation, security and transport.

The railway station, as previously mentioned, had been rebuilt and enlarged to cope with the increased volume of visitors to the area. On re-opening in 1937, the new station was of a scale such as one might expect to find in a city at that time rather than a small Alpine market town.

The postcards in the following section, numbers 297 to 328 cover the majority of these buildings, all of which remain standing today.

297. Reichs Chancellery with Watzmann and Hochkalter.

The Reich Chancellery was constructed in 1936 under the supervision of Alois Degano, the architect responsible for both the Berghof and Göring's house on the Obersalzberg. Both Hitler and Martin Bormann considered it a good idea to have a building of such status in the area performing dual diplomatic and governmental roles. The interior was in keeping with the status of the building using the finest quality materials throughout. A large bunker beneath the Chancellery provided both shelter and ample storage space for essential supplies.

297. continued

While Wilhelm Keitel and Alfred Jodl had houses close to the Chancellery, further buildings within the complex provided accommodation for staff and security personnel. These buildings survived the war undamaged. After the Second World War the complex was taken over and used by the occupying US forces for administration and accommodation of employees. The former Reich Chancellery is situated in the suburb of Stanggaß. It stands at the end of Urbanweg off Staatsstraße, approximately fifty minutes on foot from the centre of Berchtesgaden itself. The building has recently been converted into private apartments. The conversion work has been carried out sympathetically, with virtually no alterations to the exterior. While the large eagle above the main doorway has been retained, the wreath held in its claws no longer displays the swastika.

298. With the eagle still in place above the main entrance, this is how the Reich Chancellery appeared when photographed in 2012. The conversion work has been carried out sympathetically leaving the exterior of the building virtually unchanged. On turning off Staatsstraße onto Urbanweg, the small building standing alone on the right hand side is in fact the original guardhouse. All visitors to Berchtesgaden's Reich Chancellery would have been stopped by the guards at this checkpoint. Only when the relevant paperwork or security passess had been presented, and checked, would visitors be permitted access to the complex.

299. Reich Chancellery in Berchtesgaden.

This image shows the back of the Reich Chancellery as photographed from a point further left of the flagpole observed in postcard number 297. The balconies seen on the left in image number 297 appear on the right in this instance. Berchtesgaden's Reich Chancellery operated mainly as a diplomatic centre. Reich Minister and Head of the Reich Chancellery, Dr Hans-Heinrich Lammers (1879-1962) spent considerable time here. Albert Bormann (1902-89) from 1938 to 1945 *Chef, Hauptamt I, Leiter der Privatkanzlei des Führers in Führerkanzlei* (Chief of Main Office I, Personal Matters of the Führer in the Private Chancellery of the Führer), a rather grand title, also spent time at Hitler's second Chancellery.

As such, Albert Bormann, Martin Bormann's brother handled much of Hitler's routine correspondence. The relationship between the Bormann brothers was particularly strained; to a point where they barely spoke to one another. The homes of *Generaloberst* (Colonel-General) Alfred Jodl, Chief of Operations Staff and *Generalfeldmarschall* (Field Marshal) Wilhelm Keitel, Chief of Staff of the Armed Forces were located on the opposite side of the building as we see it here. Keitel's former home has been renovated and is now privately owned. The house once occupied by Jodl was demolished in 2006. A new house now occupies the former site.

300. Uncaptioned.
Hitler never forgot his old friend and early mentor, Dietrich Eckart. This postcard shows the main entrance to the Dietrich Eckart *Krankenhaus* (Hospital) at Stanggaß on the outskirts of Berchtesgaden. The now disused former hospital is situated on Sonnleitsstr; not far from where the former Reich Chancellery is located. The foundation stone was laid on 6 May 1938. A 'topping out' ceremony was held on 15 December 1939 when the hospital was officially named. This thoroughly modern hospital, named in honour of the Führer's old friend was opened by Adolf Wagner, Bavarian Interior Minister on 13 June 1942. Within weeks of opening the complex became a military hospital treating wounded German soldiers. The sign attached to the wall of the gatehouse on the right reads; *Reserve-Lazerett Berchtesgaden Dietrich Eckart Krankenhaus* (Reserve Military Hospital Berchtesgaden Dietrich Eckart Hospital).

301. The former Dietrich Eckart Hospital as it appeared when photographed from a similar angle in 2011. As we can see, nature has wasted no time in taking over the previously well-maintained grounds since the complex was abandoned.

302. Uncaptioned.

The Dietrich Eckart Hospital photographed in winter. The hospital buildings cover a large area. After the Second World War the Dietrich Eckart Hospital became the local district hospital and renamed; Klinik in der Stanggaß Berchtesgaden. Sadly, this wonderful building fell into disuse in the 1990s. The mountains in the background are the Kehlstein and the Hoher Göll. The highlighted area in the photograph shows the location of the Kehlsteinhaus (Eagle's Nest). Unfortunately the building is too far away to be visible in this instance. Even the use of a magnifying glass reveals nothing of Hitler's second teahouse in this photograph.

These next four photographs, numbers 303 to 306 were taken in 2012.

303. This beautiful and original marble fountain featuring a dolphin is set in the wall in the entrance hall of the old hospital. There have been rumours of plans to redevelop the former hospital complex as apartments.

304. A magnificent ceramic of Berchtesgaden's coat of arms. This shield is fixed to the wall high above the aforementioned marble fountain in the entrance hall.

305. Another period feature is this wonderful marble staircase located close to and behind the main reception area.

306. The quality of the workmanship and the materials used in construction were of the highest standard and quality. These huge windows at the top of the staircase look out over the rear of the main building. Looking out of these windows, the wall on the right has two enormous period murals by local artist Maria Harrich depicting traditional Alpine scenes.

307. Barracks Berchtesgaden-Strub with Hochkalter.

A view of the main gate of the Adolf Hitler Barracks as seen from the roadside; the scene remains virtually unchanged in the seventy-odd years that have passed since this photograph was taken. With gaze fixed upon the Untersberg the imposing stone lion continues to assert his authority over the approach to the complex. Designed by Munich architect Bruno Biehler, construction of the complex began in September 1937. The II Battalion, *Gebirgs-Jäger* (Mountain Rifle) Regiment 100 moved into the completed barracks on 11 November 1938; the twentieth anniversary of the 1918 armistice. The barracks are located on Gebirgsjägerstrasse, off Ramsauer Straße about thirty-five minutes walk (half of which is uphill) from Berchtesgaden, a short distance past the youth hostel.

308. Barracks Berchtesgaden-Strub with Untersberg.

This postcard shows soldiers standing in the grounds of the barracks just inside the main gate observed on the right. With members of the Nazi hierarchy spending so much time in the area and, given the mountainous terrain of the region, it made sense to have a specialist Alpine regiment based nearby. The role of these troops was to provide additional protection for the Nazi leaders and security for the area in general.

During the latter stages of the Second World War the barracks provided accommodation for high-ranking German officers. After 1945 the former Adolf Hitler Barracks were taken over by the US and put to various uses. Returned to German control in 1995, they are again home to a German Mountain Infantry Regiment, the purpose for which they were originally constructed. In recent years the barracks have been enlarged with several new blocks being constructed. However the new buildings have been constructed in the same style as those built in the 1930s thus maintaining a high degree of seamless architectural continuity.

309. Berchtesgaden, Adolf Hitler Barracks.

Although similar to the previous postcard, number 308, this image appears strangely devoid of life. Having been photographed from a point further back inside the complex it depicts some of the grounds and accommodation blocks.

310. The same scene photographed in 2004; were it not for the large trees interrupting the view these two images are virtually identical. On approaching the main gate a notice warns that the taking of photographs is strictly forbidden, however, having sought permission and explained my reasons to the officer of the day, I was kindly permitted to carry out my request, a consideration for which I remain most grateful.

311. Barracks Berchtesgaden-Strub with Göll and Brett.

Here we look across the parade ground in the direction of the Hoher Göll. A large group of soldiers can be seen in the distance behind the flagpole. A small notice near the flagpole warns; 'Keep off the Grass'. Posted on 22.5.42, the reverse of this postcard carries greetings from a young soldier stationed at the barracks to his grandmother in Linz.

312. Adolf Hitler Youth Hostel Strub near Berchtesgaden.
This charming winter study depicts the youth hostel in Strub. The hostel is located by the roadside not far from the army barracks mentioned in caption number 307. The foundation stone was laid on 20 April 1935; Hitler's birthday. The Adolf Hitler Youth Hostel opened on 18 October 1936. A speech by Baldur von Schirach during the opening ceremony was radio-broadcast to the nation. The complex would accommodate thousands of members of the various youth organizations visiting the 'Fuhrer's chosen homeland' through the following years. The youth hostel continues to perform the role for which it was originally constructed. The hostel is located on Gebirgsjägerstrasse, approximately half an hour on foot from Berchtesgaden; to reach the barracks takes another five minutes along the same road. The latter half of the journey is a steep climb, however the scenery on arrival certainly compensates for the effort.

313. The Führer and Baldur von Schirach in the Adolf Hitler Youth Hostel in Berchtesgaden.
Hitler, together with his entourage and Reich Youth Leader, Baldur von Schirach (on Hitler's left) take their leave of the youth hostel near Berchtesgaden to the excited farewells of young people gathered at the windows. The SS man behind Hitler dutifully carries the Führer's hat and coat.

314. Adolf Hitler Youth Hostel Berchtesgaden-Strub with Untersberg.
The entire region lies still and silent in the full grip of winter while the mighty Untersberg, bleak and unwelcoming, dominates the background. On the reverse the sender explains how their room is located on this side of the building, that cloud continues to obscure the view of the mountains, the depth of snow in the area and finally, how beautiful the hostel is.

315. This image shows the back of the youth hostel as it appeared when photographed in 2009. As we can see, apart from the addition of a small balcony to the window high in the eaves on the left, and the mounting of a television aerial on the roof, little has changed through the intervening years.

316. Adolf Hitler Youth Hostel, Berchtesgaden.
The towering Hoher Göll forms the backdrop for this summer view of that part of the hostel located close to the roadside. The Kehlsteinhaus, while obscured from view by the trees in this instance sits high on the mountain to the left of the Hoher Göll.

317. This is how the youth hostel appeared when photographed in 2004. The perimeter wall next to the road together with the small fence on the right, as seen in the previous postcard number 316, no longer exist. Apart from these minor alterations, little had changed at that time. In 2011 major refurbishment work began on this part of the hostel. The wing closest to the roadside with the 'Jugendherberge' sign attached has now been demolished. The original interior of the main building has been completely ripped out leaving only the external walls and the roof untouched. Regardless of how the interior is redesigned, the soul has been torn out of the building. The hostel complex is made up of three buildings; the other two stand a little further up the small road on the right, in the direction of the aforementioned 'Jugendherberge' sign. One of these blocks has been converted into private flats. The other however remains untouched and still operates as part of the youth hostel.

318. The former Adolf Hitler Youth Hostel as photographed in 2012 following refurbishment. In comparing this image with postcard number 312 we can see the changes brought about through modernization and the removal of the annex that stood on the right in earlier times. While internal refurbishment may have been necessary the external changes detract from the overall look of the youth hostel.

319. View from the terrace towards the Untersberg.
The terrace (balcony) located on the first floor at the front of the building with the Untersberg in the background. The small house observed in the centre of the image located on the opposite side of the road still stands. On the extreme left we see a flagpole with the ubiquitous *Hitlerjugend* (Hitler Youth) flag attached.

320. Part view of the woodcarvings.
Again we see part of the balcony on the front of the building. However, as the caption states, it is the carved wood panels by the larger windows on the right that are of interest. These carvings, depicting figures in traditional dress together with woodland animals are still a particularly attractive feature on the façade.

236

321. The large day-room.
This photograph shows the day-room in the Adolf Hitler Youth Hostel. Landscape paintings line the wall on the left while a large picture of the Führer hangs between the windows on the opposite wall. Despite the size of the room, the wood panelling, the heavy wooden beams of the ceiling and their equally sturdy timber supports help create a cosy, almost homely atmosphere in typical Alpine style.

322. Berchtesgaden with Main Station and Untersberg.
Photographed from a point on the Königsseer Straße, this postcard shows the new train station constructed in Berchtesgaden; the station is the long white building with numerous arches on the left. On completion in 1937 Berchtesgaden's train station was, when compared to the size of this small Alpine market town, absolutely enormous. This was, of course, in keeping with the area's status as the location of Adolf Hitler's country retreat. Many Third Reich officials and foreign diplomats made the journey to Berchtesgaden by train. Part of the town of Berchtesgaden itself can be seen higher up in the background. While the station building has changed little through the years; the Königsseer Straße looks very different today.

Photographs numbers 323 to 327 were taken in 2011 and 2012.

323. The same scene photographed in 2011. While the train station remains virtually unchanged it is obvious that the Königsseer Straße has changed beyond all recognition through the intervening years.

324. This part of the station with its three distinctive arches is where the Führer's private reception area was located. The two wall-mounted lanterns seen above the supporting columns are original.

325. This large period mosaic was produced by the firm F X Zettler of Munich. The mosaic is on the end wall of the *Postamt* (Post Office), also part of the station complex. The post office is located at the opposite end of the station to Hitler's private reception area. The wreath on the flag once encircled a swastika. The swastika was removed from the mosaic in 1945. The shield held by the figure features Berchtesgaden's coat of arms.

239

326. This small, seemingly innocuous building stands by the Schießstättsbrücke, at the junction of Bergwerkstraße and Salzbergstraße. Despite its appearance, this building was once the first of three SS guard posts that had to be passed *en route* to the Berghof. Having turned off Bergwerkstraße, all vehicles, and of course pedestrians, would have to be cleared by the guards prior to being permitted to cross the bridge over the river Ache and continue their journey up the Obersalzberg. This former guardhouse is the last of the three to remain standing.

327. The former home of *Reichsführer-SS* Heinrich Himmler at Schneewinkl near Schönau, just outside Berchtesgaden. The house, called Schneewinkllehen was built in the nineteenth century. Himmler and his wife Margarete separated soon after the birth of their daughter Gudrun, born 8 August 1929. The *Reichsführer* began an affair with his secretary Hedwig Potthast in 1940. In 1943 the NSDAP appropriated Schneewinkllehen. The house was rebuilt to include a substantial underground air-raid shelter. Himmler installed his mistress in the house. Hedwig Potthast and Heinrich Himmler had two children together; a son Helge, born in 1942, and a daughter Nanette, born in 1944. The property is now privately owned.

328. Reich's airport Bad Reichenhall-Berchtesgaden at Ainring.
Following inauguration in October 1934, the newly-opened government airport at nearby Ainring proved extremely useful to those requiring an audience with the Führer when he was residing on the Obersalzberg; upon arrival at the airfield visitors completed the journey, approximately thirty-five kilometres (twenty-two miles) to the Berghof by car. Interestingly, Hitler personally explored the region to select Ainring as the location for the new airport. While capable of handling large passenger aircraft, Ainring's use steadily decreased following *Anschluss* with Austria in March 1938; after that time the airport at Salzburg saw increased use and to some extent replaced Ainring. Postcards of the airport at Ainring are rare, this example bears a postmark dated; 29.10.39. Less than ten days later, on 8 November 1939, an unsuccessful attempt would be made on Hitler's life at the Bürgerbräukeller in Munich. Hitler, having delivered his address had left early, before the bomb exploded. The Führer had travelled to Munich to take part in the annual celebrations and combined remembrance ceremony to honour the fallen comrades of the 1923 Beer-Hall *Putsch*, to be held the following day, 9 November.

Section Four

Associates of the Obersalzberg:

Martin Bormann

Eva Braun

Joseph Goebbels

Magda Goebbels

Hermann Göring

Rudolf Hess

Heinrich Himmler

Adolf Hitler

Leni Riefenstahl

Baldur von Schirach

Albert Speer

The Obersalzberg:
Tangible Remains Today

Associates of the Obersalzberg

The following postcards, numbers 329 to 346, deal with some of those individuals with whom Hitler associated on the Obersalzberg. Whether professionally, or on a more personal level as members of the Führer's 'inner social circle', all spent considerable time in Hitler's company, both at the Berghof and in the surrounding area.

Martin Bormann

329. Opening the Party Congress.

This interesting postcard dating from the mid 1930s depicts the members of the Nazi 'Old Guard' attending the opening of the Annual Party Congress in Nuremberg.

From left to right they are: Dr Wilhelm Frick, Reich Minister of the Interior. Dr Paul Joseph Goebbels, Reich Minister for Public Enlightenment and Propaganda. Dr Hanns Kerrl, Prussian Minister of Justice and Reich Minister without Portfolio. Franz Xavier Schwarz, Treasurer of the

NSDAP. Viktor Lutze, Chief of Staff of the SA. Adolf Hitler, Führer. Rudolf Hess, Deputy Führer. Julius Streicher, owner of *Der Stürmer* (The Stormer/The Attacker), an illustrated anti-Semitic newspaper and Gauleiter (District leader) of Franconia. Behind Hess stands *Lieutnant* Wilhelm Brückner of the SA, adjutant to Hitler. Behind Streicher stands Julius Schaub, adjutant to Hitler. Finally, and on the extreme right, stands the man who has been described as 'the power behind the throne', *Reichsleiter* (Reich Leader) Martin Bormann.

Martin Ludwig Bormann was born in Halberstadt, Lower Saxony, on 17 June 1900. His father, Theodore (1862-1903) a former sergeant in a cavalry regiment and later postal worker died when Martin was barely four years old. Martin Bormann was drafted towards the end of the First World War and served as a gunner with Field Artillery Regiment 55; he saw little, if any action. After the First World War Bormann worked as an inspector in agriculture and eventually joined the *Freikorps* (Free Corps).

The *Freikorps* were paramilitary units made up of former army officers, demobilized soldiers, adventurers, nationalists, and the unemployed. These right-wing groups blamed the Social Democrats and the Jews for Germany's ills. Their main objective was to eliminate anyone whom they believed might be considered a 'traitor to the Fatherland'. The German Army, also believing in the 'stab in the back' theory secretly supported the *Freikorps*.

Martin Bormann, as a member of the Rossback *Freikorps* unit operating in Mecklenburg, was implicated in the murder of one Walther Kadow. Kadow had allegedly betrayed a *Freikorps* officer, Albert Leo Schlageter. Tried on charges of espionage and sabotage, Schlageter had been executed by the French near Düsseldorf on 26 May 1923. Bormann, for his part, was subsequently found guilty of complicity in the murder of Kadow and served one year in prison in Leipzig. Following his release, Bormann came into contact with the NSDAP and began working in the Party's press section in Thuringia. In 1928 Bormann was promoted to work for the Chief of Staff of the SA. Bormann was a good organizer and soon acquired an excellent understanding of the workings of the Party.

In 1929 Martin Bormann married Gerda Bach, the daughter of the President of the Party court. The fact that Adolf Hitler acted as a witness at the ceremony confirms Bormann's ascendancy as a rising star in the Party hierarchy. The couple would have ten children; Adolf Martin (14.04.1930), twins Ilse and Ehrengard (09.07.31) Ehrengard died in infancy, Irmgard (25.07.33), Rudolf Gerhard (31.08.34), Heinrich Hugo (13.06.36), Eva Ute (04.08.38), Gerda (23.10.40), Fred Hartmut (04.03.42) and Volker (18.09.43). The Nazi Party achieved power in Germany in January 1933; soon after Martin Bormann was promoted to the position of Chief of Staff to Deputy Führer, Rudolf Hess. Bormann, the intriguer, the manipulator, was slowly but steadily working his way into Hitler's inner circle. While Bormann had a number of extra-marital affairs, his wife Gerda, knowing of his infidelities, complained little. The film star Manja Behrens was Bormann's mistress for a considerable time. On the subject of Manja Behrens, Gerda Bormann wrote; *'See to it that one year she has a child and the next year I have a child, so that you will always have a wife who is serviceable.'* Nonetheless, it is said that Bormann remained in love with Gerda throughout. Gerda Bormann died of cancer in March 1946; she is buried in Merano, Italy. All nine Bormann children survived the Second World War.

It was Bormann who oversaw the acquisition of land and property on the Obersalzberg above Berchtesgaden when it was decided to create the *Führersperrgebiet* (Restricted Area of the Führer). This led to the creation of a fenced-in area of approximately 800 hectares (2,000 acres). Ambitious, and ruthless in his methods, Martin Bormann was hated by the local population. Indeed even his own colleagues, those in the higher echelons of the Nazi Party, neither liked nor trusted him. Martin Bormann planned and oversaw the destruction of the long-established community of Obersalzberg. By the end of 1937 the vast majority of the homes and farms on the Obersalzberg were in Bormann's hands, whether by voluntary sale or compulsory purchase. Bormann was a man of enormous energy and could survive on a mere three or four hours sleep a night. Indeed it was

Bormann who conceived the idea of building the Kehlsteinhaus (Eagle's Nest) as a gift from the Party to Hitler on the occasion of the Führer's 50th birthday. Bormann's moment came with the flight of Rudolf Hess to Britain on 10 May 1941. While it is generally accepted that Hitler was fully aware of Hess's plans, it had been agreed that if Hess were unsuccessful in his attempt to negotiate peace with Britain, the Deputy Führer had acted alone.

Martin Bormann was promoted head of the newly created *Parteikanzlei* (Party Chancellery) that same day. Bormann became so powerful that he eventually controlled virtually all access to Hitler. Even high-ranking officers could not gain an audience with Hitler without first going through Bormann. Martin Bormann did everything possible to secure his position within Hitler's inner circle. In the end, even Hitler came to realize that he had come to rely too much on Bormann. In the last days in Berlin in 1945, Hitler confided to Eva Braun that he had seen through Bormann, and, that had things been different, he would have replaced Bormann.

It is said that Bormann was so confident of his position that he would send out 'Führer Orders', orders in the name of the Führer, in the knowledge that no-one would be prepared to question their origin. Adolf Hitler married Eva Braun in the bunker of the Berlin Reich Chancellery on 29 April 1945. This time Bormann acted as witness for Hitler. The Führer committed suicide the next day, Monday 30 April 1945, at about 3.30 in the afternoon. Soon after, Bormann made his bid for freedom. Travelling in civilian clothes with a small group Bormann left the bunker. For many years it was believed that Bormann had escaped. Indeed there were numerous reported sightings of Bormann in countries in South America during the years after the Second World War. However in 1972, groundwork close to the Lehrter station in Berlin uncovered two skeletons. One of these was quite quickly identified as that of Dr Ludwig Stumpfegger, one of Hitler's physicians. As for the other, it took almost two years searching through dental records before these remains were finally identified as those of Martin Bormann. Shards of glass found lodged in Bormann's jaw led to the conclusion that he had committed suicide by means of a cyanide capsule. Bormann's decision to attempt an escape from an encircled Berlin was unlikely to succeed, but the decision to end his life was probably one forced upon him as he observed large numbers of advancing Soviet troops moving through the city. Bormann's final decision was based on a determination not to be taken alive.

Eva Braun

Throughout the period of the Third Reich the subject of Eva Braun and her relationship with Adolf Hitler, indeed her very existence, for the most part, remained secret. With the exception of the Führer's 'inner circle', to the outside world she was simply another of Hitler's secretaries. The subject of politicians maintaining mistresses is certainly nothing new; neither are their attempts to maintain secrecy or denial in such matters. Nonetheless the Führer's reputation had to be preserved; he had no wish to see his personal life investigated. When in the company of others, Hitler and Eva maintained certain formalities so as not to reveal their true relationship. In reality, all members of Hitler's 'inner circle' knew the truth, but none of these ever broached the subject in their presence. Not until after 1945 would the secret of their long love affair be revealed to the world.

Consequently it is entirely reasonable to assume that postcards depicting Eva Braun were never produced. To have done so would have given her status; this would have led to questions, explanations and all manner of unnecessary complications which in the end might have tarnished the Führer's image. Few photographs exist showing Eva Braun and Adolf Hitler together, those that do exist are generally privately taken examples and these were certainly not for public scrutiny. On those rare occasions that Eva Braun does appear in official group photographs, she is presented as, and perceived to be just another member of the Führer's staff.

Eva Anna Paula Braun was born in Munich on 6 February 1912. Eva was the second of three daughters born to Freidrich 'Fritz' Braun, a schoolteacher, and his wife Franziska, known as 'Fanny'. As a child Eva showed little interest in schoolwork but was always very keen on sports. In late 1928, when almost fifteen and by sheer coincidence, Eva attended a convent school at Simbach am Inn, (the River Inn forms a natural border between Germany and Austria) Simbach looks directly across the bridge connecting two countries towards Braunau am Inn, the birthplace of Adolf Hitler on the Austrian side.

Having spent a year at Simbach studying book-keeping and economics, Eva returned to Munich where she found employment for a short time as a doctor's receptionist. In late 1930 she answered an advert in a newspaper for a job as an assistant in a photographic studio. Heinrich Hoffmann, already Hitler's official photographer, gave Eva the job. Within a few weeks of working at the studio Eva met Adolf Hitler for the first time, on that occasion he was introduced to her as Herr Wolf. This was an alias used by Hitler during the early days; he had used the name years before around Berchtesgaden when banned from public speaking in an effort to keep his whereabouts secret.

There was an immediate attraction on both sides. Eva and Adolf began to meet and many letters were exchanged between them. Later, in 1932, as the demands of politics took up more and more of his time, Eva saw much less of Hitler. In November that year, during a spell of depression, Eva attempted suicide using her father's pistol. The attempt failed but immediately brought Hitler to her bedside in a Munich clinic. Eva later tried to dismiss the event as nothing more than an accident while examining the gun.

When Hitler was appointed Chancellor in 1933, Eva became a more frequent visitor to the Obersalzberg, under the guise of just another of the Führer's secretaries. Eva's parents, who it must be said Hitler always treated with the utmost respect, were opposed to the relationship on both personal and political grounds from the start. However, Hitler's steadily growing importance then his becoming Chancellor would eventually see this initial reluctance replaced with a much higher level of acceptance as Fritz and Fanny Braun became regular visitors at the Berghof. Hitler's half-sister Angela, had been installed as housekeeper at Haus Wachenfeld in 1928, however, she and Eva did not see eye to eye and Angela finally left in 1936. Eva, a girl who demanded nothing of Hitler other than his attention and affection, who became melancholic during his absences, then assumed the role of housekeeper on the Obersalzberg having moved into the Berghof soon after Angela's departure.

Eva's only vice was something that Hitler detested, smoking, somehow she managed to keep this a secret from him, or, he pretended never to know. Always a keen sportswoman, Eva enjoyed gymnastics, swimming, climbing and skiing which she did on the Obersalzberg and in the surrounding area. The Königssee was a favourite venue for activities like swimming and picnics. Eva maintained a keen interest in photography, something she had picked up while working for Hoffmann. Shopping was something she delighted in, particularly clothes; as a result she was probably the most fashionably dressed woman in the area. It is said she might change clothes as many as two or three times a day. Eva's closest friends on the Obersalzberg were her younger sister Gretel, her old school friend Herta Schneider (née Ostermeyer), Margerethe Speer, and Gerda Bormann; all spent much time in each others company. Her cousin, Gertrude Weisker also visited occasionally. Eva's family and friends were frequent visitors at the Berghof, and, during Hitler's absences, they often held parties where Eva took advantage of these rare opportunities to indulge her love of dancing. Her elder sister Ilse, was not a frequent visitor to the Obersalzberg. Ilse had no interest in politics and consequently spent little time at the Berghof.

While totally uninterested in politics Eva had total trust in Hitler's abilities. The Führer, it must be said, showed great affection for Eva during his many long absences through the war by way of daily telephone calls. Those who knew Eva through these years said she lost neither her naturalness nor her warm personality. Loyal to the last, and against the Führer's wishes, Eva left the relative safety of the Berghof and travelled to Berlin to be with Hitler at the end, arriving there on 15 April. There, in the Führer bunker beneath the crumbling city, the man to whom she had devoted her life finally married her in recognition of that devotion and loyalty on 29 April 1945. Joseph Goebbels and Martin Bormann acted as witnesses at the short civil ceremony presided over by Walther Wagner, a minor official from the Propaganda Ministry.

330. Uncaptioned.
This privately taken photograph shows Eva Braun at the Kehlsteinhaus with one of her two Scottish Terriers, Stasi and Negus. Hitler often teased Eva referring to the dogs as 'carpet-sweepers', a term he initiated due to their short legs and long coats. Eva is sitting on the wall at the back of the building with the entrance to the sun terrace directly behind her; a position easily located in postcard number 270.

    This is the only photograph I have of Eva Braun. Is it not somewhat uncanny that in over ten years spent collecting the images seen on these pages, I should by pure chance, stumble upon it amongst a group of postcards in an antique shop in Berchtesgaden itself while making a final effort to locate some last images prior to publication in 2004.

Eva maintained her composure to the last. The following day, Monday 30 April, Eva and Adolf Hitler said their goodbyes to those gathered in the bunker. That done they retired to their private suite. There, at about 3.30 in the afternoon, Eva and her husband committed suicide together. Both took cyanide. The Führer however, whilst biting through the thin glass vial of cyanide simultaneously shot himself through the mouth with his 7.65 Walther pistol. Within minutes Martin Bormann ordered that the door to Adolf and Eva Hitler's room be opened. SS-*Oberscharführer* Rochus Misch, who was there, states that he saw Hitler's body. The Führer, said Misch, lay slumped forward; his head face down on the low table. Eva was lying on the sofa beside him, her head leaning towards Hitler. Herr Misch told me that Eva sat with her legs drawn up close to her chest. On Hitler's prior instructions the bodies were carried up out of the bunker and burned side by side in the Reich Chancellery garden.

All the members of Eva Hitler's immediate family survived the Second World War. Her father Freidrich (17.9.1879-22.1.1964) and her mother Franziska (12.12.1885-13.1.1976) lived out their lives in the small Bavarian town of Rupholding, west of Bad Reichenhall. They are both buried in the small cemetery in Rupholding. Eva's elder sister Ilse, born in 1909, died of cancer in 1979. Her younger sister Margarethe, known as Gretel, born in 1915, who married SS-*Obergruppenführer* (Lieutenant-General) Hans Georg Otto Hermann Fegelein, gave birth to a daughter Eva Barbara on 5 May 1945. Gretel, who died in October 1987 named her daughter Eva in memory of her late sister. Eva Barbara Fegelein committed suicide in April 1975 after an unhappy love affair. Eva Barbara and her aunt Ilse are buried side by side in a Munich cemetery.

Joseph Goebbels

Paul Joseph Goebbels was born in the small town of Rheydt in the Rhineland on 29 October 1897. Goebbels suffered polio as a child; this left him with a crippled left foot and weakened leg for the rest of his life. An extremely bright boy, Goebbels compensated for his physical weakness by indulging an almost insatiable appetite for reading. It was in Munich in 1922 that Joseph Goebbels heard Adolf Hitler speak for the first time. So impressed was Goebbels that he immediately joined the Nazi Party. This was the beginning of a journey that would see Goebbels become a dedicated follower of Hitler, almost without exception, for the remainder of his life.

Like Hitler, Goebbels was a very gifted speaker. The unexpected success of the Communists in Berlin through 1926 prompted Hitler to dispatch Goebbels to the capital in an effort to re-organize the Party there, and to win back the city from the Communists. At the same time the political infighting amongst the Party leadership in the capital was a cause of great concern to Hitler. On his arrival in Berlin Goebbels encountered abject apathy, generated for the most part by a conflict-ridden leadership and a lack of organization. Nonetheless within twelve months Goebbels had broken the supremacy of the Strasser brothers in northern Germany and had turned the Party's fortunes around. As *Gauleiter* (District Leader), Goebbels' gifts for inflammatory speechmaking and innovative campaigning methods proved a successful combination. Notwithstanding the winning of numerous street battles that regularly took place between the SA and the Communists.

In July 1927 Goebbels established *Der Angriff* (The Attack) in Berlin. This was the Nazi Party's weekly newspaper, which he edited. The aim of *Der Angriff* was to attack and discredit all political opponents in the capital. Later, following the announcement of the *Nürnberger Gesetze* (Nuremberg Laws) at the 1935 Party Rally, Goebbels used *Der Angriff* to urge all Party members to take violent action against the Jews. This was done for two reasons; firstly, it was hoped that in stirring up further hatred of the Jews that this would turn the attention of a now grumbling public and faltering Party support towards a 'common enemy.' Secondly, it was intended to increase pressure on the Jews to consider leaving Germany.

Joseph Goebbels was undoubtedly a brilliant propagandist; as time passed he would be instrumental in creating the idea of the Hitler myth, presenting the Führer as Germany's Messiah. As

331. Reich Minister Dr Goebbels.
Dr Joseph Goebbels, Hitler's Minister for Public Enlightenment and Propaganda. This fine Hoffmann study certainly portrays Goebbels as an extremely confident man who, while appearing relaxed in front of the camera, also displays the calm authority of one who is obviously well aware of the considerable extent of his far-reaching power.

332. The family of Reich Minister Dr Goebbels.
Probably taken in early 1938, this particularly captivating photograph shows Joseph and Magda Goebbels together with four of their six children; behind Goebbels stands Magda's son from her first marriage, Harald. While beautifully posed and photographed this image communicates the impression of a happy and united family.

250

a reward for winning Berlin back for the Party, Hitler appointed Goebbels head of propaganda. The 'little doctor' set about introducing crowd-pleasing dramatic effects at Nazi rallies and meetings. Goebbels played an important role in the campaigns that eventually led to the Nazis achieving power in Germany in 1933. In recognition of his efforts, Hitler appointed Goebbels; Minister for Public Enlightenment and Propaganda. Goebbels then poured his considerable energy into gaining control over the press and radio. His next move was to bring cinema, publishing, and the theatre under his control. Goebbels' power over what was seen, heard, and thought, was considerable.

Joseph Goebbels married Magda Quandt, a divorcee with a ten-year-old son Harald, on 19 December 1931. Johanna Maria Magdalena 'Magda' Quandt, nee Behrend, was born in Berlin on 11 November 1901. On 4 January 1921 she had married Günther Quandt, a wealthy German industrialist twice her age. Their only son Harald was born on 1 November 1921. Magda and Günther Quandt divorced in 1929. Magda joined the NSDAP in September 1930. She came into contact with Joseph Goebbels in the course of her work for the Party. Goebbels was completely taken with the attractive young blond and pursued her relentlessly. Magda Goebbels tolerated her

333. The Führer and Dr Goebbels with his little daughter Helga.
This photograph was taken by the entrance to the Goebbels family home on the island of Schwanenwerder. Dr Joseph Goebbels bought number 8/10 Inselstraße on Schwanenwerder from banker Oscar Schlitter in 1936 as a summer residence. Schwanenwerder lies off the eastern shore of the Wannsee west of Berlin. This exclusive island is accessed via a small bridge. No trace of Goebbels' former summer residence remains. Helga, whom Goebbels is holding was a particular favourite of the children with Hitler.

FÜHRER u. Dr. Goebbels mit Töchterchen Helga

husband Joseph's numerous affairs. But when Goebbels took up with the Czech actress Lida Baarova, Magda had had enough. She spoke to Hitler and threatened to divorce her husband. The Führer intervened, and Goebbels ended his affair with Baarova. Lida Baarova died in Salzburg, Austria, on 27 October 2000, aged 86.

Constantly striving to ensure that the public were continuously subjected to an endless diet of propaganda, in 1933 the Nazis introduced the *'Volksempfänger'* (Peoples Radio). The Rundfunkgerät model VE 301 W, was an affordable radio that was produced in large numbers with the idea that no-one should be beyond the reach of the Führer's spoken word, or the Party's message. Again, the Party introduced the latest technological advances, including television. Television sets were placed in community centres in the knowledge that this latest media innovation would attract mass public attention. Indeed, the Nazis introduced the world's first public service broadcasts.

Goebbels was not in favour of war, but when war came, he did everything in his power to inspire the people. He was one of but a few of the Nazi leaders who continually visited areas devastated by Allied bombing as the Second World War progressed to its inevitable conclusion. In the final days, Joseph Goebbels, his wife Magda and their six children took refuge in the bunker beneath the Reich Chancellery in Berlin. Following the suicide of Adolf and Eva Hitler on 30 April 1945, Goebbels quickly determined that he had no wish to continue living in a Germany without his Führer. Magda fully agreed with her husband in that regard. On considering what might happen to their children if they fell into Russian hands, Joseph and Magda Goebbels arrived at the terrible decision that their children should share their own fate; all six Goebbel's children died by their mother's hand.

This gruesome, terrible act accomplished, Magda and her husband exited the bunker. Joseph and Magda Goebbels ended their lives in the Reich Chancellery garden close to the bunker entrance, not far from where the remains of Adolf and Eva Hitler lay. Magda took cyanide while Joseph Goebbels shot himself. Their bodies were then set alight with the remaining fuel that had been collected for the purposes of burning the bodies of Hitler and his wife the previous day. The Russians discovered the remains on taking the Reich Chancellery soon after.

Versions of how Magda and Joseph Gobbels' lives ended differ considerably. I recently discussed the matter with *SS-Oberscharführer* (Technical Sergeant) Rochus Misch who was in the Berlin bunker. Misch was in the 5th Company, 1st SS Panzer Division – *Leibstandarte-SS Adolf Hitler*. He served on the Führer's staff as bodyguard, courier, and telephone operator from May 1940 until April 1945. According to Sergeant Misch, both Joseph and Magda Goebbels committed suicide inside the bunker using cyanide capsules. He continued by telling me that attempts were then made to burn the bodies inside the bunker, but this proved unsuccessful owing to a lack of oxygen. Misch said that the partly burned remains of Joseph and Magda Goebbels were carried up out of the bunker and burned in the garden. The Russians took the Reich Chancellery approximately two hours later.

Magda Goebbels

Magda Goebbels was born in Berlin on 11 November 1901. Her mother, Auguste Behrend, although some controversy surrounds the issue, was unmarried, her father, Oskar Ritschel was an engineer. The child, christened Johanna Maria Magdalena, was raised and educated from the age of five in a convent at Thild in Belgium, in 1908 she moved to the convent at Vilvoorde just north of Brussels. When the First World War began in 1914, Magda returned to Germany. At the age of eighteen she met and married Günther Quandt, a wealthy businessman twenty years her senior. The marriage produced one child, Harald, however the relationship was not a happy one and the couple divorced amicably in 1929.

In 1930 Magda Quandt attended a Nazi election campaign meeting at the Sportpalast in Berlin. Joseph Goebbels was one of those speaking at the event. Magda, completely overwhelmed by

Dr. GOEBBELS

334. The family of Dr Goebbels.

This delightful studio image shows Magda Goebbels surrounded by her children, all the children from her marriage to Joseph Goebbels were given names beginning with the letter 'H' in honour of Hitler.

Front row left to right; Hellmut (02.10.35), Hedda (05.05.38), Heidi, on mothers knee (29.10.40), Holde (19.02.37) and Helga (01.09.32). Back row; Hilde (12.04.34) and Harald Quandt the son from her first marriage born in 1921. The Goebbels children absolutely adored Harald their elder half-brother.

Harald, a lieutenant in the Luftwaffe was wounded and captured in Italy in 1944. Subsequently he spent the remainder of the Second World War as a POW in North Africa. Harald Quandt went on to become a successful and wealthy businessman in post-war West Germany. He died on 22 September 1967 when his personal aircraft crashed in Italy. Harald left a wife, Inga, and five daughters.

335. Uncaptioned.
Yet another image from the same photographic session. This time Hitler's devoted Propaganda Minister, Joseph Goebbels joins Magda and their children in an image where some of the children are finding it rather difficult to contain their restlessness; typical of all children on such occasions.

Goebbels' oratory, left the meeting a convert to the Nazi cause. They were to meet a short time later at one of the Party's offices where Magda had then found employment. Goebbels immediately showed an interest in the attractive young blonde, as time passed he realized that Magda would be a very good catch, her background and contacts would bring an air of respectability to the Party. Magda offered access to areas of the upper classes where the Nazis still struggled to make a favourable impression.

Magda Quandt and Joseph Goebbels were married on 19 December 1931. Adolf Hitler acted as witness. The Führer was actually very fond of Magda; she was intelligent, confident, charming, and showed an interest in the Party. Hitler realized these valuable attributes could be of great use. Magda represented the perfect Nazi image of German womanhood, as such she supported Hitler acting as hostess at parties and official functions. In time her role became that of unofficial first lady. The six children from her marriage to Goebbels were filmed and photographed in and around their home at Schwanenwerder; these images were used in a promotional way to impart the Party's idea of the model Nazi family, with Magda representing the ideal mother and homemaker.

In 1938 the continuing womanising of her husband finally brought Magda to breaking point. Goebbels had declared his love for Lida Baarova, a twenty-two-year-old Czech actress, his latest conquest. On hearing that he planned to leave her and the children Magda threatened divorce and went straight to Hitler. The Führer would not hear of his Propaganda Minister getting divorced thus shattering the perfect image of Nazi family life. Hitler fully realized the value of Goebbels devotion to him and the abilities he possessed. Goebbels finally bowed to the Führer's wishes and the scandal was averted.

Madga Goebbels also remained totally loyal to Hitler; in the end neither she nor her husband could see any point in a life without their Führer, or the Party. Magda feared for her children; if captured they might be the victims of a terrible revenge, and given that it was the Russians who were surrounding Berlin, this fear may not have been unjustified. With the end fast approaching, Magda penned a letter to her son Harald, then serving in the Luftwaffe. In the hope that somehow Harald would receive the letter, Magda wrote, *My dear son I've stayed with Papa against his will. Last Sunday the Führer wanted to help me leave. You know your mother well. We have the same blood. I had no second thoughts. Our magnificent idea has died along with every beautiful, noble, good thing I've ever known. The world after the Führer's death and after National Socialism is no longer worth living in. That's why the children are here. They are too good for what will come. A merciful God will understand me for giving them redemption.*

On 1 May 1945, the day after Hitler's suicide, Magda and the children were in the bunker. Having discussed this point with former *SS-Oberscharführer* Rochus Misch, a witness to these events, Herr Misch told me how he saw one of Hitler's physicians, Dr Ludwig Stumpfegger give the Goebbels' children something to drink; some kind of sugary drink. It is now clear that this drink contained a strong sedative. Magda stayed with the children as they fell into a deep sleep. Then, with Dr Stumpfegger's assistance, Magda proceeded to go around the room to carefully place a cyanide capsule into the mouth of every child. Each child died as Magda carefully and deliberately forced their mouths closed to break the small glass capsule to release the cyanide. A truly desperate decision taken in desperate circumstances; one cannot begin to imagine the anguish, the sense of total loss of a mother driven to such an act. More than an hour passed before Magda came out of the room where the children lay. Herr Misch could see she was crying. Then, perhaps as a form of distraction, Magda, sitting at a table, got out some cards and began playing patience. Both Magda and Joseph Goebbels committed suicide later that same day.

Hermann Göring

Hermann Wilhelm Göring was born in Rosenheim east of Munich on 12 January 1893. When he was only twelve years old Hermann Göring went off to the military academy at Karlsruhe. He left Karlsruhe aged sixteen with good results. Göring then attended the officer cadet training college at Lichterfelde near Berlin. On successful completion of his exams, Göring left Lichterfelde, aged nineteen, to join the 112th Prince Wilhelm Regiment. Hermann Göring was twenty years old when the First World War began. Göring's dearest wish was to join his friend, Bruno Loerzer in the Imperial Air Corps. He submitted an application, and, following certain irregularities, and a degree of string-pulling, his wish was granted. Hermann Göring quickly earned a reputation as a brave and competent pilot.

In 1917 he was appointed commander of a new squadron, *Jagdstaffel 27*, based in Flanders. A *Jagdstaffel* is a formation consisting of between nine and twelve aircraft. Göring went on to win the *Pour le Mérite,* Germany's highest military honour. The *Pour le Mérite* was normally awarded to pilots who had shot down twenty-five enemy aircraft. However with only fifteen victories to his credit at the time, Hermann Göring received the prestigious award for his leadership qualities and

336. The Reich Marshal.
Göring behind his desk at *Luftwaffe* headquarters in the Wilhelmstrasse in Berlin. The building stands today virtually unchanged.

professionalism. Göring was given command of the famous 'Richthofen Squadron' following the untimely death of its commander, Manfred Freiherr von Richthofen (1982-1918) better known as the 'Red Baron'. Hermann Göring ended the First World War with twenty victories.

After the war Göring spent considerable time travelling in Denmark and Sweden demonstrating Fokker aircraft. It was while working in Sweden that Göring met his first wife Carin von Kantzow. Despite the fact that Carin and her husband were already living apart, her relationship with Hermann Göring caused a scandal. Again, the fact that this lady was still legally married and had a son made no difference to Göring. Having obtained a divorce, Carin von Kantzow and Hermann Göring were married on 3 February 1923. Sadly, Carin died of tuberculosis on 17 October 1931. Göring was devastated at the loss of his wife.

It was in 1922 while in Munich that Hermann Göring encountered Adolf Hitler for the first time. Soon after this encounter, Göring joined the NSDAP. Göring was well connected; he knew influential people and could arrange introductions that would prove beneficial to the Party. On taking part in the Munich Beer-Hall *Putsch* on 9 November 1923, Göring was badly wounded. He received treatment in Austria, unfortunately the amounts of morphine he received during his recovery led to an addiction from which he would never fully recover. Additionally the treatment had affected his glands; this in turn led to a substantial increase in body weight.

Göring was elected to the Reichstag in 1928. Following Nazi electoral success during the 1932 elections Hermann Göring became President of the Reichstag. When the Nazis came to power in 1933, Göring received a number of important appointments. He became; Reich Minister without

337. Hermann Göring, General Field Marshal.
Göring's demeanour is that of a man set on his course, determined, unyielding, immovable.

Most of the medals and awards he proudly wears were earned during the First World War while in command of *Jagdstaffel 27* (Fighter Squadron 27), and later the famous Richthofen 'Flying Circus' following the death of the 'Red Baron'.

338. Reich Minister Göring.

Postcards depicting Göring in civilian clothes are rare; here was a man who much preferred being photographed in uniform. In this instance, Göring more resembles a film star of the period rather than a minister in Hitler's government; nevertheless this is certainly a striking image.

REICHSMINISTER
GÖRING

Portfolio, Reich Commissioner for Air, Prussian Minister President, and Prussian Minister of the Interior. As Reich Commissioner for Air, Göring initiated plans to build a strong air force for Germany. This was carried out in secrecy as the terms of the Versailles Treaty denied Germany the right to an air force. Nonetheless, by the time Hitler announced the existence of this new German *Luftwaffe* to the world in March 1935; the Allied powers stood by and barely reacted.

On 10 April 1935 Hermann Göring married the actress Emmy Sonnemann. Adolf Hitler acted as best man. The much publicized wedding was a high point in the Nazi calendar at the time. The couple's only child, Edda, was born on 2 June 1938. Göring adored the little girl. Both mother and daughter survived the Second World War. Edda and her mother spent four years in an Allied prison camp after the war. Emmy Göring died in Munich on 8 June 1973. She is buried in Munich's Waldfriedhof – *Neue Teil* (New Section). Many well-known former Nazi's are buried in this particular cemetery.

Hermann Göring rightly believed that Germany could not win a protracted war. When the Second World War began in September 1939, Göring tried to impress upon Hitler the importance of defeating England prior to any thoughts of invading the Soviet Union. Hitler, however, held to the belief that peace could and would be negotiated with Britain, eventually. Göring was right; he knew that the *Luftwaffe* was not strong enough to fight a war on two fronts. With the fall of France in June 1940, Hermann Göring was promoted Field Marshal. As the war situation deteriorated, and with defeat staring them in the face, Hitler and a number of the Nazi hierarchy took refuge in Berlin. The Allies had received information to suggest that Hitler might leave Berlin on 20 April 1945 and make his way to the Obersalzberg above Berchtesgaden. Indeed an aircraft did leave Berlin on 20 April and fly down to Bavaria, but it was Hermann Göring, not Adolf Hitler who made his way to the Obersalzberg. On 23 April, Göring sent a telegram to Hitler in Berlin. The telegram proposed the following; that he, Göring, given that he enjoyed a greater level of freedom of movement than Hitler in Berlin, should assume leadership of the Reich. Furthermore, Göring suggested the idea of his making efforts to contact the Western Allies to explore the possibilities of arriving at some form of a negotiated surrender.

Hitler's initial reaction was one of relative calm. However, Göring's arch-enemy Bormann lost no time in deliberately twisting and misrepresenting the entire content of the telegram to a point where Hitler believed that Göring had betrayed him. Hitler immediately ordered Göring's house arrest; and so Hermann Göring was held under guard in his own home on the Obersalzberg. Two days later, on 25 April, an Allied air-raid consisting of 375 Lancaster and Mosquito bombers attacked the Obersalzberg. Most of the buildings on the mountain, including Hitler's Berghof, suffered considerable damage. Göring and his guards sat out the air-raid in the bunker beneath the Göring home. When the raid was over, Göring and his guards re-emerged to an unrecognizable landscape. The guards, following a private discussion, decided there was little point in remaining on scene and promptly left.

Hermann Göring was picked up on 9 May 1945 by US forces near Salzburg in Austria. He subsequently stood trial alongside the remaining Nazi leaders at Nürnberg. Göring was the one man who stood out amongst the defendants during the trials. Nonetheless, he was found guilty and sentenced to death by hanging. Hermann Göring's request that, as a military man he should be shot by firing-squad was denied. Göring, like so many other Nazi leaders, denied the hangman. He was found dying in his cell on 15 October 1946, just a matter of hours before the sentence was due to be carried out. Only in recent years has the information explaining exactly how Hermann Göring acquired the cyanide capsule with which he killed himself been released. The young GI who was standing guard before the door to Göring's cell, had Göring's fountain pen in his possession. Göring had pleaded for the pen to write some final letters. Hermann Göring went so far as to offer a trade; his wristwatch for the pen. Eventually the trade took place; Göring got his fountain pen, and the cyanide capsule hidden inside it.

Rudolf Hess

Walter Richard Rudolf Hess was born in Alexandria, Egypt on 26 April 1894. Rudolf was the eldest son of Fritz Hess, a successful German businessman who had immigrated to Egypt. When in 1908 his father bought property in Bavaria, Rudolf Hess returned to Germany to continue his studies at a school in Godesberg-am-Rhein. Coming as he did from an upper middle class family background Hess was well educated. Rudolf Hess served as a lieutenant with the 16th Bavarian Reserve Infantry Regiment during the First World War. He was wounded three times; the last time seriously. On his release from hospital Hess joined the Imperial Air Corps. He had just completed his pilot training when the First World War came to an end. Hess was demobilized in December 1918.

His right-wing leanings led Hess to join the *Freikorps* in 1919. In 1920 Hess entered the university in Munich to study economics, history, and geopolitics – the study of the influence upon the politics of a country through its geographical position. Hess maintained an interest in

339. Rudolf Hess. Deputy Führer.
Rudolf Hess photographed wearing SS uniform. Hess held the honorary rank of *Obergruppenführer* (Lieutenant-General) in the SS.

340. Reich Minister Rudolf Hess Deputy Führer with his son Wolf-Rüdiger.
This truly fabulous image sees Hess, the family man, playing with his small son, Wolf-Rüdiger (born on 18 November 1937) at the family home at Harlaching on the outskirts of Munich. Displaying all the affection of a father for his son, one can only speculate as to the number of times Hess would have reflected on such moments as he languished in Spandau Prison until his death in 1987.

politics over many years. It was through a chance encounter in 1920 that Hess heard Hitler speak for the first time. The young Hess was so impressed that he joined the fledgling NSDAP soon after. Rudolf Hess quickly became a constant companion of Adolf Hitler. Hess often fought alongside the SA in the numerous street battles against the Communists.

Hess marched beside Hitler on the morning of 9 November 1923 during the Beer-Hall *Putsch*. Somehow in the aftermath of the debacle Hess managed to escape across the border into Austria. Following the trials held in Munich in 1924 and Hitler's resulting prison sentence, Hess returned, and was himself imprisoned for his part in the revolt. Hess joined Hitler in Landsberg Prison where most of his time was occupied acting as secretary to Hitler; he was of great help to Hitler during the writing of *Mein Kampf*. The two men developed a close bond during the period of their incarceration.

Hess married Ilse Pröhl, the daughter of a wealthy physician on 20 December 1927. The couple had one child, a son Wolf-Rüdiger, born on 18 December 1937. Ilse Hess died in Lilienthal on 7 September 1995. Rudolf Hess played an important part in the electoral campaign that would eventually see Hitler appointed Chancellor on 30 January 1933. His reward was to be appointed Deputy Führer on 21 April 1933. Hess spent considerable time on the Obersalzberg, and at Hitler's country home, the Berghof. Those amongst the Party hierarchy, that is those who did not have their own homes on the Obersalzberg, people like Hess and Goebbels, were accommodated in the Party guesthouse, Villa Bechstein, just below the Berghof. Hitler and Hess spent many hours together discussing politics and other subjects during the long periods spent on the Obersalzberg.

The flight of Hess to Scotland on 10 May 1941 remains something of a mystery to this day. The idea that Hitler knew nothing of Hess's planned flight is most unlikely. The two men spent four hours in private conversation just days prior to the Deputy Führer's departure. Hess had planned to meet with the Duke of Hamilton, whom he already knew. Suffice to say that at that stage of the conflict there were still a number of highly placed individuals in Britain, amongst them members of the then British government, who were still disposed to a negotiated settlement with Germany. Hess took off from Augsburg in a Messerschmitt Bf 110 fitted with auxiliary fuel-tanks on 10 May 1941. Hess failed in his mission. Had he been successful, Germany would probably have won the Second World War by not having to fight a war on two fronts, against Britain and her allies in the west, and the Soviet Union in the east. Hess was held at various locations around Britain until the Second World War ended, he was then brought back to Germany to stand trial alongside the other surviving Nazi leaders.

Rudolf Hess was found guilty and sentenced to life imprisonment. So it was, that when all other Nazi leaders had either been executed, or had been released having served jail sentences, that Rudolf Hess, prisoner number 7, was the last man to be held in Spandau Prison in Berlin. Thus a prison of six hundred cells was home to just one man, a very expensive undertaking. Eventually, Britain, France and the United States would agree that Hess might be released on humanitarian grounds. The Russians however, would never agree, they would continually veto such a move. Much controversy and speculation surrounds the mysterious death of Rudolf Hess. He was found hanged in a summer house in the grounds of Spandau Prison on 17 August 1987. At the time of his death Hess was almost 93 years old and in poor health. He walked with the aid of a stick and could not rise from a chair unaided. Nonetheless, despite these infirmities, Rudolf Hess still managed to hang himself with a piece of electric wire.

The affidavit of Abdallah Melaouhi, the civilian male nurse who had attended Rudolf Hess during the last five years of his life makes most interesting reading. What information did Hess have that might embarrass or even destroy the reputations of so many people that it would for ever prevent his release. Why have so many successive governments refused to release the paperwork surrounding his capture and subsequent interrogation. Many unanswered questions surround the imprisonment and death of the former Deputy Führer, Rudolf Hess.

341. Reich Minister Rudolf Hess, Deputy Führer, with his son Wolf-Rüdiger.
Joyful and carefree, Hess expects his son may fall from the shutter at any moment and, like any loving father, he is prepared to catch the boy instantly should this happen. These photographs were taken just a short time before Hess's fateful flight to Britain on 10 May 1941.

Heinrich Himmler

Heinrich Luitpold Himmler was born in Munich on 7 October 1900. His father, Joseph, was a secondary school teacher. Heinrich had two brothers, Gebhard, born on 29 July 1898 and Ernst, born on 23 December 1905. As a student Himmler did well at school. Towards the end of 1917 he began officer training with the 11th Bavarian Infantry Regiment. Himmler never managed to see action during the First World War; this would remain a source of irritation to him for the rest of his life. Having left the army Heinrich Himmler became a student of agriculture at the Munich Technische Hochschule in 1919.

In 1920 Himmler met Captain Ernst Röhm. Röhm recruited Himmler to the NSDAP and introduced him to Adolf Hitler. Having successfully completed his studies Himmler found employment as an agriculturist in Schlessheim. Himmler took part in the unsuccessful Beer-Hall

342. The Reichsführer-SS visiting SS-Panzer-Grenadier-Regiment 'Der Führer'.
Heinrich Himmler, Head of the SS, the police, and the Gestapo.
This postcard shows Himmler (centre) in discussion with *Brigadeführer* (Major-General) Dr Otto Wachter and *Brigadeführer* Friedrich Freitag while visiting SS-Panzer-Grenadier-Regiment - *Der Führer*. *Der Führer* was a combat unit of the 2nd SS-Panzer-Division - *Das Reich*, this Division produced more Knights' Cross winners than any other, sixty-nine in total.

A typical SS Division consisted of some 15,000 fighting men together with between 5,000 and 6,000 support personnel. The reverse of this postcard bears a large contemporary regimental stamp that has subsequently been completed by hand recording the details of the event.

Putsch on 9 November 1923. Amazingly, Himmler, somehow managed to avoid both injury and arrest. In July 1928 Himmler married Margarete Boden, almost eight years his senior. The rather unhappy marriage produced one child, a daughter, Gudrun, born on 8 August 1929, whom Himmler adored. The couple separated soon after the birth of their child. Gudrun Himmler was presented as the perfect German child and spoiled by her adoring father. Something rather odd is the fact that Gudrun occasionally accompanied her father when he visited the concentration camps.

Himmler had a reputation as paying great attention to detail; he adopted a methodical approach to all tasks. In January 1929 Hitler appointed Himmler head of a recently formed small group existing within the much larger SA, the SS. Himmler brought his considerable organizational skills into play and set about building up the SS and introducing strict recruitment criteria. Hitler, for his part, took little interest initially, but he approved Himmler's plans. By 1933 the SS had grown to a force of about 50,000 men. In 1940 Himmler began an affair with his secretary, Hedwig Potthast; she bore him two children, a son Helge, born in 1942, and a daughter Nanette, born in 1944.

During the Second World War the *Waffen-SS* (Military SS) fought on every front. The men of the *Waffen-SS* quickly earned a reputation for being very tough soldiers. Himmler had created an élite force, one to be feared on the battlefield. In the end the Waffen-SS consisted of thirty-eight divisions, almost one million men. In April 1934 Himmler was given control of the *Geheime Staatspolizei* (Gestapo; Secret State Police). In June 1936 he became Chief of German Police with the title *Reichsführer-SS*. In 1943 he replaced Wilhelm Frick as Reich Minister of the Interior. Himmler had far reaching powers. He oversaw the setting up and running of the first concentration camps prior to the outbreak of the Second World War with his usual efficiency and meticulous attention to detail.

By 1944 Himmler realized that Germany could no longer win the war. This realization eventually led to thoughts of self-preservation. In February 1945 Himmler had a private meeting with Count Folke Bernadotte, a representative of the Swedish Red Cross. The meeting took place to discuss the possible release of Danish and Norwegian prisoners held in the concentration camp system. This was the first stage in Himmler's bid to gain favour with the Allies. Later, and as the military situation deteriorated, his efforts became more frantic. He went so far as to ask Folke Bernadotte to attempt to arrange a meeting with Eisenhower. His efforts came to nothing. Hitler, on learning of Himmler's actions commented, that this was the worst act of treachery he had ever known.

With the Führer dead and the war over, Himmler attempted to evade capture. Shaving off his moustache and wearing an eye-patch he further attempted to disguise himself by wearing a tattered sergeant's uniform. Himmler and his travelling companions were picked up near Bremervörde, west of Hamburg on 21 May 1945. Himmler's downfall was the fact that he presented brand new identification papers to British troops manning a checkpoint at a time when hardly anyone could produce any papers at all, let alone newly issued and complete. He was subsequently arrested and brought to Lüneburg for questioning. Two days later on 23 May 1945, having admitted his identity and while being medically examined, Heinrich Himmler bit down hard on a cyanide capsule hidden in his mouth and died on the spot. His remains were buried in an unmarked grave on Lüneburg Heath on 26 May 1945.

Adolf Hitler

Adolf Hitler was born in the small Austrian border town of Braunau am Inn on 20 April 1889. It was there that his father, Alois, worked as an Inspector of Customs along the Austrian/German border. Alois Hitler, (1837-1903) despite rather humble beginnings, had done well to achieve a position of which he was justly proud. A strict disciplinarian, Alois administered physical punishment to his rebellious son Adolf on an almost daily basis. Hitler's mother, Klara, (1860-1907) on the other hand always tried to protect her son. Where his father failed to gain obedience through toughness and beatings, Hitler's mother proved the more successful with her gentle ways, appeals, and persuasion. Needless to say, Adolf Hitler adored his mother. On retiring from the Customs Service, Alois Hitler moved the family to Leonding just outside Linz. It was there on the morning of 3 January 1903 while out for his morning walk that Hitler's father suddenly felt unwell. He made his way into his local inn, Gasthaus Stiefler, where he died of a pleural haemorrhage. Klara Hitler moved the family to Urfhar, a suburb of Linz soon after her husband's death.

Since he had been a boy Adolf Hitler had dreamed of being an artist; a subject upon which he and his father continually disagreed. With his father now dead, Hitler moved to Vienna in the hope of pursuing that dream. He sat the entrance exam to the Academy of Fine Arts in Vienna in October 1907, but was rejected on the grounds that it was felt his work lacked imagination. This was a great blow to the would-be artist, nonetheless Hitler remained in Vienna. Towards the end of November that year Hitler received word that his mother was unwell and that he should return home. Hitler returned to Linz to find that his mother was in fact dying of breast cancer. Taking charge, Adolf Hitler tenderly nursed his mother through her final weeks; she died on 21 December 1907. Hitler was emotionally devastated.

Adolf Hitler returned to Vienna soon after his mother's passing. He had a small allowance, and this combined with what money he earned from selling small, postcard-sized drawings and watercolours that he produced of the better known buildings around the city provided enough to rent a room and to feed himself. Towards the end of 1908 Hitler returned to the Academy of Fine Arts with the intention of sitting the entrance exam a second time. Unfortunately for him, some of those who had judged his work the previous year, recognized him, and he was not allowed to sit the exam. While Hitler continually sent some of his own small allowance to help his younger sister Paula, his own financial situation got steadily worse. In the end he could no longer afford the room and he was forced to live on the streets. It was through this situation, while he was living in the city's homeless men's hostels, that Hitler first came into contact with those possessed of extreme political views.

Turning his back on Vienna, Adolf Hitler left the city in 1913 and made his way to Munich. It has been said that Hitler made this move to avoid the draft. Apparently he had received notification from the Austrian authorities that he was required to do military service. However, in February 1914 Hitler presented himself in Salzburg, Austria, for medical examination. His lifestyle prior to this point had been one of living rough and irregular eating habits for the most part with the result that he was considered unfit for military service. The medical report concluded with the line; 'too weak to bear arms'. Hitler returned to Munich.

With the outbreak of the First World War in August 1914, Hitler immediately volunteered. However, as an Austrian, he had to seek permission to be allowed to serve in the German Army. To his great delight, permission was granted. Adolf Hitler served through the entire period of the First World War with the 16th Bavarian Reserve Infantry Regiment (List Regiment). Hitler proved a brave and able soldier. During four years he took part in no less than forty-seven battles, often in the thick of the fighting. He was wounded in the leg in October 1917 and the victim of a gas attack in late 1918. Adolf Hitler would win the Iron Cross, both first and second class during the conflict. The gas attack in 1918 left Hitler temporarily blinded. It was while he was recovering from these injuries in hospital at Pasewalk that the First World War came to and end. Adolf Hitler, like many

343. Uncaptioned.
The reverse of this fine Hoffmann study of the Führer bears a commemorative stamp and postmark celebrating the annexation of Austria to German Reich. It reads; 10 April 1938 Wien (Vienna) *Ein Volk • Ein Reich • Ein Führer* (One People • One State • One Leader). Two days later, on 12 April 1938, Hitler announced the establishment of the Greater German Reich in a speech in the Rathaus in Linz, Austria.

of his comrades, felt that the German army, while it had not been defeated on the battlefield, had been dealt a stab in the back by the weak politicians at home.

Hitler was finally released from hospital but he remained in military service. In 1919 he underwent training as a 'political officer'. Having completed his training, Hitler's job was to ensure that the troops were not influenced by those advocating socialist, pacifist, and even democratic ideas. Again in 1919 the head of the political section of the army gave Hitler a specific task. He was instructed to attend, in civilian clothes, the meetings of both left and right-wing political groups around the city of Munich. His job was to go along to these meetings, listen to what was being said, and then report his findings to his superiors. In this way it was hoped to learn what was happening at a grass-roots level on the then turbulent political scene.

It was while doing this work that Adolf Hitler first came in contact with a particular small right-wing group, the *Deutscher Arbeiterpartei* (German Workers' Party) in September 1919. Going along to the meetings Hitler discovered that the views of this party were actually very similar to his own views. Hitler joined the German Workers' Party as member number 55. When Hitler joined the German Workers' Party's Executive Committee his original membership number 55 would be altered; Hitler then became number 7. It was only then that Hitler discovered that he could hold an audience through the power of his oratory. He was soon addressing the meetings of the German Workers' Party on a regular basis and encouraging new membership. Hitler finally left the army in April 1920. Undoubtedly Hitler's greatest attribute was his natural ability as a great orator, but also his uncanny ability to attune to the expectations and needs of his audiences. Additionally he had a fantastic memory; Hitler could accurately recall minute details from conversations and events that had taken place many years before.

By July 1921 Adolf Hitler had won the internal battle for control of the party, now renamed the *Nationalsozialistische Deutsche Arbeiterpartei* (NSDAP; National Socialist German Workers' Party). On 9 November 1923 the Nazis attempted to seize power in Bavaria when they carried out the Munich Beer-Hall *Putsch* (Revolt). The attempt failed, and Hitler subsequently stood trial on a charge of treason. If convicted, and given the maximum penalty under the law, Hitler was in fact facing a death penalty. The trials began on 28 February 1924. Of the accused, Adolf Hitler would dominate the proceedings. Thanks to the intervention of powerful friends in the Justice Ministry, and while highly irregular, Hitler was permitted to cross-examine witnesses. Additionally, he was allowed to make what amounted to speeches and proclamations promoting the Party's ideals during the trials. Again, thanks to the intervention of these same powerful friends and a judge who was not unsympathetic towards the Nazis, Hitler was sentenced to five years imprisonment on 1 April 1924. This, in fact, was the minimum sentence that could be handed down to a person convicted of treason.

The trials attracted great media attention. The press reported the trials throughout Germany and beyond on a daily basis. Hitler seized upon the interest of the press, here was his opportunity, and he made the most of it. By the end of the proceedings Hitler had emerged as both victim and patriot. He and his party had achieved a level of publicity they might otherwise never have dreamed of. The *Putsch* had not been a failure after all. It was around this time that Adolf Hitler decided that all further attempts to achieve power would be by legal means. In the meantime, he was dispatched to the prison fortress at Landsberg am Lech to serve his sentence. On his arrival at Landsberg, Hitler found he was treated as something of a celebrity. His cell door was left open most of the time, he had the freedom of the prison grounds, and he could receive visitors. It was during this period of incarnation that Hitler wrote the first part of his book; *Mein Kampf* (My Struggle). His friend and fellow-prisoner, Rudolf Hess, acted as secretary to Hitler during this time.

Adolf Hitler was released from Landsberg Prison on 20 December 1924. He had in fact served less than twelve months of the five year sentence. Upon his release he immediately returned to Berchtesgaden where he stayed with friends and benefactors. One of the terms of Hitler's early prison release was a ban on public speaking. But that did not stop Adolf Hitler; he still found opportunities to speak to local people and those in the surrounding areas. He did however keep quite a low profile, should the authorities back in Munich get wind of his public speaking activities he might just find himself back in prison. It was during this time, while renting a small hut on the Obersalzberg above Berchtesgaden that Hitler wrote the second part of *Mein Kampf.*

Notwithstanding the charismatic, almost magnetic personality and oratory of its leader, Adolf Hitler, many ordinary Germans were drawn to the Nazi Party simply because it opposed Communism. Nonetheless, while the Party attempted to assume the mantle of respectability, the existing mainstream political parties viewed the NSDAP as upstarts not to be taken seriously. This failure to recognize what was really happening would be their undoing. While never able to achieve an overall majority in the Reichstag, the NSDAP achieved great electoral success during the many elections held in Germany through the late 1920s and early 1930s. The elections held in November 1932 saw the Nazis emerge as the single strongest political party in Germany. In the end the NSDAP came to power through legal means. No longer able to exclude Hitler and the Nazis, and seeing their own position weakened, German Chancellor Franz von Papen and Field Marshal Paul von Hindenburg, the ageing German President did a deal; they offered Hitler the Chancellorship with von Papen as Vice-Chancellor, believing in this way they might contain and control Hitler. They were wrong. Once in power, Hitler, the skilled politician, easily outmanoeuvred his soon-to-be bewildered would-be keepers with ease.

Adolf Hitler acted quickly in his bid to gather all power unto himself. The Enabling Act that was passed on 24 March 1933 gave him independence from both the Reichstag and the President. Previous Chancellors had been dependent on the President's power to issue emergency decrees under Article 48 of the Constitution. Hitler now reserved that right for himself; furthermore, he now had the right to set aside the Constitution itself. President von Hindenburg died on 2 August 1934. Within a matter of hours of his passing it was announced that henceforth the office of President would be merged with that of Chancellor. Effectively Adolf Hitler would become Head of State and Commander-in-Chief of the German Armed Forces. Later that day the men of the German Army swore an oath of allegiance to their new commander, Adolf Hitler.

On 19 August 1934 the German people went to the polls to vote on the amalgamation of the powers of the President's office with those of the Reich Chancellor, 95.7 per cent of the electorate went to the polls. Of over forty-five million voters who turned out, thirty-eight million, 89.93 per cent voted in favour. Hitler was jubilant; he had achieved everything he had set out to. The following years were spent openly defying the terms of the much-hated Versailles Treaty imposed on the German nation in 1919. Hitler set about regaining many of the former German territories lost following the First World War. Again, apart from some diplomatic protesting on the part of the Western Allies, chiefly Britain and France, there was no action taken. Even when German forces entered Czechoslovakia in 1939 the European powers sat idly by. Hitler's popularity at home was now immense. German national pride had been restored. The injustices of the Versailles Treaty had been redressed.

The Führer would soon turn his attention towards Poland and the east, leading his reinvigorated country into a world war that would spell disaster for millions. Adolf Hitler would shoot himself in his Berlin bunker on 30 April 1945 as the great empire he had built crumbled around him. Eva Hitler would end her life at her husband's side, taking cyanide. The Führer had left instructions as to what should take place after his death, and these were followed to the letter. Hitler had previously ordered that fuel should be collected and brought to the Reich Chancellery. The two bodies were carried up out of the bunker, and under almost continuous Russian artillery bombardment, the remains were placed side by side in a shell crater close to the bunker entrance. Fuel was poured into the crater and over the remains; then set alight.

Hitler's reasoning for not having married as a younger man was in part explained in a conversation he had with his valet, Heinz Linge. The Führer explained that from a propaganda viewpoint he was anxious to maintain the appearance of a statesman who dedicated all his energy to the German nation. He went on to question the role and achievements of the children of great men through history. He continued by stating that the people's expectation of the children of those who achieve greatness, often, if not always, fell far short of the expectation. Hitler concluded, 'A son of mine would only be a burden and accordingly an unhappy person or a danger.' However, the possibility that Hitler may have had a son remains vague and unanswered. It was said that a liaison between Hitler and a French girl, Charlotte Lobjoie in 1917 had produced a son, Jean-Marie, born in March 1918. Linge believed that a private meeting between Hitler and Himmler in July 1940 concluded with Himmler being instructed to do everything possible to trace the mother and child. On the other hand, having personally discussed this matter with a former member of Hitler's staff, and someone who spent considerable time in his presence, I am reliably informed by this person that they never heard any talk amongst Hitler's intimates of the Führer having fathered a child.

To unravel and to begin to understand the complex personality that was Adolf Hitler is a subject worthy of several volumes in its own right. However, understanding Hitler's immense popularity through the 1930s is somewhat easier. While we know that innovative propaganda was instrumental in bringing about Nazi electoral success. A number of contributing factors beyond Hitler's control also played their part in bringing the Nazis to power. The humiliation of defeat in 1918; the deeply resented Versailles Treaty; the loss of national pride; the perceived weakness and subsequent resentment of the democratic Weimar government; world economic depression; high unemployment; lawlessness and general misery; all these things were continually played upon by the Nazis. By the end of 1932 the establishment had lost all credibility in the eyes of the public. An ageing German President, Field Marshal Paul von Hindenburg and Chancellor Franz von Papen concluded that a Hitler in government would be more easily controlled than a Hitler outside government. These would-be controllers soon became the controlled.

In less than four years in power it seemed that Hitler got to grips with many of the country's ills. The almost 'Godlike' image of the Führer, in no small part manufactured by Nazi propaganda, reflected the expectations and sentiments of the vast majority of the population. The Führer's perceived success in rebuilding much of the infrastructure and the economy, not to mention his successes in foreign policy made Hitler extremely popular. High unemployment had been addressed. Law and order had been re-established, if at the cost of certain civil liberties. Above all, national pride had been restored. Any shortcomings were put down to the actions of subordinates; they were not the fault of the Führer. Hitler, it seemed was beyond reproach. Even foreign governments of the day stood in awe and admiration of Hitler's achievements in the 1930s. The German Führer was perceived as a talented visionary. At home the life of the average German had improved beyond all recognition. Notwithstanding the as yet unknown terrible hidden agenda, why would they not support the Führer and the Nazi Party?

Leni Riefenstahl

Helene Bertha Amalie 'Leni' Riefenstahl was born in Berlin on 22 August 1902. Following a successful career as a dancer with the Russian ballet, Leni Riefenstahl was somehow drawn to the world of film acting. Founding her own film company in 1931, Riefenstahl received recognition for her work almost immediately. *Das blaue Licht* (The Blue Light) which she wrote, produced, and directed, with Riefenstahl herself playing the lead role won a gold medal at the Venice Biennale in 1932, establishing her name and paving the way to future success.

In February 1932, Fräulein Riefenstahl, on attending her first ever political meeting heard Hitler speak in the Berlin Sportpalast. Shortly after the event she wrote to Hitler requesting a meeting; this took place soon after. Hitler admired the charming, beautiful perfectionist and suggested that when the Nazis achieved power she must make his films. Riefenstahl replied that she could not make politically-motivated films; furthermore, she would not join the Party. Hitler would not be put off. While continuing to declare his enormous respect for her as an artist, and employing his not to be underestimated power of persuasion, Leni Riefenstahl finally succumbed and was duly appointed Director/Producer for Party Film-making.

344. Leni Riefenstahl.
A delightful studio study of the glamorous Leni Riefenstahl dating from the 1920s.

At Hitler's request Riefenstahl produced the film *'Der Sieg des Glaubens'* (Victory of Faith) a documentary covering the 1933 Nürnberg Party Rally. However, Riefenstahl's best known work during the Third Reich period is undoubtedly *'Triumph des Willens'* (Triumph of the Will) covering the 1934 Nürnberg Rally. This documentary-style film is testament to the quality of her work and expertise. It remains the single, greatest, directly politically-motivated film of all time, a three-hour-long spectacular which even today stands apart as an incredible feat for the period. Riefenstahl overcame many technical difficulties to produce a masterpiece that captured the event superbly.

Needless to say, Hitler was delighted with the result. Riefenstahl's newfound status meant she was invited to many Party functions and went on outings with Hitler and his inner circle, including visits to the Obersalzberg and the Berghof. It has been suggested that Reifenstahl and Hitler had a personal relationship, this she always denied and no proof that any such relationship took place has ever been produced. Joseph Goebbels, strangely and for some unexplained reason, perhaps jealousy, always seemed to resent Riefenstahl's direct access to Hitler and her friendly relationship with him. Leni Riefenstahl may have accurately identified the reason for some of the resentment she sometimes felt directed towards her by certain members of the Nazi hierarchy when she said, 'Hitler thought very highly of me. And that's why the Party hated me. Because sometimes Adolf Hitler set me up as an example to his men, as someone they could learn from.'

Riefenstahl continued to work in film after the Second World War, but never again quite so successfully. She could never quite shake off the memories of her connection to the Third Reich. However she insisted on her having had no knowledge of any wrongdoing during the period of her film work under Hitler. Leni Riefenstahl died quietly at her home in Pöcking on the Starnberger See southwest of Munich, on 9 September 2003. She was 101 years old. Riefenstahl is buried in Munich's Waldfriedhof.

Baldur von Schirach

Baldur Benedikt von Schirach was born in Berlin on 9 March 1907. His father, Carl, had been an officer in the Garde-Kürassier-Regiment Wilhelm II until 1908, when he left the army to become a theatre director. Baldur von Schirach began studying Germanic folklore and art history in Munich in 1924. It was there that he fell in with a group of National Socialists. Finding that the views of this group were very similar to his own views von Schirach joined the NSDAP in 1925. He was active in recruiting students to the Nazi movement and in 1931 he was appointed *Reishsjugendführer der NSDAP* (Reich Youth Leader of the NSDAP). A law enacted on 1 December 1936 made the Hitler Youth the only legal organization open to German youth aged ten to eighteen years. Hitler decreed that all German youth must become members of this new youth organization. By the end of 1938 the Hitler Youth had about eight million members. That said, a large number of German children managed to avoid becoming members despite the risk of fines and possible imprisonment to their parents.

As head of the Hitler Youth von Schirach oversaw the introduction of the indoctrination programmes designed to influence young people throughout the Reich. Von Schirach married Henriette Hoffmann, the daughter of Heinrich Hoffmann, Hitler's personal photographer on 31 March 1932. The couple were members of the Führer's inner circle; as such they were often guests at Hitler's private residence, the Berghof on the Obersalzberg. The von Schirach's had four children, one daughter and three sons, born between 1933 and 1942.

Baldur von Schirach organized the evacuation of many thousands of children from German cities in the face of anticipated Allied bombing. In early 1940 von Schirach volunteered. He joined the army and saw service on the western front where he won the Iron Cross. The fall of France in June 1940 and a reduction in the fighting in the west saw von Schirach recalled to Berlin. Hitler

345. Reich Governor Baldur v. Schirach.
Baldur von Schirach, Head of the Hitler Youth and later *Gauleiter* (District Leader) of Vienna. This absolutely superb postcard image simply screams the name 'Hoffmann' from the printed page; it is as fine an example of that Munich photographer's work as can be found. The postmark on the reverse reads; *Wien 17.9.42 Europaeischer Jugendverband Gründungstagung* (Vienna 17.9.42 European Youth Association Foundation Conference).

feared that von Schirach might become too powerful if he returned to his former post as head of the Hitler Youth. As a result Hitler appointed von Schirach *Gauleiter* (District Leader) of Vienna. Artur Axmann replaced von Schirach as Hitler Youth Leader. Axmann took up the position following his appointment on 8 August 1940.

As *Gauleiter* of Vienna, von Schirach oversaw the transportation of some 65,000 Jews from the city to the concentration camps in Poland. In 1943 his wife Henriette visited the Netherlands. While in Amsterdam she witnessed the rounding up of Jews in the city. Absolutely horrified, she was determined to bring the matter to Hitler's attention at their next meeting. Following her return to Germany and on visiting the Berghof soon after Henriette von Schirach, perhaps unwisely, tentatively touched upon the subject with Hitler. The Führer fell silent. Henriette continued, describing what she had seen. Hitler flew into a rage, telling her not to pursue the subject. This created a terrible atmosphere in the room, no-one knowing what to say. The von Schirach's made their excuses and left the Berghof. This incident led to a breakdown in the relationship between the Führer and the von Schirachs; so much so that they never visited the Berghof again.

Baldur von Schirach remained *Gauleiter* of Vienna until the end of the Second World War. He was tried at Nürnberg and sentenced to twenty years imprisonment. He was released together with Albert Speer on 30 September 1966. Their release would leave Rudolf Hess alone, the last of the Nazi leadership to remain in Berlin's Spandau Prison. Baldur von Schirach died at Kröv, a town in the Rhineland on 8 August 1974. His wife Henriette divorced him while he was in prison in 1946. She died on 27 January 1992.

Albert Speer

Berthold Konrad Hermann Albert Speer was born in Mannheim on 19 March 1905. His father, also Albert, was an architect. Under pressure from his father, the young Speer gave up his wish to study mathematics and instead followed family tradition to study architecture. Through the 1920s Speer studied in Karlsruhe, Munich and Berlin. On passing his exams in 1927 Albert Speer worked as assistant to Professor Heinrich Tessenow from 1927 until 1930. Speer, who had previously shown little interest in politics, encouraged by some of his students attended a political meeting in Berlin in late 1930. There he would hear Adolf Hitler speak for the first time. The meeting hall was packed with students and the young architect came away much impressed by Hitler. Albert Speer joined the Nazi Party soon after.

Despite family opposition, Albert Speer married Margarete Weber on 28 August 1928 in Berlin. Speer's mother Luise, in particular, disapproved of his choice believing his wife's family were of a lower class. The couple would have six children, Albert, Hilde, Fritz, Margarete, Arnold and Ernst. However in early 1931 financial constraints led to the young architect losing his job. Speer, now unemployed began looking for work. Fortunately, Speer had good contacts within the NSDAP. He was offered work renovating the Party's office building in Berlin. Soon after the Nazis came to power in 1933, Speer received a commission from Dr Joseph Goebbels to carry out the renovation work on the Propaganda Ministry building on Berlin's Wilhelmplatz.

Speer was later commissioned to submit designs for the Nürnberg Stadium. This led to a first meeting with Adolf Hitler. Many such meetings followed. Hitler warmed to the young architect. It has been said that Hitler may have seen many of his own youthful aspirations reflected and fulfilled in Albert Speer. The Führer, himself something of a frustrated architect, admired and respected Speer for his flair, skill and imagination. Speer soon became one of Hitler's inner circle. The Führer would describe Speer as a 'kindred spirit'. The young architect was invited to live on the Obersalzberg above Berchtesgaden. Speer designed and constructed his own studio close to his new home on the Obersalzberg. Hitler and Speer would spend many hours discussing plans and building projects in the studio during Hitler's numerous impromptu visits, where the Führer often presented his own sketches and drawings.

346. Professor Speer.
Albert Speer, Hitler's favourite architect then later Reich Minister for Armaments and War Production as photographed by Heinrich Hoffmann. While Speer turns up frequently in 'press type' photographs, postcard images of the man are quite rare.

In 1934 Albert Speer received his most important commission to date. The Führer asked Speer to design and construct a complex of huge structures at the Party Rally Grounds in Nürnberg. Hitler was extremely pleased with Speer's work at Nürnberg and at the beginning of 1937 he told Speer of his plans for the remodelling and rebuilding of Berlin. Berlin was to be renamed Germania. As such it would be the new capital of Hitler's planned 'Thousand-Year-Reich'. In 1938 the Führer instructed Speer to construct a new Reich Chancellery in Berlin. Speer had just one year to complete the task. The project was completed on time and Hitler was both impressed and delighted with the new Chancellery. In recognition, the Führer awarded Speer the Nazi Golden Party Badge in appreciation of his work on the Chancellery.

Professor Paul Ludwig Troost, allegedly Hitler's favourite architect died on 21 January 1934. Albert Speer, friend and confidant of the Führer succeeded Troost. Speer could do no wrong in Hitler's eyes. When on 8 February 1942, Dr Fritz Todt, Minister for Armaments and Munitions was killed in a plane crash on leaving the Wolf's Lair, the Führer's eastern headquarters near Rastenburg in East Prussia, it was to Speer that Hitler turned, appointing him Todt's successor. Albert Speer proved more than equal to the task. Production increased across the board reaching its high point in 1944, despite the damage inflicted on German industry by Allied bombing. Speer's 'central planning programme' certainly enabled Germany to continue the war for much longer than would otherwise have been possible. In the final months of the Second World War it was Speer and Goebbels who were seen in public attempting to maintain morale and inspire the people. Virtually without exception these two men were the only members of the Nazi hierarchy then to be seen in public.

Speer's last meeting with Hitler was on 20 April 1945 in the Berlin bunker. He came to celebrate the Führer's fifty-sixth birthday. Albert Speer said goodbye to Adolf Hitler for the last time as he left the bunker early on the morning of 24 April 1945. Speer was captured by the Allies and stood trial at Nürnberg. He was sentenced to twenty years imprisonment. Speer was released with Baldur von Schirach in 1966, the last two Nazi prisoners to be released from Spandau Prison. On his release Speer returned to his home town of Heidelberg where he spent the remainder of his life writing. In 1981 Speer travelled in England to take part in a television programme with the BBC. Albert Speer died in London on 1 September 1981 following a heart attack. He is buried in Heidelberg, Germany.

The Obersalzberg: Tangible Remains Today

The numbered sites on the map indicate the locations of buildings from the Nazi period, whether in a complete state or offering identifiable remains only. At the time of writing, with the exception of Hitler's Berghof and the former teahouse at Mooslahnerkopf, now both site only with minimal remains, most sites are identifiable regardless of their current state using the postcards in this book as a reference aid.

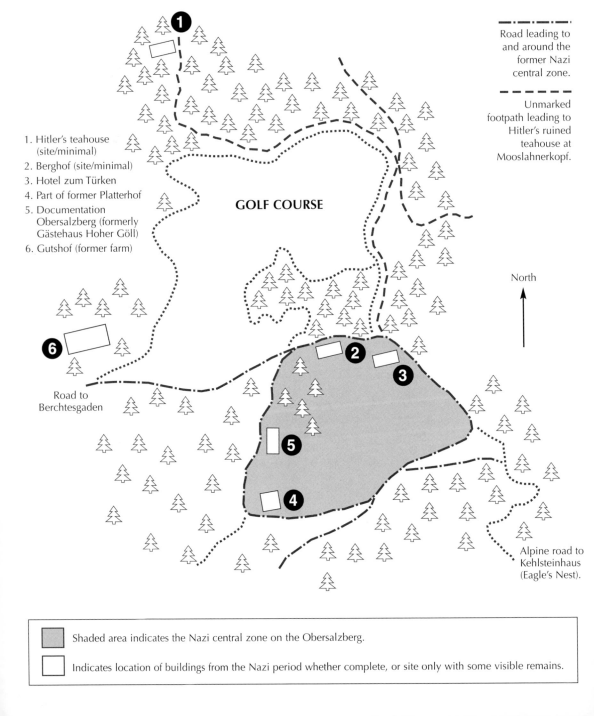

1. Hitler's teahouse (site/minimal)
2. Berghof (site/minimal)
3. Hotel zum Türken
4. Part of former Platterhof
5. Documentation Obersalzberg (formerly Gästehaus Hoher Göll)
6. Gutshof (former farm)

GOLF COURSE

Road leading to and around the former Nazi central zone.

Unmarked footpath leading to Hitler's ruined teahouse at Mooslahnerkopf.

North

Road to Berchtesgaden

Alpine road to Kehlsteinhaus (Eagle's Nest).

Shaded area indicates the Nazi central zone on the Obersalzberg.

Indicates location of buildings from the Nazi period whether complete, or site only with some visible remains.

Acknowledgements

There are those who deserve a great deal of thanks for their kind assistance and indulgence while I was carrying out the research and planning for this book.

David and Christine Harper, Eagle's Nest Historical Tours, Kurdirektion, Berchtesgaden, for their tolerance and kindness during the period that I worked with them as tour guide through the 2009/2010 seasons; a delightful experience that I fully intend to repeat at some point in the future. Gerhard Bartels, Bartels Alpenhof, Hintersee, Berchtesgaden, for his kindness and for taking the time to share his memories with me.

The **Bayerische Staatsbibliothek München/Fotoarchiv Hoffmann** who now own part of the Heinrich Hoffmann Picture Archive, including the reproduction rights to those images in their possession. A number of postcard images appearing in *Hitler's Alpine Headquarters* belong to the **Bayerische Staatsbibliothek München/Fotoarchiv Hoffmann.**

Everyone at Pen & Sword Books Limited for their continued support.

Finally, Lena, for having endured further hours of neglect while I was absorbed on this latest project.

Bibliography

The following is a list of books that have proved useful in the preparation of this work.

Beierl, Florian M, *History of the Eagle's Nest,* Verlag Plenk, Berchtesgaden, 2001.
Bullock, Alan, *Hitler a Study in Tyranny,* C. Tinling & Co. Ltd., 1954. Originally published by Odhams Press Ltd.
Die tödliche Utopie, Verlag Dokumentation Obersalzberg im Institut für Zeitgeschichte, München – Berlin. © Institut für Zeitgeschichte, München – Berlin 2008.
Evans, Richard J, *The Coming of the Third Reich,* Penguin Books, 2003.
Evans, Richard J, *The Third Reich in Power,* Penguin Books, 2005.
Hess, Wolf Rüdiger, *My Father Rudolf Hess,* W.H. Allen & Co. Plc, 1986.
Kershaw, Ian, *Hitler, 1936-45: Nemesis,* Allen Lane, The Penguin Press, 2000.
Linge Heinz, *With Hitler to the End,* LangdenMüller in der F.A. Herbig Verlagsbuchhandlung GmbH, 1980. Frontline Books, 2009. (Frontline Books is an imprint of Pen & Sword Books Ltd.)
Semmler, Rudolf, *Goebbels – the man next to Hitler,* John Westhouse (Publishers) Ltd., 1947.
Schöner, Hellmut, und Irlinger, Rosl, *Der alte Obersalzberg bis 1937,* Verlag Berchtesgadener Anzeiger 1989.
Schroeder, Christa, *He Was My Chief,* LangdenMüller in der F.A. Herbig Verlagsbuchhandlung GmbH, 1985. Frontline Books, 2009. (Frontline Books is an imprint of Pen & Sword Books Ltd.)
Shirer, William L, *The Rise and Fall of the Third Reich,* Pan Books Ltd., 1964. First published by Secker & Warburg, 1960.
Snyder, Louis L, *Encyclopaedia of the Third Reich,*The Promotional Reprint Company Ltd., 1995.
Thomas, Hugh, *Hess: A Tale of Two Murders,* Hodder & Stoughton, 1988.
Toland, John, *Adolf Hitler,* Ballantine Books, 1977.

Appendix

The following information has been taken from the reverse of the postcards shown throughout this book (together with dates of postmarks where these exist); it is offered by way of acknowledgment and credit to the original photographers and publishers of these postcards. This information may be cross-referenced by using the corresponding number that relates directly to each postcard caption. The reverse of some of the more interesting postcards are also shown on these pages.

1. Fot. Ernst Baumann, Bad Reichenhall. Echt Foto.
2. Fot. Ernst Baumann, Bad Reichenhall.
3. Reichs-Bildberichterstatter der NSDAP, Heinrich Hoffmann.
4. HDK. 193 – Verlag Heinrich Hoffmann, München.
5. Photo-Hoffmann, München, Friedrichstr. 34. Echte Fotografie.
6. Photo-Hoffmann, München, Freidrichstr. 34. Echte Fotografie.
7. Alleinvertrieb Walter Preuß, Berlin Friedenau. Stamped: 8.4.38.
8. Eduard Doppler, Braunau am Inn, L&H.
9. Eduard Doppler, Braunau am Inn, L&H. Echte Photographie.
10. JLL - Echte Photographie.
11. Echte Photographie.
12. Photo-Hoffmann, München, Theresienstraße 74. Echt Foto.
13. Photo-Hoffmann, München, Theresienstr. 74. Echte Fotografie.
14. Photo-Hoffmann, München, Theresienstr. 74. Echte Fotografie.
15. Photo-Hoffmann, München, Theresienstr. 74. Echte Fotografie.
16. Badisch Pfälzische Flugbetrieb A. G., Mannheim. Freigeg vom RLM. Posted: 16.8.41.
17. Reverse unmarked - source unknown.
18. Max Stadler, Kunstverlag, München, Welfenstrasse 39.

53

Photo-Hoffmann, München, Theresienstr. 74

Nachdruck verboten

71

19. Photo-Hoffmann, München, Theresienstr. 74. Echte Fotografie.
20. Ottmar Zieher, München. Fotokarte. Echte Photographie.
21. Südd. Kunstverlag M. Seidlein, München 8. Posted: 2.4.40.
22. A. Lengauer, München.
23. Verlag Carl Krueck, München, Kaufingerstr. 25. Echte Photographie. Posted: 13.5.42.
24. A. Lengauer, München. Echte Fotografie. Posted: 12.11.39.
25. Photograph by author.
26. A. Lengauer, München. Echte Fotografie.
27. Photograph by author.
28. A. Lengauer, München. Echte Fotografie.
29. A. Lengauer, München. Posted: 17.8.36.
30. A. Lengauer, München.
31. Verlag Carl Krueck, München, Kaufingerstrasse 25. Echtes Foto.
32. Photo-Hoffmann, München, Theresienstr. 74. Vitacolor.
    Reverse bears commemorative postmark celebrating; Day of German Art 16.7.1939.
33. Photo-Hoffmann, München, Friedrichstr. 34. Posted: 27.6.40.
34. Photograph by author.
35. Photokarte v. H. Gürtler, Salzburg, Faberstraße 30.
36. Reverse unmarked - source unknown. Posted: 24.1.23.
37. Photograph by author.
38. Aufnahme und Verlag F. G. Zeitz, Königssee / Obb. Posted: 12.9.42.
39. Photograph by author.
40. Verlag: L. Ammon, Schönau-Berchtesgaden.
41. Alpiner Kunstverlag Hans Huber, Garmisch-Partenkirchen. Deutsche Heimatbilder.
    Posted: 16.9.41.
42. Verlag: L. Ammon, Schönau-B'gaden. Posted: 14.8.41.
43. Photohaus J. Schmid, Berchtesgaden, Fernruf 254. Echt Foto.
44. Alpiner Kunstverlag F.G. Zeitz Königssee Ob.Bay. Posted: 9.12.30.
45. Phot. L Ammon. Verlag L Ammon, Schönau-B'gaden. Posted: 21.10.32.
46. Verlag von Karl Ermisch, Berchtesgaden.

47. Verlag von Karl Ermisch, Berchtesgaden.
48. Orig.-Aufn. v. Hans Huber, Alpiner Verlag, Garmisch-Partenkirchen. Deutsche Heimatbilder.
49. Gebirgsaufnahme von Michel Lochner, Berchtesgaden. No postmark but dated: 14.7.29.
50. L Monopol, Kunst u. Verlagsanstalt A. G. Schöllhorn, München-Innsbruck. Posted: 22.8.35.
51. Verlag A. Gg. Schöllhorn München 2. S O. Echte Photographie.
52. Photo-Hoffmann, München, Theresienstr. 74.
53. Photo-Hoffmann, München, Theresienstr. 74.
54. Photo-Hoffmann, München, Theresienstr. 74.
55. Photo-Hoffmann, München, Theresienstr. 74.
56. Photo-Hoffmann, München, Theresienstr. 74.
57. Photo-Hoffmann, München, Theresienstr. 74.
58. Photo-Hoffmann, München, Theresienstr. 74.
59. Photo-Hoffmann, München, Theresienstr. 74.
60. Photo-Hoffmann, München, Theresienstr. 74.
61. Reverse unmarked – source unknown. Posted: 21.8.33.
62. Verlag: Theodor Fritsch jun., Leipzig C 1. Ges. gesch. Bromüra.
63. Heinrich Hoffmann, Verlag nationalsozialistischer Bilder, Düsseldorf, Wilhelmplatz 12.
    Echte Fotografie.
64. Gebirgsaufnahmen von Michael Lochner, Berchtesgaden. Echte Fotografie.
65. Kunstverlag Friedrich Schmidt jr., Frankfurt a. M., Kleiner Hirschgraben 11.
    Photo Reinelt. Echte Fotografie.
66. Aufnahme und Verlag v. M. Lochner, Berchtesgaden. Echte Photographie.
67. Graph. Kunst und Verlagsanstalt Jos. C. Huber, Diessen vor München.
    Phot. E. Schmauß, München.
68. Foto Böhm, Verlag Michael Lochner, Berchtesgaden. Posted: 29.12.33.
69. Aufnahme von Michael Lochner, Berchtesgaden. Echte Fotografie.
70. Alpiner Kunstverlag Hans Huber, München 19. Deutsche Heimatbilder. Posted: 16.6.34.
71. Alpiner Kunstverlag Hans Huber, München 19. Deutsche Heimatbilder.
72. Alpiner Kunstverlag Hans Huber, München 19. Deutsche Heimatbilder. Posted: 27.7.33.
73. Alpiner Kunstverlag Hans Huber, München 19. Deutsche Heimatbilder.

Rear jacket (bottom)

74. Photograph by author.
75. Photo-Hoffmann, München, Theresienstr. 74. Echte Fotografie.
76. Gebirgsaufnahmen von Michael Lochner, Berchtesgaden. Echte Fotografie.
77. Photo-Pfingstl, Berchtesgaden. Echte Photographie.
78. Photohaus J. Schmid, Berchtesgaden, Fernruf 254. Echt Photo.
79. Alpiner Kunstverlag Hans Huber München 19. Deutsche Heimatbilder.
80. Aufn. u. Verlag M. Lochner, Obersalzberg, Berchtesgaden. Posted: 10.9.35.
81. Photo-Hoffmann, München, Amalienstr. 25. Uvachrom.
82. Verlag von Karl Ermisch, Berchtesgaden. Posted: 1935.
83. Photo-Hoffmann, München, Theresienstr. 74. Echte Fotografie.
84. Photo-Hoffmann, München, Friedrichstr. 34.
    Commemorative postmark: Nürnberg Reichsparteitag der NSDAP 12.9.38.
85. Photo-Hoffmann, München, Friedrichstr. 34. Posted: 14.5.40.
86. Photo-Hoffmann, München, Theresienstr. 74. Commemorative postmark:
    Reichsparteitag der N·S·D·A·P in Nürnberg 5-10 Sept. 1934. Posted: 9.9.34.
87. Photo-Hoffmann, München, Friedrichstr. 34. Echte Fotografie.
88. Photo-Hoffmann, München, Theresienstr. 74. Echte Fotografie.
89. Photo-Hoffmann, München, Friedrichstr. 34. Echte Fotografie.
90. Cosy Verlag, Alfred Gründler, Zweigstelle Freilassing. Posted: 26.5.35.
91. Verlag von Karl Ermisch, Berchtesgaden. Posted: 8.8.35.
92. Photo-Hoffmann, München, Theresienstr. 74.
93. Photo-Hoffmann, München, Theresienstr. 74. Echte Fotografie.
94. Photo-Hoffmann, München, Theresienstr. 74. Echte Fotografie.
95. Photo Brandner, unterhalb Haus Wachenfeld, Telef. 83. Echt Foto.
96. Photo-Hoffmann, München, Friedrichstr. 34. Echte Fotografie.
97. Photo-Hoffmann, Berlin SW 68, Kochstr. 10.
98. Photo-Hoffmann, Berlin SW 68, Kochstr. 10.
99. Orig.-Aufn. v. Hans Huber, Alpiner Verlag, München 19.
100. Photo-Hoffmann, Berlin SW 68, Kochstr. 10.
101. Alpiner Kunstverlag Hans Huber, Garmisch-Partenkirchen. Deutsche Heimatbilder. Posted: 11.6.35.

102. Cosy-Verlag, A. Gründler, Freilassing. Echte Photographie. Posted: 1934.
103. Orig.-Aufn. v. Hans Huber. Alpiner Verlag, Garmisch-Partenkirchen. Deutsche Heimatbilder. Posted: 1.8.35.
104. Photo-Hoffmann, München, Theresienstr. 74. Echte Fotografie.
105. Photo-Hoffmann, München, Amalienstr. 25. Uvachrom.
106. Photo-Hoffmann, München, Friedrichstr. 34. Echte Fotografie.
107. Verlag: L. Ammon, Schönau-B'gaden. Echte Fotografie.
108. Photo-Hoffmann, München, Theresienstr. 74. Uvachrom.
109. Emil Köhn, Kunstverlag, München. Echte Photographie.
110. Orig.-Aufnahme Kunst und Verlagsanstalt Martin Herpich, München. Echte Photographie.
111. Freig. D. Prüfst d. R.L.M. Hersteller: Helff & Stein GMBH, Leipzig C 1. Echte Fotografie.
112. Photo-Hoffmann, München, Theresienstr. 74. Echte Fotografie.
113. Photo-Hoffmann, München, Theresienstr. 74. Uvachrom.
114. Original-Aufnahme Walter Hahn, Dresden – A. 24, Godeffrov Str. 26. Fernruf: 42222. Posted: 28.2.34.
115. Photo-Hoffmann, München, Theresienstr. 74. Uvachrom.
116. Photo-Hoffmann, München, Theresienstr. 74. Uvachrom.
117. Photo-Hoffmann, München, Theresienstr. 74. Echte Photographie.
118. Photo-Hoffmann, München, Theresienstr. 74. Uvachrom.
119. Photo-Hoffmann, München, Theresienstr. 74. Uvachrom-Aufnahme. Posted: 29.5.37.
120. Photo-Hoffmann, München, Theresienstr. 74.
121. Aufnahme und Verlag: M. Lochner, Berchtesgaden. Echte Photographie.
122. Verlag Photo Böhm, Deutsche Buchhandlung, Berchtesgaden. Echt Foto.
123. Photo-Hoffmann, München Theresienstr. 74. Echte Fotografie.
124. Photo-Hoffmann, München, Friedrichstr. 34. Echte Fotografie. Not posted but dated: 6.9.43.
125. Rudolf Schneider-Verlag. Reichenau (Ga.). Aufn. P. J. Hoffmann.
126. Photo-Hoffmann, München, Friedrichstraße 34. Echte Fotografie.
127. Orig.-Aufnahme Kunst und Verlagsanstalt Martin Herpich, München. Echte Fotografie.

112

128. Bilddruck der Rückseite: Brendamour, Simhart & Co. München.
Commerorative stamp reads: *Werbeschau der KdF-Sammlergruppe 20.4.1941 Hannover.*

129. Photohaus J. Schmid, Berchtesgaden, Fernruf 254. Echt Foto.

130. Photo-Hoffmann, München, Friedrichstr. 34. Posted: 6.12.42.

131. Cosy-Verlag, Salzburg, Getreidgasse 22. Echte Photographie.

132. Verlag: L. Ammon, Schönau-B'gaden. Posted: 22.10.36.

133. Photo Jul. Hillebrand, Königssee (Ob.-Bayern). Echt Foto.

134. Verlag L. Ammon, Berchtesgaden-Schönau. Echte Photographie.

135. Aufnahme und Verlag F. G. Zeitz, Königssee Obb. Echte Photografie.

136. Photo-Hoffmann, München, Theresienstr. 74. Echte Fotografie.

137. Photo-Hoffmann, München, Friedrichstr. 34. Echte Fotografie.

138. Photo-Hoffmann, München, Theresienstr. 74. Echte Fotografie.

139. Photo-Hoffmann, München, Theresienstr. 74. Echte Fotografie.

140. Photohaus J. Schmid, Berchtesgaden, Fernruf 254. Posted: 13.7.37.

141. Aufnahme und Verlag F. G. Zeitz, Königssee / Obb. Posted: 25.10.38.

142. Photo-Hoffmann, München, Friedrichstr. 34. Echte Fotografie.

143. Aufnahme und Verlag F. G. Zeitz, Königssee / Obb. Original Zeitz-Photo.

144. Photo-Hoffmann, München, Theresienstr. 74.
Commemorative postmark: 10.4.38 (Plebiscite on *Anschluß* of Austria and the German Reich).

145. Photohaus J. Schmid, Berchtesgaden, Fernruf 254. Posted: 18.9.37.

146. Photohaus J. Schmid, Berchtesgaden, Fernruf 254. Echt Photo.

147. Photohaus J. Schmid, Berchtesgaden – Fernruf 254. Posted: 16.1.41.

148. Photo-Hoffmann, München, Friedrichstr. 34. Echte Fotografie.

149. Orig.-Aufn. v. Hans Huber, Alpiner Verlag, Garmisch-Partenkirchen. Deutsche Heimatbilder.

150. Aufnahme und Verlag M. Lochner, Berchtesgaden. Echte Photographie.

151. Photo-Haus J. Schmid, Berchtesgaden. Echte Photographie.

152. Photograph by author.

153. Photograph by author.

154. Photograph by author.

155. Aufnahme und Verlag F. G. Zeitz, Konigssee / Obb. Posted: 18.8.41.

156. Deutsche Kunst und Verlagsanstalt, G.m.b.H., Dortmund, Stubengasse 29. Posted: 6.10.42.
157. Verlag: L. Ammon, Schönau-B'gaden.
158. Photo-Hoffmann, München, Friedrichstr. 34. Echte Fotografie.
159. Photo-Hoffmann, München, Friedrichstr. 34. Echte Fotografie.
160. Verlag M. Bauer, München 13. Echt Foto.
161. Verlag Heinrich Hoffmann, München. Vitacolor.
162. Photo-Hoffmann, München, Theresienstr. 74.
163. Photo-Hoffmann, München, Friedrichstr. 34. Echte Fotografie.
164. Photo-Hoffmann, München, Friedrichstr. 34. Echte Fotografie.
165. Verlag Heinrich Hoffmann, München.
166. Photo-Hoffmann, München, Friedrichstr. 34. Echte Fotografie.
167. Photo-Hoffmann, München, Friedrichstr. 34. Echte Fotografie.
168. Photo-Hoffmann, München, Theresienstr. 74. Echte Fotografie.
169. Photo-Hoffmann, München, Friedrichstr. 34. Echte Fotografie.
170. Verlag Heinrich Hoffmann, München.
171. Verlag M. Bauer, München 13. Echt Foto.
172. Photo-Hoffmann, München, Theresienstr. 74. Echte Fotografie.
173. Photo-Hoffmann, München, Friedrichstraße 34. Vitacolor.
174. Photo-Hoffmann, München, Theresienstr. 74. Posted: 1.7.37.
175. Photo-Hoffmann, München, Theresienstr. 74. Echte Fotografie.
176. Köhler-Tiftze Bad Elster. Ergo.
177. Photo-Hoffmann, München, Theresienstr. 74. Echte Fotografie.
178. Photo-Hoffmann, München, Theresienstr. 74. Echte Fotografie.
179. Photo-Hoffmann, München, Theresienstr. 74. Echte Fotografie.
180. Cramers Kunstanstalt, Dortmund. Cekade. Originalfoto.
181. Cramers Kunstanstalt, Dortmund. Cekade. Originalfoto.
182. Photo-Hoffmann, München, Theresienstr. 74. Echte Photographie.
183. Aufnahme und Verlag F. G. Zeitz, Königsee / Obb. Posted: 26.8.34.
184. Photo-Hoffmann, München, Friedrichstr. 34. Echte Fotografie.

183

185. Photo-Hoffmann, München, Theresienstr. 74. Posted: 19.10.38.
186. Photo-Pfingstl, Berchtesgaden. Aufgenommen auf Agfa Isochrom-Film.
187. Photo-Hoffmann, München, Theresienstr. 74. Echte Fotografie.
188. Photo-Hoffmann, München, Theresienstr. 74. Echte Fotografie. Posted: 18.8.36.
189. Nordd. Städte-Verkehrs-Werbung, Hannover-Hainholz. Ruf: 32020.
190. Photograph by author.
191. Photo-Hoffmann, München, Friedrichstr. 34. Echte Fotografie.
192. Photo-Hoffmann, München, Theresienstr. 74. Echte Fotografie.
193. Alpiner Kunstverlag Hans Huber, München. Deutsche Heimatbilder. Posted: 5.10.33.
194. Photo-Hoffmann, München, Theresienstr. 74. Echte Fotografie.
195. Photo-Hoffmann, München, Amalienstr. 25. Echt Photo.
196. Photo-Hoffmann, München, Theresienstr. 74. Echte Fotografie.
197. Photo Jul. Hillebrand Nachf., Königssee (Ob.-Bayern). Posted: 12.8.38.
198. Photograph by author.
199. Photo-Hoffmann, München, Amalienstr. 25. Echt Photo.
200. Photograph by author.
201. Photo-Hoffmann, München, Friedrichstr. 34. Posted: 8.10.38.
202. Photo-Hoffmann, München, Friedrichstr. 34. Commemorative postmark: 18.6.40.
203. Photo-Hoffmann, München, Friedrichstr. 34. Echte Fotografie.
204. Photo-Hoffmann, München, Friedrichstr. 34. Echte Fotografie.
205. Photo-Hoffmann, München, Friedrichstr. 34.
    Commemorative postmark: München • Hauptstadt der Bewegung • 9.11.23 - 9.11.1938.
206. Photo-Hoffmann, München, Friedrichstr. 34. Commemorative postmark: 21.9.38.
207. Photo-Hoffmann, München, Friedrichstr. 34. Commemorative postmark: 3.10.38.
208. Photo-Hoffmann, München, Friedrichstr. 34. Commemorative postmark: 29.9.38.
209. Photo-Hoffmann, München, Friedrichstr. 34. Echte Fotografie.
210. Monopol. A. G. Schöllhorn.
211. Verlag: L. Ammon, Schönau-B'gaden. Echte Fotografie.
212. Deutsche Kunst und Verlagsanstalt, G.m.b.H., Dortmund, Stubengasse 29.
213. Verlag von Karl Ermisch, Berchtesgaden. Echte Fotografie.
214. Verlag von Karl Ermisch, Berchtesgaden. Echte Fotografie.
215. Deutsche Kunst und Verlagsanstalt, G.m.b.H., Dortmund, Stubengasse 29. Posted: 10.6.42.
216. Deutsche Kunst und Verlagsanstalt, G.m.b.H., Dortmund, Stubengasse 29. Echte Fotografie.
217. Photograph by author.
218. Deutsche Kunst und Verlagsanstalt, G.m.b.H., Dortmund, Stubengasse 29. Posted: 29.5.42.
219. Deutsche Kunst und Verlagsanstalt, G.m.b.H., Dortmund, Stubengasse 29. Echte Fotografie.
220. Deutsche Kunst und Verlagsanstalt, G.m.b.H., Dortmund, Stubengasse 29. Echte Fotografie.
221. Deutsche Kunst und Verlagsanstalt, G.m.b.H., Dortmund, Stubengasse 29. Echte Fotografie.
222. Deutsche Kunst und Verlagsanstalt, G.m.b.H., Dortmund, Stubengasse 29. Echte Fotografie.
223. Deutsche Kunst und Verlagsanstalt, G.m.b.H., Dortmund, Stubengasse 29. Echte Fotografie.
224. Deutsche Kunst und Verlagsanstalt, G.m.b.H., Dortmund, Stubengasse 29. Echte Fotografie.
225. Deutsche Kunst und Verlagsanstalt, G.m.b.H., Dortmund, Stubengasse 29. Posted: 2.12.42.
226. Deutsche Kunst und Verlagsanstalt, G.m.b.H., Dortmund, Stubengasse 29. Echte Fotografie.
227. Deutsche Kunst und Verlagsanstalt, G.m.b.H., Dortmund, Stubengasse 29. Posted: 8.6.44.
228. Deutsche Kunst und Verlagsanstalt, G.m.b.H., Dortmund, Stubengasse 29. Echte Fotografie.
229. Ross Verlag. Foto Clausen.
230. Alpiner Kunstverlag Hans Huber, Garmisch-Partenkirchen. Deutsche Heimatbilder.
231. Photo-Hoffmann, München, Friedrichstr. 34. Echte Fotografie.
232. Aufnahme und Verlag: M. Lochner, Berchtesgaden. Echte Photographie.
233. Ross Verlag. Foto Clausen. Posted: 10.7.40.
234. Verlag: L. Ammon, Schönau-B'gaden. Echte Fotografie.

235. Cosy-Verlag, Salzburg, Getreidegasse 22. Echte Photographie.
236. Foto Rosemarie Clausen. Ross-Verlag, Berlin SW 68. Posted: 7.2.41.
237. Aufnahme und Verlag U. Bornemann, Blankenburg-Harz. Echte Photographie.
238. Photo-Hoffmann, München, Theresienstr. 74.
239. Photo-Hoffmann, München, Theresienstr. 74.
240. Photo-Hoffmann, München, Theresienstr. 74.
241. Photo-Hoffmann, München, Theresienstr. 74.
242. Photohaus J. Schmid, Berchtesgaden. Tel. 254. Posted: 18.7.32.
243. Photo-Hoffmann, München, Friedrichstr. 34. Echte Fotografie.
244. L. Monopol, Kunst u. Verlagsanstalt A. G. Schöllhorn. München-Innsbruck. Echte Fotografie.
245. Photohaus J. Schmid, Berchtesgaden. Fernruf 254. Echt Foto.
246. Aufnahme und Verlag: M. Lochner, Berchtesgaden. Echte Photographie.
247. Photograph used courtesy of Verlag Plenk, Berchtesgaden.
248. Aufnahme und Verlag: M. Lochner, Berchtesgaden. Echte Photographie.
249. Reichs-Bildberichterstatter der NSDAP, Heinrich Hoffmann.
250. Aufnahme und Verlag F. G. Zeitz, Königssee/Obb. Posted: 9.7.41.
251. Photograph by author.
252. Photograph by author.
253. Photograph by author.
254. Photograph by author.
255. Photograph by author.
256. Photograph by author.
257. Photograph by author.
258. Photograph by author.
259. Photograph by author.
260. Photograph by author.
261. Photograph by author.
262. Photograph by author.
263. Photograph by author.
264. Reverse unmarked - source unknown.
265. Ansichtskartenfabrik Schöning & Co., Lübeck. Echte Fotografie.
266. Ansichtskartenfabrik Schöning & Co., Lübeck. Echte Fotografie.
267. Foto L. Ammon, Berchtesgaden-Schönau. Echt Foto.
268. Aufnahme u. Verlag: F. G. Zeitz, Königssee/Obb. Original-Zeitz-Photo.
269. Aufnahme u. Verlag: F. G. Zeitz, Königssee/Obb. Original-Zeitz-Photo.
270. Aufnahme u. Verlag: F. G. Zeitz, Königssee/Obb. Original-Zeitz-Photo.
271. Alpiner Kunstverlag Hans Huber, Garmisch-Partenkirchen.
272. Alpiner Kunstverlag Hans Huber, Garmisch-Partenkirchen.
273. Privately taken photograph, source unknown, reverse unmarked.
274. Privately taken photograph, source unknown, reverse unmarked.
275. Ernst Baumann, Bad Reichenhall. Echt Foto.
276. Privately taken photograph. Reverse unmarked – source unknown.
277. Privately taken photograph. Reverse unmarked – source unknown.
278. Privately taken photograph. Reverse unmarked – source unknown.
279. Privately taken photograph. Reverse unmarked – source unknown.
280. Privately taken photograph. Reverse unmarked – source unknown.
281. Privately taken photograph. Reverse unmarked – source unknown.
282. Privately taken photograph. Reverse unmarked – source unknown.
283. Privately taken photograph. Reverse unmarked – source unknown.
284. Privately taken photograph. Reverse unmarked – source unknown.
285. Privately taken photograph. Reverse unmarked – source unknown.

286. Photograph by author.
287. Photo-Hoffmann, München, Friedrichstr. 34. Echte Fotografie.
288. Photo-Hoffmann, München, Friedrichstr. 34. Echte Fotografie.
289. Photo-Hoffmann, München, Friedrichstr. 34. Echte Fotografie.
290. Photo-Hoffmann, München, Friedrichstr. 34. Echte Fotografie.
291. Verlag Heinrich Hoffmann, München.
292. Photo-Hoffmann, München, Friedrichstr. 34. Echte Fotografie.
293. Photo-Hoffmann, München, Friedrichstr. 34. Echte Fotografie.
294. Photo-Hoffmann, München, Friedrichstr. 34. Echte Fotografie.
295. Photo-Hoffmann, München, Friedrichstr. 34. Echte Fotografie.
296. Photograph by author.
297. Verlag: L. Ammon, Schönau-B'gaden.
298. Photograph by author.
299. Aufnahme J. Schmid, Berchtesgaden. Echte Fotografie.
300. Photohaus J. Schmid, Berchtesgaden.
301. Photograph by author.
302. Aufn. u. Verlag J. Schmid, Berchtesgaden. Echte Fotografie.
303. Photograph by author.
304. Photograph by author.
305. Photograph by author.
306. Photograph by author.
307. Aufnahme und Verlag: M. Lochner, Berchtesgaden. Echte Photographie. Posted: 8.12.40.
308. Aufnahme und Verlag: M. Lochner, Berchtesgaden. Echte Photographie. Posted: 10.9.40.
309. Aufnahme Dr. Wiedemann. Herausgegeben vom Generalkommando VII. A.K.
310. Photograph by author.
311. Aufnahme und Verlag M. Lochner, Berchtesgaden. Echte Photographie. Posted: 22.5.42.
312. Aufnahme und Verlag F. G. Zeitz, Königssee / Obb. Original-Zeitz-Photo.
313. Photohaus J. Schmid, Berchtesgaden, Fernruf 254. Posted: 28.1.39.
314. Aufnahme und Verlag: M. Lochner, Berchtesgaden. Echte Photographie.
315. Photograph by author.

316. Verlag: L. Ammon, Schönau-B'gaden. Dated: 28.8.32.
317. Photograph by author.
318. Photograph by author
319. Reverse unmarked - source unknown.
320. Reverse unmarked - source unknown.
321. Reverse unmarked - source unknown.
322. Aufn. u. Verlag M. Lochner, Berchtesgaden. Echte Photographie.
323. Photograph by author.
324. Photograph by author.
325. Photograph by author.
326. Photograph by author.
327. Photograph by author.
328. Kunst u. Verlagsanstalt Martin Herpich, München.
    Foto Karl Kruse, Bad Reichenhall – Kirchberg. Freigegeben d. RLM. 5.4.35. Posted: 29.10.39.
329. Photo-Hoffmann, München, Theresienstraße 74.
330. Privately taken photograph. Reverse unmarked – source unknown.
331. Photo-Hoffmann, München, Theresienstr. 74. Echte Fotografie.
332. Phot. Rob. Röhr. Echte Photographie.
333. Reverse unmarked – source unknown.
334. Photo-Hoffmann, München, Friedrichstr. 34. Echte Fotografie.
335. Sandau, Berlin. Film . Foto . Verlag, Berlin SW68. Echt Photo.
336. Foto Rosemarie Clausen. Film-Foto-Verlag, Berlin SW68. Zur Veröffentlichung freigegeben.
337. Photo-Hoffmann, München, Theresienstr. 74. Echte Fotografie.
338. Photo-Hoffmann, München, Amalienstr. 25. Echte Photographie.
339. Photo-Hoffmann, München, Theresienstr. 74.
340. Phot. Rob. Röhr, Magdeburg. Echte Photographie.
341. Phot. u. Verlag Rob. Röhr, Magdeburg. Echte Photographie.
342. Contemporary official stamp on reverse reads; SS-Panzer-Grenadier-Regiment 'Der Führer'.
343. Photo-Hoffmann, München, Theresienstr. 74.
    Commemorative postmark: Wien 10 April 1938 'Ein Volk – Ein Reich – Ein Führer'.
344. Atelier Kiesel, Berlin phot. Verlag 'Ross' Berlin SW 68.
345. Photo-Hoffmann, München, Friedrichstr. 34. Posted: 17.9.42.
346. Photo-Hoffmann, München, Friedrichstr. 34. Echte Fotografie. Not posted but date
    stamped: 6.6.43.

Jacket images (front).
Top: Adolf Hitler after a painting by Hans Toepper (1885-1956).
             F. A. Ackermanns Kunstverlag, München.
Main image: Haus Wachenfeld, country house of the Reich's Chancellor in Berchtesgaden
             (Obersalzberg). Photo-Hoffmann, München, Amalienstr. 25.
Jacket images (back).
Top left: Deutsche Heimatbilder. Orig.-Aufn. V. Hans Huber.
             Alpiner Verlag, Garmisch-Partenkirchen.
Middle left: Berghof Wachenfeld, country house of the Reich's Chancellor in Berchtesgaden
             (Obersalzberg). Photo-Hoffmann, München, Theresienstr. 74.
Top right: Berghof Wachenfeld, country house of the Reich's Chancellor in Berchtesgaden.
Main image: Haus Wachenfeld, country house of the Reich's Chancellor in Berchtesgaden
             (Obersalzberg).Photo-Hoffmann, München, Theresienstr. 74.
Jacket images (inside).
             Haus Wachenfeld, country house of the Reich's Chancellor in Berchtesgaden
             (Obersalzberg). Photo-Hoffmann, München, Amalienstr. 25.